Cities and Governance: New Directions in Latin America, Asia and Africa

Cities and Governance

NEW DIRECTIONS IN LATIN AMERICA, ASIA AND AFRICA

EDITED BY
PATRICIA L. McCARNEY

CENTRE FOR URBAN & COMMUNITY STUDIES
UNIVERSITY OF TORONTO

© 1996
   Centre for Urban and Community Studies
   Printed in Canada by University of Toronto Press Incorporated
   Cover design and interior by Opus House

Canadian Cataloguing in Publication data

   Main entry under title:
Cities and governance: new directions in Latin America, Asia and Africa

   ISBN: 0-7727-1407-X
   1. Municipal government — Developing countries.
   I. McCarney, Patricia L. (Patricia Louise). II. University of Toronto.
   Centre for Urban and Community Studies.

JS67.C57 1996   320.8'5'091724 C96-930560

Centre for Urban and Community Studies
University of Toronto
455 Spadina Avenue
Toronto M5S 2G8 Canada
TEL 416-978-2072/FAX 416-978-7162
E-MAIL CUCS@epas.utoronto.ca

Contents

Preface

The importance of urban research in the developing world was recognized by the Urban Poverty Program of the Ford Foundation in 1990. In response, a global network of urban researchers, NGO activists and planners was formed, calling itself GURI (the Global Urban Research Initiative). This network is the largest, and one of the most successful, networks of developing country urban researchers to have emerged in recent years. The identification of the need for this research basis and the evolution of GURI is due to the keen insight and dedication of Robert Curvin, Mark Elliott and Anne Kubisch (the latter, formerly) of the Ford Foundation. Their tremendous intellectual and financial support over these years is gratefully acknowledged. The contribution of the World Bank, and in particular of Michael Cohen, to the second phase of this work is also recognized with thanks.

An urban research agenda for the 1990s developed from the first phase of the project (1991–93) which identified a number of key themes for the 1990s: urban governance, globalization, the urban environment and sustainability, poverty, finance and the economy of cities, and urban social structure. From this agenda, one topic — *urban governance* — was agreed to be the single most critical theme for urban research in the 1990s. As a consequence, the work of the second phase of the project (1993–95) has focused on this theme, with researchers throughout Latin America, Asia and Africa actively addressing the evolving nature of urban governance in their local contexts. The results of this research on urban governance were presented in Mexico City at the GURI Annual Meeting in October 1995 and are contained in this volume.

While the coordinating "team" of the GURI network, under the pivotal and tireless leadership of Richard Stren in the Centre for Urban and Community Studies at the University of Toronto, has lent its editorial support to putting this volume together, it is the intellectual dedication of the twelve GURI researchers which is responsible for this work. Over the past few years, they have identified the theme of governance, prepared papers on the topic, and disseminated their ideas through public discussion, publication and numerous meetings. They have travelled to international fora to present their ideas and exchanged knowledge on this subject with many parts of the development community. In the course of these activities they have built a strong network in GURI, and together, as a network, these individuals are strategically positioned to have a significant impact on governance in the cities we all inhabit.

PATRICIA L. McCARNEY

Contributors

KOFFI ATTAHI is an Ivorian planner trained in Canada where he obtained his doctorate in urban planning from the University of Montreal. He was previously in the department of geography and director of the *Centre de recherches architecturales et urbaines* (CRAU), University of Abidjan. He is currently Regional Advisor at the Regional Office for Africa of the United Nations Development Programme (UNDP)/World Bank Urban Management Programme in Accra, Ghana. He has carried out extensive research on urbanization and urban management in Francophone sub-Saharan Africa, and has worked as a consultant for United Nations Centre for Human Settlements (UNCHS-Habitat), the World Bank and the overseas development agencies of Canada, Germany and the United States. He has contributed to two of Habitat's monographs on urban management: *Metropolitan Planning and Management in the Developing World, Abidjan and Quito* (1992), and *The Management of Secondary Cities in Sub-Saharan Africa* (1991); and to *African Cities in Crisis* (1986), edited by Richard Stren and Rodney White.

MAGDA PRATES COELHO is a researcher at the *Instituto Universitário de Pesquisas do Rio de Janeiro* (IUPERJ). Her graduate studies were undertaken in political science, and undergraduate studies in sociology, at the Federal University of Minas Gerais. Since 1972 she has been involved in different research projects conducted by IUPERJ, covering such themes as the urban labour market, housing policies and urban social movements and, more recently, urban violence in Rio de Janeiro. She is at present executive secretary of the journal *Revista do Rio de Janeiro*, published by CEPRIO, the State University of Rio de Janeiro. Her involvement with GURI started in 1992 as a close collaborator of Licia Valladares.

EMILIO DUHAU is a sociologist with post-graduate degrees in urban development (*Maestria en Desarrollo Urbano*, El Colegio de México) and urbanism (*Doctorado en Urbanismo*, UNAM). He is a full professor and researcher at the Universidad Autonoma Metropolitana, Mexico City, where he teaches urban sociology, and was appointed National Researcher by Mexico's *Sistema Nacional de Investigadores* in 1989. He conducts research in the fields of urban and social policy, urban management and planning. He has published widely on these subjects and on theoretical and methodological problems in urban studies and sociology. He is the author, co-author and editor of the following books: with R. Coulomb, *La ciudad y sus actores*, 1988; *Mercado Interior y Urbanización en el México Colonial*, 1989; with R. Coulomb, *Políticas Urbanas y Urbanización de la Política*, 1989; with A Azuela, *Gestión Urbana y Cambio Institucional en la Ciudad de México*, 1993; and with A. Azuela, *Evictions and the Right to Housing* for IDRC, Ottawa (forthcoming). Since 1992 he has coordinated the research programme *Observatorio Urbano de las Ciudad de México* (OCIM).

MOHAMED HALFANI is currently a Senior Lecturer in the Institute of Development Studies, University of Dar es Salaam, Tanzania. He has a PhD in Political Science from the University of Toronto, Canada. His field of research is institutional revitalization and local governance, with a special focus on urban development. He has published several articles on urban development, civil society, urban research and administrative reforms. His writing includes *Empowering People: Building Community, Civil Association and Legality in Africa* (edited, with Richard Sand-brook); and *Vitalizing African Public Administration for Recovery and Development*. Dr. Halfani is working at present on a research project which examines the mechanisms for interfacing urban management and the informal sector in Tanzania.

NAZRUL ISLAM is Professor of Geography at the University of Dhaka and Director of the Centre for Urban Studies, Dhaka. He has also taught at the Asian Institute of Technology, Bangkok. He received his MA in Geography from the University of Dhaka in 1962 and subsequently attended the University of Western Ontario, London, Canada, and the Development Planning Unit, London, England. His major publications include *Dhaka Metropolitan Fringe Land and Housing Development*, *Upgrading a Slum Settlement in Dhaka*, *Urban Land Management in Bangladesh*, *Urban Poor in Bangladesh*, and *Urban Research in Bangladesh*. He is also Editor of *Bangladesh Urban Studies*, *Dhaka University Studies* (Bengali), and Member of the Board of Directors, *The Habitat International*.

MUHAMMAD MOHABBAT KHAN is a professor of public administration at the University of Dhaka. He received his MA in 1969 from the University of Dhaka, MPA from Syracuse in 1974, and MPA and PhD in 1976 from the University of Southern California. He has taught at universities in Nigeria and Jordan, and he was a Senior Fulbright Fellow in 1989–90 at the University of Texas at Austin. He has published ten books, six monographs, and over 100 papers in professional journals. He was the editor or the Dhaka University Press *Social Science Review* from 1993 to 1995. His major publications include: *Bureaucratic Self-Preservation: Failure of Major Administrative Reform Efforts in the Civil Service*, 1980; and *Politics of Administrative Reform: A Case Study of Bangledesh*, 1991.

MOSTAFA KHAROUFI is joining the *Centre National Marocain pour la Jeunesse et L'Avenir* in Rabat. He was previously a researcher at the *Institut de Recherches sur le Maghreb Contemporain* in Tunis, and prior to that at the *Centre de Documentation Economique, Juridique et Social* in Cairo, and coordinator of a programme on economic, social and cultural changes and internal migration in Egypt and the Sudan. He received a *Doctorat* in sociology, a *Maîtrise* in geography, a *Licence* in educational science and a *Diplôme d'Etudes Approfondies* in political science from the Universities of Toulouse I and Toulouse II. Besides the issue of migration in the Arab world, Dr. Kharoufi has conducted field work in urban areas in Egypt, Sudan and Tunisia. He is preparing a book on the issue of migration and urbanization in North Africa and the Middle East.

OM PRAKASH MATHUR is currently HDFC Professor of Housing and Urban Economics at the National Institute of Public Finance and Policy, New Delhi. Prior to taking up this position, he was Director of the National Institute of Urban Affairs, New Delhi. Dr. Mathur has worked as a Senior Economist with the United Nations Centre for Regional Development, Nagoya (Japan), and as the UNDP Project Manager of a Regional Planning Project in Iran. He has served as a short-term consultant to the United Nations University, Asian Development Bank, UNESCAP, and UNICEF. Dr. Mathur is an economist by discipline. He has been a visiting fellow at the Massachusetts Institute of Technology.

PATRICIA MCCARNEY is an Assistant Professor of Political Science and an Associate of the Centre for Urban and Community Studies in the University of Toronto. She received her PhD in International Development from the Massachusetts Institute of Technology (MIT) in 1987, and worked in a number of international agencies including the International Development Research Centre (IDRC), the World Bank and UNCHS (Habitat). Much of her research is in the field of urban development and politics in the developing world, her main interests being in governance, the shifting agendas of international development agencies, the urban sector of the World Bank, the urban environment and gender issues. Dr. McCarney has worked in many countries of the developing world, particularly in Africa, and in 1992 led a mission to South Africa to assist the democratic movement in the development of an urban policy framework. She is associate coordinator of GURI, and is a member of the board of directors of the Canadian Urban Institute in Toronto.

ADEPOJU G. ONIBOKUN holds MA and PhD degrees in Urban and Regional Planning from the University of Waterloo in Canada. His extensive professional contributions to the urban field include participation in many Nigerian federal and state government advisory committees on urban matters. He is the first Nigerian Professor of Urban and Regional Planning, and has taught in a number of universities in Nigeria and elsewhere, including for many years as Professor of Urban Planning at the University of Illinois at Urbana and at the University of Ibadan in Nigeria. He has also served as consultant to the World Health Organization, the World Bank and the United Nations on matters relating to urban and regional planning, infrastructure development and institution building. Professor Onibokun founded and is chief executive of the Centre for African Settlement Studies and Development (CASSAD), a non-governmental organization. He has published over a hundred books and articles.

ALFREDO RODRIGUEZ is Director of SUR, Centre for Social Studies and Education in Santiago, Chile. He trained as an architect at the Catholic University of Valparaiso, Chile, and received his MSc in City Planning from Yale University. He has worked for over 25 years in non-governmental research institutions: DESCO in Lima, CIUDAD in Quito, and SUR. His work has centred on the themes of urban poverty, democracy in the city and low-income housing. He has consulted for the United Nations Development Programme (UNDP), the Urban Management Programme in Latin America (UMP/LAC) and the Organization of American States (OAS). He is the coordinator of the Urban and Regional Commission of CLACSO. His most recent publications include *Municipio y servicios públicos* (as co-editor) and *Por una ciudad democrática*.

MARTHA SCHTEINGART is an architect and urban sociologist who received her graduate education at the Universities of Buenos Aires and Paris. She is now Research Professor in the Centre for Demographic and Urban Development Studies (CEDDU) of El Colegio de México, where she teaches in the masters programme in urban development. She is also a senior national researcher of the National System of Research of Mexico. Dr. Schteingart has carried out extensive research on urbanization, poverty, health, environment and housing. Her many publications include ten books, the most recent of which are: *Los productores del espacio habitable: Estado, empresa y sociedad en la Ciudad de México; Espacio, y vivienda en la Ciudad de México; Servicios urbanos, gestión local y medio ambiente* (with Luciano d'Andrea); and (with M. Solis)*Vivienda y familia en México* (forthcoming). Among her other activities Dr. Schteingart is a member of the Ford and MacArthur Foundations, and a member of the Mexico and Central America Scholarship Committee.

MARK SWILLING is Director of the School of Public and Development Management, Faculty of Management, University of Witwatersrand, Johannesburg. He was previously a development project worker in PLANACT, and before that a lecturer in the Department of Political Studies and a Research Officer in the Centre for Policy Studies, both at the University of the Witwatersrand. His achievements include participation in the design and establishment of PLANACT, the School of Public and Development Management, the Community Bank, Metropolitan Chamber, and numerous development NGOs involved in the delivery of mass housing. He has published several books and over 50 articles on the nature of the South African state, community movements, the politics of the independent trade union movement, the South African local government system and policy alternatives, the management of urban transition, transport policy, South Africa's international relations and the dynamics of non-revolutionary transitions to democracy. He recently completed a PhD in the Department of Sociology at the University of Warwick entitled "Urban Control and Changing Forms of Political Conflict in the Western Cape with Special Reference to Uitenhage, 1979–1986." His work now focuses on the management of change in state administrations and the structuring of new forms of democratic governance in the public and community sector.

YUKUN WANG co-ordinated the China sub-region for the first phase of the Urban Research in the Developing World project in his position as Associate Professor at the Development Research Centre of the State Council, People's Republic of China. Mr. Wang has worked on the second phase of the GURI project through the Grand Development Company, Beijing. He has been active in a wide range of policy formulation and analysis activities, particularly in the housing, urban land, pricing, development and financial fields. He has published six books, five papers in English, and more than 70 papers in Chinese.

LUCY WINCHESTER is a researcher/analyst at the Urban Studies Programme in SUR, *Centro de Estudios Sociales y Educación* in Santiago, Chile. She received a Bachelor of Arts degree in Economics in 1982 from the State University of New York and an MSc in Agricultural Economics from Michigan State University in 1991. Since 1993 she has been involved in different research projects conducted by SUR covering such themes as local institutional framework and political context for public policy development and implementation. She has consulted for the US Peace Corps, for the Latin American Bureau of DANIDA and for USAID. Her main fields of interest include public policy analysis and marketing alternatives.

Section I

Introduction

1 Considerations on the Notion of "Governance" — New Directions for Cities in the Developing World

PATRICIA L. McCARNEY

I INTRODUCTION

In a global context of profound change, many countries in the developing world are undertaking extensive state reforms which create pressure, and potential, for new forms of governing cities. Many countries for example are undertaking government and civil service reorganization, are engaged in processes of decentralization of state structures and functions, and are initiating critical transitional steps to democratization. These reforms raise questions not simply of "governance" as it is often considered, merely in terms of national state structures and practices, but also of "urban governance" and the nature of local government as an important element in the governing relationship. This is particularly true since in many countries local government has been a neglected tier in the overall development effort.

As a result of these reforms, it has become critical for the development community concerned with cities to reconsider the urban management paradigm that has dominated the period of the 1980s to the present. It is important now to consider the changing nature of local government in the arena of urban politics. This re-casting of the urban field is as yet not well understood and is certainly under-researched. The cities of Latin America, Asia and Africa are facing profound changes as a result of the shifting global context. The importance of research on local government has therefore never been greater; it is needed to provide insight into the changing nature of urban governance in the developing world. This is the central objective of this volume in bringing together the research results on urban governance in the cities of Latin America, Asia and Africa.

This chapter will not provide any detailed overview of the 12 chapters which follow, because of space limitations. Rather, the objectives of this chapter are to position the notion of governance within the shifting context in which cities of the developing world now find themselves. It will also identify new challenges facing these cities and their local governments if a new form of governance is to be created. The structure of this chapter is divided into four parts. The next section presents an evolving definition of governance, as viewed from the perspective of this author, in an urban context within the developing world. The third section traces the emerging perspectives on urban governance, resulting from the changing global, national and local contexts as well as the shifting terrain of the international donor community. Finally, the fourth and concluding section addresses the new challenges confronting the development community — governments, civic groups, researchers and international donors — if a strong and potent form of governance is to emerge in cities of the developing world.

II EVOLVING DEFINITIONS OF GOVERNANCE IN AN URBAN CONTEXT

An understanding of urban governance stems from a definition of governance itself. Good and workable definitions of governance have been difficult to find. Existing usage seems to fall into two traps. First, *governance* is simply equated too often with *government*, and second, governance often focuses on the state side of the picture, concentrating on accountability, transparency and management, and ignoring the role of groups in civil society in the governing relationship. Unlike much of the literature on government, one political scientist, Michael Lofchie, describes governance as not prejudging the locus or character of real decisional authority (Lofchie 1989). In a paper by Mohamed Halfani, Patricia McCarney and Alfredo Rodriguez where urban governance was first examined,[1] this dimension of governance was recognized as valuable since it broadens the space to include the critical role played by organizations in civil society where formal state structures are weak and unable to provide basic services:

> As we increasingly recognize that civil society organizes into new associational arrangements, often to pursue survival strategies in this changing state-civil society nexus, it becomes important to reconsider our thinking about government within a broader dimension. Hence the increased attention to the concept of governance (McCarney, Halfani and Rodriguez 1995, 94–95).

In recognition of the prevalent weaknesses in usage of the term, these authors defined governance as referring to "the *relationship* between civil society and the state, between rulers and the ruled, the government and the governed." It is this "relation of civil society to the state . . . that distinguishes the study of governance from other studies of government" (McCarney, Halfani and Rodriguez 1995, 95–96).

When this definition is applied to the local level, a notion of urban governance helps to shift thinking away from state-centred perspectives which have predominantly focused on urban management to include elements which, in conventional terms, are often considered to be outside the public policy process. These include civic associations, private sector organizations, community groups and social movements, all of which in fact exert an indelible impact on the morphology and development of urban centres (Castells 1983; Mabogunje 1990; Turner 1990). As Hernando De Soto has pointed out in the case of Lima, Peru, the more informal aspects of urban development activities constitute exceedingly large portions of the urban process. He states that 83 percent of the markets are informal sector ones, 95 percent of the public transport is run by the informal sector, and between 50 and 75 percent of the housing occupied by urban dwellers is informal (De Soto 1989). In addition, in the absence of strict planning legislation and enforcement of local zoning ordinances, larger private sector organizations and commercial interests have also had a significant impact on land use and development in cities. Once we recognize that the bulk of housing activities, transportation, infrastructure services, land development, employment creation and commercial trading takes place outside formal state institutions, the traditional management paradigm becomes something of an anomaly.

In addition, when we further consider civil society within this local context, the overall "fit" of these activities into a market context is even less well understood. The concept of market within the urban context is further complicated by the interplay of the unregulated sub-markets, particularly in the purchase, development and sale of urban land. The interrelationships between the more traditional formal market operations in urban development and the extensive informal sub-markets in land and housing development, constitute horizontal linkages between actors in civil society that demand investigation if urban governance is to be effective. It is the failure to concede to these structural features of the urban development process which has been the main cause of market inefficiencies, fiscal incapacities and management dysfunctions in Third World cities.

A critical question is posed: How do newly empowered local governments, established along traditional lines to regulate, administer and manage the local environment and the delivery of services, and ensure sound land-use practices and orderly development of urban spatial systems, operate within a non-traditional city built largely outside of any regulatory framework? Critical new relationships and patterns of engagement are required between newly empowered local governments and thriving groups in civil society that are led by strong local actors who have been responsible for the bulk of urban construction in the past. This dictates both a better understanding of urban politics within this emergent arena and a reconsideration of the relationship between local government, local commercial interests, and local communities as traditionally construed.

Urban governance thus allows us to reconsider local government as more than just a technical or administrative arm of central government in the developing world. In the context of decentralization, governance permits an understanding of local government as more than just a bureaucratic structure with new autonomous powers and functions. When urban governance is introduced as the relation between actors in civil society engaging with local state structures, new territory is opened up for reviving local government. Recognition of the importance of the local level in discussions of democratization focuses new attention on this tier of government in the development dialogue. The chapters which follow contribute to this dialogue in that they offer an in-depth examination of urban governance in 12 areas of Latin America, Asia and Africa. Each chapter is an investigation of the emergent governing relationship at the local level.

III THE CHANGING CONTEXT FOR GOVERNANCE IN CITIES
OF THE DEVELOPING WORLD

Local Governance and Global Restructuring

At a global level, the increasing role of transnational corporations within the cities of Third World countries, the construction of newly integrated trading blocs, the globalization of economic and socio-cultural development spheres, and the persistence of international debt and the attendant austerity measures, all find expression in the city.

There does not appear to be any single definition of globalization, although the internationalization of economies is a common trait discussed in most efforts to define the process (Dicken 1992). Globalization may be said to refer to the internationalization of capital, production, services and culture. A new economic system is emerging as economic transactions and integration of the systems of production occur on a worldwide basis. The information age together with the strategic logic inherent in the operations of transnational corporations are pushing us towards something called "the globalized economy." A central question facing urbanists is what impact this process of globalization has on cities.

This global context in which cities now find themselves as key actors, is further altered by the creation of new trading blocs and new post-industrial alignments. North-South trade patterns were originally concentrated around resource extraction and later industrial and manufacturing industries, which relied heavily on port and other transport facilities and heavy infrastructure. However, the emerging post-industrial alignments and integrated South-South and North-South trade agreements are producing new modern office towers, commercial free trade zones and enterprise development areas, increasingly connected by sophisticated information systems and global telecommunications. In order to attract and retain multinational and transnational corporations, increased pressure is placed on local governments to provide a high standard of services which will improve the efficiency of, and quality of life in, their cities.

Ironically, persisting and, arguably, worsening global debt patterns in the developing countries, and nationally and internationally imposed austerity measures have also dictated deep cuts in both new and recurrent spending for urban infrastructure. With new investments being effectively ruled out, and maintenance to existing infrastructure being postponed, the overall urban decline becomes more and more endemic. When infrastructure investment suffers in general, the situation for urban infrastructure targeted to the urban poor worsens commensurately. For urban residents living in poverty, an already acute situation — seen as a lack of urban services, in particular of clean drinking water, sewerage and solid waste removal — deteriorates further. The physical duality of extreme poverty and extreme wealth therefore becomes even more evident in the "indebted globalized city." Local governments are faced with increased competition for basic services to serve the needs of the general population and the poor, versus investment in those specialized services which initially are of use to more sophisticated international business interests. This situation has placed serious pressures on local governments and continues to pose, in an unflagging way, the persistent question of service delivery.

Debt-ridden governments throughout the world, not just those of the developing world, are examining ways of reforming the state, or "reinventing" themselves (Osborne and Gaebler 1992) In Canada, for example, massive cut-backs in the civil service and self-imposed austerity programmes in senior levels of government vastly limit the transfer of funding support to lower tiers of government. These changes have dictated a new line of questioning on how best to restructure local government in order to improve efficiency and create more effective governance. The municipalities in Toronto, for example, are currently engaged in debate over proposals to restructure the old boundaries of Metropolitan Toronto and create a Greater Toronto Area (GTA) with not only broader boundaries but also a reformed tax base.

The "less government" movement in Canada and developing countries alike, spawned by austerity measures in senior levels of government, has resulted in expanded local responsibilities not just for better services but for improved fiscal capacity and more efficient revenue generating capabilities. This greater responsibility is necessarily coupled with a heightened need for local government accountability and, ultimately, for improvements in the urban governance relationship.

When urban governance is considered within this shifting global context, the notion needs to be broadened. This expansive perspective of governance must include groups in civil society, not only those who are acting for survival in their situation of poverty, but also other private-sector actors who hold increasingly higher stakes in the cities. These groups will be more actively engaging with the local levels of government in the future, especially in the field of urban infrastructure and land development. While this implies new forms of civic action vis a vis local government, it also suggests new horizontal relationships across groups in civil society.

Local Governance and National Restructuring

At a national level, many countries are taking transitional steps towards democratization, and implementing extensive programs of state reform and structural adjustment with its accompanying decentralization strategy. These initiatives have all recently introduced dramatic changes within the urban territories managed by local governments in the developing world.

As many countries of the developing world undertake the initial steps necessary for democratic transitions, the role of local government is being reformulated and specified. This may stem from the Tocquevillian notion that local government is a training ground for democracy or simply from the assumption that government closer to the people is part and parcel of democratic reform. In either case, the emergence of local government as an important actor in the democratization movement is significant. The importance of addressing the notion of urban governance at the local level is thus at a critical point. Many of the chapters in this volume point to the need for a better understanding of the nature of urban politics. They also contribute knowledge on the nature of the governing relationship at the local level, and in the context of democratic reform. This comparative knowledge and exchange of experience is crucial at this time if this process of reform is to be furthered.

The emergence of structural adjustment programmes in many countries is creating new pressures on the city and causing new local government reforms to be initiated. Together with the usual elements — currency devaluation, trade liberalization, interest rate increases, removal of price controls/supports and other state subsidies, and privatization — it is the reform of state structures (including the decentralization of state powers and duties to sub-national governments and local authorities) that accompanies structural adjustment which make it one of the most significant forces affecting the role of local government.

Operating under structural adjustment programmes and suffering serious debt problems, central governments are examining ways to decentralize some of the burdens of service provision to the local level. Until only recently in many parts of Africa, Asia and Latin America, highly centralized states have been the norm. In certain instances, centralism is understandable as a condition perceived to be particularly important after struggles for independence and during periods of domestic and regional conflict. In other situations, centralism is embodied in the very nature of authoritarianism.

The results for the local level are the same nevertheless: local government has usually been the weak partner in the governing relationship within the developing world, lacking both political and financial power to act. Now, however, the World Bank reports that the decentralization effort has become far-ranging. Of the 75 developing countries with populations over five million, all but 12 have initiated some form of transfer of power to local governments (World Bank 1995, vii). The record of successful decentralization strategies is incomplete, as the chapters which follow will demonstrate more clearly.

In some cases, problems have been identified from early decentralization efforts. For example, while authority to deliver services is often transferred from central to local levels of government, the financial revenues are not. Intergovernmental transfer payments remain unreliable, and the powers to raise revenues locally are not in place. In general, real financial autonomy — the power to act on newly acquired local functions — remains weak. In addition, the need to train local government officials, to strengthen the civil service workplace and to make that sufficiently attractive to bring in and retain qualified staff, have been recognized as key elements if decentralization strategies are to be successfully implemented. These lessons from past experience are directing increased attention to ways of strengthening local government in order to improve the success rate in decentralization efforts.

Studies on decentralization have not been well integrated with studies on democratization, nor with the more recent discussions on governance. It has become clear that decentralization in no way guarantees more representative and accountable, nor more democratic, government at the local level. If better governance is to be achieved in cities throughout the world, the linkages between the various streams of research on democratization, decentralization and urban governance now need to be re-focused through a single lens.

Local Governance and the New Urban Setting

At a local level, the urban context for considering governance is also shifting. In addition to the persistent and rapid growth of Third World cities, urban violence, worsening poverty and other social costs all are aggravated by the adjustment process. This situation, as well as the seemingly perpetual incapacities of local governments to meet the demand for basic infrastructure, are focusing attention on the need for strengthening local government. At the same time, and in response to the state's inability to address these local problems, organizations in civil society are expanding. These associations are engaging in self-help programmes, building social networks and mutual support groups, and creating other forms of associational life in order to meet their needs for basic services.

The concept of urban governance allows us to address these two realities — the declining capacity of state structures, and the growing capacity of civil associations — in a connected and more meaningful way within the local political context. This new understanding goes beyond considerations of political participation in the traditional sense to prompt investigations into the new meaning of participation coupled with local action. Ideally, this scrutiny will help to promote new channels of engagement among actors in civil society, local government politicians and bureaucrats.

The rapid rate of urban growth in the developing world is well documented and need not be detailed here. There are two basic demographic facts which suggest that local government's strategic role in governance merits a heightened awareness. First, over half of the developing world will be urbanized by the year 2020. Second, the majority of the world's largest cities soon will be found in the developing world (UNCHS 1987; World Bank 1995).

Local service failures and deficiencies also call attention to the need to strengthen the local level of government. It is now estimated that "at least 170 million people in urban areas lack a source of potable water near their homes, and the water supplied to those who have access is often polluted. Access to basic sanitation, collection of solid wastes, and urban transport, as well as education and health services, pose similar problems" (World Bank 1995, 1).

In response to state incapacity to address these local problems, organizations in civil society have entered the void, often out of necessity, and have organized to meet these un-met needs and demands. There are now organizations for squatter communities, tenants' associations, savings and credit associations, area development committees, security committees, women's associations, and even independent research and management advisory bodies:

> It is not simply the breakdown of public infrastructure, service deterioration, or managerial inefficiency . . . It is the remarkable resilience of non-state agencies to challenge the monopoly of state institutions in shaping the character of cities today, which is of striking importance. In most Third World cities, the bulk of housing, transportation, employment and trade takes place outside formal state institutions (McCarney, Halfani and Rodriguez 1995, 101–2).

Associations in Latin American, Asian and African cities are no longer simply striving for subsistence needs. Their organizational mandate with respect to their local constituencies has broadened over time. Their own management capacity has deepened and become more sophisticated, and now extends into creating local policy. The civic organizations are imposing fees and taxes and/or membership fees to fulfil their mandates, and establishing organizational rules, procedures, and systems of accountability and transparency in their operations. As a result of the trust they have gained in their respective communities, their ability to organize their constituencies as political voice has also expanded. Therefore, these groups, together with other, more formal, private sector organizations, constitute an urban civil society which has increased its political and economic space and created a power block in the urban centres. While it is easy to view these forms of associational life in a positive way as a politically active and socially cooperative civil society, some reticence is also needed so as to not romanticize the role of urban civil society. In many instances these local actors have been moved to organize in order to access essential services that governments have opted out of providing, either intentionally or by default. This may be due to fiscal or management incapacity or it may be due to an overt policy choice by political officials as to which areas of the city will receive priority attention for services. Questions need to be more sharply posed: are the local associations, NGOs, CBOs and others unduly burdened in their activities? More specifically, if affluent neighbourhoods are receiving water, sewerage and solid waste collection services from government, are civil groups in the low-income neighbourhoods that are active in providing these same essential services, unfairly burdened? To what extent are these activities especially burdening women's groups? What are the opportunity costs of poor households participating in these community organizations for accessing services? In recognition of the constraints on time of households living in poverty, particularly female headed households, these questions need to be addressed when considering the evolution of new state societal relations in the urban governance effort.

Another constraint or "brake" on the tendency towards a romantic view of civil society is that concerned with fragmentation. When local government is weak in providing services and regulating the urban context, considerable fragmentation results in how urban services function across the city, and in how largely unplanned land use patterns become entrenched in the urban form. This physical fragmentation that occurs in the context of an active civil society vis a weak state at the local level can also lead to ungovernable cities in the long term. A local tax base necessary for the delivery of services becomes untenable, legitimacy in local government authority is undermined and increasing vulnerability in local government occurs which could in fact undermine democratic capacity at the local level. This local context leads us to reconsider the nature of politics at the local level and to reexamine the essence of state societal relationships in cities and the role of local government as a significant tier in the governing relationship.

Local Governance and Development Assistance

Within the international donor community, there is also a shifting context which affects the evolution of urban governance in the developing world. Over the past few years, the subject of "governance" has been increasingly addressed by the donor agencies. There have been notable movements in policy and programming within the urban sector of the World Bank and other agencies. These changes reveal a progression from projects in housing and infrastructure targeted to the poor during the 1970s, to city-wide urban management activities in the 1980s, to an increasing emphasis on strengthening local governments and creating "good governance" at the local level in the 1990s.

This recent transition in projects and programming reflects a deeper shift from the more technical aspects of managing cities to the more political aspects of governing cities. This movement heightens an awareness of the importance of local government, not just in terms of management capacity but also in terms of the community being served, its role in service delivery, and the nature of representative local government structures. As with previous shifts (McCarney 1994), the World Bank is arguing that these current shifts in emphasis are the product of learning from the experiences of their own project work over this same period (World Bank 1995).

Other international agencies have, in recent years, adopted the notion that local governments should "facilitate" rather than deliver shelter and urban services (UNCHS 1987). This reflects a broader trend to improve local government, not so much as the builder and supplier of local infrastructure and services, but as the body best equipped to create an "enabling" environment to facilitate others in the private sector and the community in such efforts.

The World Bank recently produced a major report, entitled *Governance: The Experience of the World Bank*, in which the term "governance" is defined as "the manner in which power is exercised in the management of the economic and social resources for development" (World Bank 1993, 2). While not addressing the local level of government specifically, other documents from the urban sector of the World Bank have begun to focus less on those traditional and technocratic concerns with urban management which were common to their work in the 1980s, and more on governance-related issues in the 1990s. Currently, the issues being discussed are related more to local government, covering aspects like "community action" and the degree to which local elections function as "referenda on local government perfor-mance." According to the World Bank, local participation can be made more effective:

> [L]ocal governments could take measures to ensure more regular consulta-tion with constituents, develop stronger channels for monitoring user satis-faction with local services, and link career progression of civil servants more strongly to their responsiveness to constituents (World Bank 1995, 7).

IV NEW CHALLENGES IN THE FIELD OF URBAN GOVERNANCE

Amidst these changes arising from the evolving global, national and local context, cities in the developing world are being confronted with critical challenges of governance. Enormous potential is being created for new frameworks within which to govern cities. Local government, considered here as the often neglected tier in the governing relationship, requires more in-depth analysis on a local basis if appropriate structures are to be created to ensure dynamic urban systems in the future. Based on the fore-going analysis, it is possible to point to new directions for future work on urban governance.

New Questions on Decentralization: Beyond the Technocratic and Administrative Perspective

A number of studies of decentralization programmes have documented the problems associated with mismatched financial authority and functional responsibility. This is a common trait in many of the decentralization expe-riences, cited both here in the chapters which follow and elsewhere (see, for example, Stren [1989] and Laleye and Olowu [1989] on Africa; El Sam-mani [1989] on the Sudan; and Kulaba [1989] on Tanzania).

As experience is gained in decentralization experiments, the need for a deeper analysis is also recognized. Not only are the structural and adminis-trative aspects of decentralization important to address, but even when these are in place, local government is not necessarily effective, nor representative. The more technocratic side of decentralization does not automatically instill a system of local government which is accountable and responsive to the needs and demands of the local citizens. If local government structures are to be developed which are representative of the local citizenry and have more open channels of communication and participation, then what is also required is an improved understanding of local political organizations, how they are organized and how they are linked to their own constituencies on the ground.

There is also a need to deepen our understanding of the intergovernmental relationships required to support the newly decentralized schemes being established. Is there a continuing role for senior levels of government in a context of strengthened local government with an empowered civil society engaging as active partners in the urban development process? Should a new role for senior levels of government with respect to local government be prescribed in the current reform era when austerity measures are dictating the nature of the decentralization exercise? To what extent in this trend towards "less government" is it also politically expedient to decentralize conflict to the local government level? To what extent should senior levels opt out of the governing relationship in a country's cities?

Since decentralization has not necessarily led to democratization at the local level, investigations which re-think the relationships among decentralization, democratization and governance need to be undertaken (McCarney, Halfani and Rodriguez 1995). The research which is presented in the chapters in this volume is an important first step in addressing this nexus and in considering these broader intergovernmental relationships.

New Forms of Engagement

A number of important studies have recently been completed on the problematic interface between socially based institutions and formal systems of government. For example, in *Strong Societies and Weak States: State Society Relations and State Capabilities in the Third World*, Joel Migdal (1988) identifies the dynamism of civil society which makes it strong — often resulting from actively organizing to meet the real and daily challenges of survival — and the conservatism and non-innovative aspects of the state which makes it weak — stemming from outmoded bureaucratic structures leftover from colonial periods. Another major inquiry of this nature by Akin Mabogunje (1995) examines the role of local political, economic and social institutions in cities. He traces numerous examples of these institutions, like the Hometown Voluntary Associations (HVAs) of the West Africa Region, the remarkable take-off of the community banking system in Nigeria, and the *harambee* schemes for local self help in Kenya. Due to their indigenous nature — having their growth based in, and development derived from, the local needs and concerns of their respective communities — they have gained the trust of the citizens they serve and people contribute money and labour to keep them in existence.

When formal local government structures meet these local institutions on the ground, however, problems of state-society engagement follow:

> It is thus not surprising that one of the problems of many cities in developing countries is the poor status of their management. By not giving appropriate legal status to the institutional structures familiar to the generality of the populace and to which they can relate, the peoples' participation has been considerably emasculated. By denying the people this participation, the formal imported institution denies itself the legitimacy to raise the revenue required for effective services in the city. But this in turn serves the purpose of some vested interests in the administration of urban centres that prefer a lack of accountability and transparency. The result is that many functions of urban administration continue to be provided by "informal" institutions that are recognized by the generality of the urban inhabitants, to which they are prepared to make significant financial contributions, and which are transparent and accountable to the people (Mabogunje 1995, 32).

These studies reflect a line of inquiry which demands new research on this interface as well as research on both sides of the state-society relationship. This three-pronged approach is necessary if the engagement, or in some cases re-engagement of the state and civil society is to be better understood and assisted. The chapters in this volume contribute to our understanding of the dual nature of the local system but they also point to the need for new research on the expected problems of engagement between civil institutions and the yet-evolving structures of local government. This knowledge is essential if, ultimately, Western models of local government in the developing world context are to be challenged and more indigenous models of local government are to be constructed. New directions in the field of urban governance currently hold tremendous potential for cities and future development progress.

Reconsidering Notions of Social Capital and Civil Society from a Global Perspective

At the same time that developing country scholars and the broader development community are examining current transitions to democracy in many countries, a significant inquiry in the developed world has been undertaken into the reasons for the success of some democratic governments and the failure of others. The project, conducted by Robert D. Putnam and two colleagues, Robert Leonardi and Raffaella Y. Nanetti, undertook an extensive case study of regional governments across Italy over a 20-year period. The book which resulted, *Making Democracy Work: Civic Traditions in Modern Italy* (1993) has become widely read and frequently quoted by scholars and practitioners. Its findings point to the critical importance of civic community for democracy to work best, with the most successful democracies being found in those regions of Italy with a legacy of civic engagement — in some instances traceable to the early Middle Ages. According to Putnam and his collaborators this engagement includes neighbourhood associations, choral societies, cooperatives, sports clubs, and mass-based parties. The central idea which emerges from this study is that strong horizontal networks of civic engagement help to foster social capital. In other words, they foster trust, reciprocity, community cooperation and mutual help.

Putnam's principles stressing the importance of civic engagement at the local level and the role of social capital in the governing relationship find much in common with those emerging in other spheres of the development community. These arguments emerge from studies in the developed-country context but reinforce the critical importance of local government and new concepts of governance for democratic transitions occurring within the developing world. Whereas Putnam is stressing the importance of social capital and its longevity, as it is nurtured over time by strong groups in civil society within the developed world, it has been shown in the foregoing that these same elements already exist in many cities of the developing world. The challenge is to preserve these elements which Putnam cites as being essential to making democracy work, while also strengthening the state side of the relationship in ways which enhance a city's social capital.

The risks are high. Stronger local governments can inadvertently weaken the role of groups in civil society, thereby destroying social capital essential for democratic function and preservation. The role of local government as an essential actor in the governing relationship cannot be underestimated either. Local associations have been active and have grown in strength because of weaknesses in state capacity. In some instances, these associations are unduly burdened to supply essential services that ought to be the responsibility of local governments. In other instances their activities in attempting to fill this void lead to chaos and fragmentation in city services. This physical fragmentation points to the potential of a parallel fragmentation in the governance of cities which will eventually put the democratic project itself in jeopardy. A new alignment between the state and civil society — a challenge embodied in the very notion of governance itself — constitutes the core challenge now facing cities in the developing world. The dual possibility for fundamental change in local government and empowerment of the urban community, creates potential and space for new and potent forms of governance in the future.

Note

1　The paper referred to (by Halfani, McCarney and Rodriguez) was prepared in 1991 at the suggestion of the Ford Foundation to add to the thematic discussion on urban research at the Annual Meeting of the GURI network in Cairo in 1992. Since governance was so poorly defined in 1991, the paper reviewed the then-current usage of the term governance, considered how it could be applied to the local level, and developed a working definition of governance (stressing the *relationship* between government and civil society to overcome the state-centric approach dominating the literature at the time).The draft paper was then distributed to the GURI network for consideration by the urban researchers, as the theme of governance had been selected for more detailed investigation for the project's second phase. The paper has since been published in final form in Volume 4 of the GURI project volumes and appears in the reference list to the present chapter as McCarney, Halfani and Rodriguez (1995).

References

Castells, Manuel. 1983. *The City and the Grassroots*. Berkeley: University of California Press.

De Soto, Hernando. 1989. *The Other Path: The Invisible Revolution in the Third World*. London: I.B. Taurus, and New York: Freedom House.

Dicken, Peter. 1992. *Global Shift: The Internationalization of Economic Activity*. London: Paul Chapman.

El Sammani, Mohamed O. et al. 1989. "Management Problems of Greater Khartoum." In Richard Stren and Rodney R. White (eds.), *African Cities in Crisis: Managing Rapid Urban Growth*. Boulder, Colorado: Westview Press, pp. 247–75.

Kulaba, Saitiel. 1989. "Local Government and the Management of Urban services in Tanzania." In Richard Stren and Rodney R. White (eds.), *African Cities in Crisis: Managing Rapid Urban Growth*. Boulder, Colorado: Westview Press, pp. 203–45.

Laleye O. and Dele Olowu. 1989. "Decentralization in Africa." In World Bank and Instituto Italo-Africano, *Strengthening Local Governments in Sub-Saharan Africa*. An EDI Policy Seminar Report (No. 21). Washington, DC: Economic Development Institute of the World Bank

Lofchie, Michael F. 1989. "Perestroika Without Glasnost: Reflections on Structural Adjustment." In *Beyond Autocracy in Africa*. Working Papers from the Inaugural Seminar of the Governance in Africa Programme, The Carter Centre of Emory University, Atlanta, Georgia, February 17–18.

Mabogunje, Akin L. 1995. "Local Institutions and an Urban Agenda for the 1990s." In Richard Stren with Judith Kjellberg Bell (eds.), *Urban Research in the Developing World: Vol. 4, Perspectives on the City*. Toronto: Centre for Urban and Community Studies, University of Toronto.

Mabogunje, Akin L. 1990. "Urban Planning and the Post-Colonial State Africa: A Research Overview." *African Studies Review* 33(2): 121–203.

McCarney, Patricia L. 1994. "Shifting Agendas Inside Donor Agencies." Paper presented to the Special Program for Urban and Regional Studies of Developing Areas (SPURS) at MIT, Cambridge, MA, April 27.

McCarney, Patricia L., Mohamed Halfani and Alfredo Rodriguez. 1995. "Towards an Understanding of Governance: The Emergence of an Idea and its Implication for Urban Research in the Developing Countries." In Richard Stren with Judith Kjellberg Bell (eds.), *Urban Research in the Developing World: Vol. 4, Perspectives on the City*. Toronto: Centre for Urban and Community Studies, University of Toronto.

Migdal, Joel S. 1988. *Strong Societies and Weak States: State Society Relations and State Capabilities in the Third World*. Princeton: Princeton University Press.

Osborne, David and Ted Gaebler. 1992. *Reinventing Government: How the Entrepreneurial Spirit is Transforming the Public Sector*. Reading, MA.: Addison-Wesley.

Putnam, Robert D. with Robert Leonardi and Raffaella Y. Nanetti. 1993. *Making Democracy Work: Civil Traditions in Modern Italy*. Princeton, NJ: Princeton University Press.

Stren, Richard. 1989. "Urban Local Government in Africa." In Richard E. Stren and Rodney R. White (eds.), *African Cities in Crisis: Managing Rapid Urban Growth*. Boulder, Colorado: Westview Press, pp. 20–36.

Turner, John F.C. 1990. "Barriers, Channels and Community Control." In David Cadman and Geoffrey K. Payne (eds.), *Living City: Towards a Sustainable Future*. London: Routledge, pp.181–91.

UNCHS (Habitat). 1987. *Global Report on Human Settlements 1986.* New York: Oxford University Press.

World Bank. 1993. *Governance: The World Bank Experience.* Washington, DC: The Bank.

_____. 1995. *Better Urban Services: Finding the Right Incentives.* Washington, DC: The Bank.

Section II

Latin America

2 The Challenges for Urban Governance in Latin America: Reinventing the Government of Cities

ALFREDO RODRÍGUEZ AND
LUCY WINCHESTER

I INTRODUCTION

The Latin American city, a key nucleus in the development of the region, is experiencing fundamental transformations in its political, social and economic structures. One relevant aspect of this process is the renewal of the relative importance of local space in relation to the central state and national spaces. The expression of discontent and conflicts related to urban poverty and social problems — inequality, the instability of the work force, and the impoverishment of the city — appear to be generated and experienced locally. These problems represent unsatisfied demands and unresolved conflicts derived from the competitive nature of economic, social and political interests in the urban setting.

In addition to constituting the physical space where the majority of Latin Americans live — Latin America, as a region, has the highest level of urbanization in the world — the city is a physical and symbolic matrix of the modernization of our societies (Urban Management Programme 1995, 1). Global phenomena (globalization, democratization and the consumption of global images) and national phenomena (structural adjustment, the reform of the state and the specificity of the historical development of each nation-state) are locally manifested in the city. These local expressions include social disintegration, economic segregation and exclusion, violence, environmental degradation, poverty, and the reconstitution of the collective actors of society, to name a few. Collectively, they constitute major challenges for urban inhabitants and urban development decision-makers alike.

In the 1990s, the poor in Latin America — persons with income below the poverty line — are concentrated in cities. This is a new demographic reality and a growing phenomenon, one that has deepened over the past 20 years. Although the total percentage of poor in the region has only slightly

increased, the poor passed from 29 percent to 39 percent of the urban population between 1970 and 1990. Over the same period, the poor rural population decreased from 67 to 61 percent (CEPAL 1994, 157). The major concentrations of poverty are now situated in urban areas, which indicates that
the situation has practically reversed in two decades. While 63 percent of the
poor in Latin America were found in rural areas in 1970, today, 59 percent
of them live in urban areas. In absolute numbers, it also signifies an increase
in urban poor from 44 million to 115 million persons (CEPAL 1994, 157).
This concentration of poverty in urban areas has created new and growing
demands for urban land, infrastructure and services.

In Latin America, the effects of the economic crisis of the late 1970s and
structural adjustment of the 1980s have been much stronger in urban areas
than in rural areas. The poor face a far more complicated social situation in
urban areas; there is a greater concentration of poverty and, at the same
time, a greater inequality in income distribution. Moreover, the opening of
Latin American economies and structural adjustment reforms have had significant effects on the urban labour market. According to Ricardo Infante
(1993, 6) there are two dimensions of the labour market, employment and
salaries, which have been negatively affected by these transitions. Infante
(1993, 7–10) suggests that the nature of employment problems has
changed in three ways: there has been an increase in the available urban
labour force, a decrease in the quality of occupations, and an increase and
change in the composition of unemployment. The economic reforms have
also signified a deterioration in urban incomes in the region, due to salary
adjustments and a contraction in real incomes in the urban informal sector.
CEPAL (1994, 35–45) indicates that this tendency has been maintained
even in cases where there has been a recovery. In such cases, low-income
social sectors have increased their participation in the labour market in
occupations with very low wages, while the professional and technical sectors have achieved comparatively greater increases in their real wages.

The clearest result of these changes in the labour market is an impoverishment of the urban labour force. It is now a labour force with high
rates of unemployment and instability, with unregulated work conditions,
with reduced minimum wages and high levels of informality. This impoverishment generates new social and economic demands in the city's public space. Just as there have been increases in the concentration of the poor
in the city, and in income inequalities (due to working conditions) of the
urban inhabitants, the city itself has become impoverished over the last
two decades (Herzer 1992; Prates Coelho and Diniz 1995, 37–40).

In the case of Argentina, Alberto Minujin and Gabriel Kessler (1995, 21–2) estimate that the whole of society lost almost 40 percent of its income between 1980 and 1990. They point out that "by impoverishing ourselves as a society we have also lost goods and services that collectively belonged to us as citizens: deteriorated hospitals, overloaded schools, toll roads that replace free ones, privatized places that once were public, a neglected environment, more expensive services, new taxes without an increase in income." These are just some of the terms of a society's collective impoverishment. This decline is expressed by a reduction of the general capacity of cities to maintain public services and physical infrastructure and, in extreme cases, to maintain public security. A city in extreme poverty is a city in crisis in the endowment of its collective goods and services.

The cities function because different social groups — neighbourhood organizations, the poor, fathers of families, NGOs, centres for mothers — assume the compensating tasks of lending public services (Pírez 1994a, 2). However, there are cases in which the users go beyond the realization of compensating or complementary activities, and the services become autonomous. For example, transportation and electrical energy (from individual generators) in the city of Santo Domingo (Dominican Republic) are at least partially supplied in this manner (Douzant and Faxas 1991). Similarly, there are cooperatives in Buenos Aires (Argentina) that provide potable water as an autonomously delivered service (Brunstein 1991; Montaño and Coing 1991; Rodríguez 1991).

Clearly, the collapse of urban services has distinct effects on the physical and social structure of the city and on the efficiency of productive urban activities. When public services disintegrate, urban sectors break off from the city and become autonomous. Eventually, the city stops functioning as an interrelated entity (Pírez 1994a). When public services do not exist, literally, the urban conglomeration stops making sense and limits the competitiveness of the activities located within it. For example, Coing (1989) indicates that the development of modern economic activities in cities makes it impossible to assure an electrical service that can avoid daily power failures.

A key condition for the sustainability of the city is its capacity to combine the different demands originating in the market, civil society and the state, and distribute benefits and costs without impairing the stability and continuity of the society's development. We consider it important to investigate the range of conflict resolution strategies and their implications that could, and do, operate in our cities. In short, we are interested in how we may incorporate the demands of the city's social sectors into a functional strategy for urban governance. The sustainable development of the city, and that of Latin American countries, depends on their effective management, and that, in turn, depends on the form and process of governing the city.

II HOW ARE THE POOR INCORPORATED INTO THE CITIES?

In response to the question how social demands may be effectively incorporated in the new urban setting, different responses emerge.

The Municipality

Many see in the institution of the municipality, the instance of urban government with the capacity to articulate and join together the different emerging demands from the civil society, the marketplace and the state. Thus, they assign an active and positive role to the municipality in the sustainable development of the Latin American cities.

It is true that municipalities have gained political importance during the last 10 to 15 years and will take on more importance in the future. This revaluation of the municipality is a result of the democratization processes of the 1980s, other reforms to the state, administrative decentralization and deconcentration, and the application of compensatory social policies to alleviate poverty, amongst many other factors. Nevertheless, the Latin American municipality is not yet consolidated, and is now undergoing a process of institutional change. Decentralization has strengthened the administrative aspects of governance, but the assignment of responsibilities which this signifies has frequently been made without a corresponding transfer of effective authority, and without access to adequate financial resources (Prates Coelho and Diniz 1995, 41–2). The process of democratization has begun with the establishment of participatory politics and mechanisms for citizen and community participation. However, the municipality remains limited in its response to expressed demands. Municipalities are generally weak institutions, with little economic, political and ideological power. They are limited in their autonomy, authority, legitimacy and management capacity (Prates Coelho and Diniz 1995, 25–30). Furthermore, municipalities sometimes act with little clarity as to their role in local political life — as the social uprisings in different cities seem to indicate.[1]

Participation

There is some suggestion that a greater democratization of local decision-making apparatuses is needed, such that civil society might better share the management of development and more clearly express its real needs to its administrators. This reflects a recognition of the strong social movements which have been instrumental in the impulse towards democracy all over the world — especially in Latin America. During the 1980s, these movements were political agents, with concrete agendas and with a horizontal relation to the state. They, and "the third wave" organizational NGOs that supported them, formed a real political opposition to the power of the state.

There is currently another reality. The implementation of the new public management model — decentralized but vertical, contract oriented and privatized in the delivery of services — has made NGOs more state-like. They are now contracted and financed by the state to deliver a social service; a phenomenon observed in the contracting of NGOs by publicly supported "social funds."[2] Their ability to be contracted rests on their efficiency and their capacity to compete. In this model, participation typically becomes passive and of an informative nature and does not resemble, as a rule, the active participation and democratic revindication of the 1980s (Gaete 1995, 2).

Politics and the Market

Another dimension of urban governance refers to the relationship between politics and the economy. In theory, political parties are one of the "authentic" channels for the expression, negotiation and resolution of social demands. However, the political parties in Latin America have become discredited. This is clearly expressed by the president of the International Christian Democracy, Panamanian Ricardo Arias, who stated: "the fight for the democratization of our countries was by far the most important goal of our people. Now the people have other necessities, and it is these that are so difficult for us to recognize" (*El Mercurio* 1995, 11).

For many, the market also appears to contain the solutions to social problems. However, as we saw with the effects of adjustments in the urban labour market, the free market does not solve all problems. Furthermore, the market produces distortions, production itself is problematic. There are always external conditions related to the decisions of production, whether these decisions are generated by the state or by the market. Robert Heilbroner (1992, 89) suggests that, while production occurs primarily in the private sector, the conflicts generated by these external conditions originate in the marketplace. However, the costs and consequences of those conflicts are shared by civil society, individuals and the various social sectors. How, then, can we govern our cities and effectively incorporate emerging social demands in the cities?

It is a difficult question because its answer demands the empowerment of the citizenry and a parallel change and strengthening of our institutions. In order to achieve this, it is vital to have a true understanding of every city's local political life. Otherwise, any changes will not be able to incorporate the cultural characteristics and specific operating mechanisms of the local society into its system of management.[3] To disclaim or ignore these details is, by definition, bad governance. A blind eye to this message will create problems of governability and might require another re-invention of a city's government.

Pedro Pírez (1994a, 4–5) also considers the problem of incorporating society's demands in local governance. He maintains that the poor are treated in two ways: through formal and political means, in the case of democratic strategies; or through repression and territorial exclusion, in the case of authoritarian strategies. These strategies do not refer only to the incorporation of "the poor" but also to other social sectors and problems. He suggests that democratic governing strategies tend to develop experiences based, in some way, upon integration. This could be derived from the processes of political representation, symbolic representation, forms of political clientelism, and/or direct participation (Pírez 1994a, 5).

The cases of effective participation of the popular social classes in government are rare. Taking into account diverse experiences of popular participation in Latin America, Hilda Herzer and Pedro Pírez (1988, 139) identify two fundamental conditions which must be present for this to occur: (1) the existence of popular organizations with some presence at the local level; and (2) the occupation of positions in the municipality by parties or individuals favourable to community participation.[4]

In conclusion, they indicate that, of these two conditions, the second is determinant. In order for participation to exist, a favourable attitude of local government is necessary (Prates Coelho and Diniz 1995, 32–40). This conclusion is important to us because it shows, in the broadest terms, that the relationship between civil society and the state is not dichotomous, but instead that it is mutually reinforcing. Thus, Franz Hinkelammert

(1992, 199) affirms that the state and civil society "are directly coordinated, there is no civil society if there is no state that accepts and promotes it."

Identifying two ways of incorporating the city's social sectors — democratic and authoritative — does not mean that only one of these will prevail, nor that they do not intermix. In this sense, Pírez (1994a) reveals that the city, and its economic, social and political processes, fluctuates between legality and illegality, and between political confrontation and consensus.

III URBAN GOVERNANCE

The urban governance approach allows us to understand how Latin American cities are governed. Governance refers to the pattern of formal and informal relationships between the agents that operate within and throughout a city, and how these agents make urban development decisions.[5] These include government institutions and their roles — the municipality, regional government, local representations of central government. It also includes all the agents that function outside the sphere of the state — local, national and international businesses, political parties, social movements, NGOs and so on. It encompasses their official and legal relationships, and their informal relationships based on local culture and political life (United Nations 1995, 4–10). Our empirical knowledge is limited in this field in Latin America; urban studies typically do not analyze the city from this perspective. Thus, this is an important research area, both in the search for solutions to the problems manifested in cities, as well as in the need to manage the city strategically from a global, national, regional and local perspective.

The perspective of governance allows us to see that the government of the city is not represented exclusively by the institution of local government. Coalitions of different social sectors — including the business community, labour unions and social movements — and other branches and institutions of international and national government also influence how the city is governed, sometimes decisively. The final distribution of the costs and benefits related to social conflict resolution depends on the capacity of these coalitions and institutions to influence and act in the public space of the city.

In order to reinvent the government of the city, it is first necessary to understand the city. Our hypothesis is that social discontent, social problems, poverty and so on, are conflicts that emerge because political, administrative and social structures have not adapted to the reality of Latin American cities. This reality is expressed as much by an increasingly globalized urban economy as by the impoverishment and polarization of urban civil society resulting from these worldwide economic changes and adjustments. It is also expressed in the cultural dimensions of local life — political and otherwise — in the city. The sustainable development of the Latin American city implies an effective incorporation of social conflicts, and the consequent demands, into the decision-making process. This requires the construction of an appropriate apparatus for the management of urban development, which amounts to no less than the re-invention of city governments. This is the political dimension of the construction of a democratic city. The other dimension is economic, but a discussion of this component escapes the reach of this article.[6] The part of the economic element of governance that is worthy of note here is that it provides for a confluence of social and economic policy:

> Its application presupposes overcoming the tradition of isolated interventions or homogenous policies as well as the techno-bureaucratic urban planning models directed at maintaining a platform for exports. Rather, the policies must be directed at the conformation of a third economic pole as well as creating an adequate environment for globally oriented business (Coraggio 1994, 252–3).

Reinventing the government of the city involves a city project: a collaboration between municipalities, citizens, other social actors, political parties, the business community and other representatives of national government and its institutions. The development and implementation of this project consists of an effective democratization of the public space of the city, where the different interests have equal access to, and real participation in, the decision-making processes with regards to the administration, production and reproduction of the city.[7] Above all, reinventing the government of the city means creating a shared vision of the city and a long-term commitment to it. It is a project built on the foundation of a continuous process of strategic planning and, as such, it empowers local democratic institutions — the citizenry, municipalities, political parties and other local government institutions (Borja 1995).

This is a process of institutional and cultural change that, as with all processes of social change, awakens certain resistance along many fronts:

- Among agents of central governments that lack trust in regional and local governments and their management capabilities, or fear that the process will fall prey to clientelism;
- Among the traditional political actors, whose power was always supported by a central state and who see a possible loss or redistribution of their political clout;
- Among local political actors who oppose the participation of new actors with political power;
- Among municipal employees who see the change as a threat to their style of public administration;
- Among the social actors whose point of reference, through networks of clientele, was always the central government (Velásquez 1994).

Accordingly, we wish to highlight two dimensions that require attention in the re-invention of local government in Latin America (Stren and Gombay 1995, 7). The first is in reference to the political dimension of local governments, particularly political participation. This is a relationship between civil and political society, which at the local level is expressed through the development of an active citizenry (Prates Coelho and Diniz 1995, 44). The second refers to the structural dimension of local governance, related to the reform of the state in Latin America and the development of new models of intergovernmental relations at the local level.

In the following section, we will suggest a number of specific proposals — related to the two dimensions mentioned above — for strengthening the three local level institutions necessary for the democratization of the public space of the city: the citizenry, the municipality and metropolitan areas.

The Citizenry

In general, there are four particular circumstances, among others, under which Latin America's latent citizenry becomes visible. It is exposed in extreme situations, such as natural disasters, local emergencies, political crises and periods of extreme scarcity. It surfaces for elections. It is also revealed in occasional, symbolic identifications with places of birth or residence — the town, neighbourhood, the corner. Finally, it is present as well in urban social movements.

How can citizens be stimulated and developed? First the people must be made to identify positively with the place where they live. There are several influencing factors. One is that the place must offer a decent standard of living, satisfying the basic need for infrastructure, services, landscape and so on, and that this living standard is recognized by other communities. Another factor is that the place has a history in which the inhabitant feels to be an actor or heir. Still another is that the place has its own identifiable local culture, or an "imaginary" one that gives it a valuable symbolic identity. Where this positive identification does not exist, it must be created. For this, there are a variety of approaches. It is necessary to create a physical identification with spatial landmarks, like plazas, monuments, public spaces, green areas and shopping centres. It is necessary to modify a negative history, or create a history through activities and rites that generate a culture of their own, such as campaigns, parties, festivals or other events. Of course, a minimum level of public goods and services must be insured (García 1995, 89–90).

Second, it is necessary to develop an interest in participating in local affairs. For some, this interest is taken as the personal satisfaction attained through actions which positively influence the community, regardless of the actual impact. This feeling must be positive, and it must be considered a civic value. However, this sentiment and moralization alone do not necessarily create citizenship. Interest in affecting or influencing local affairs is directly related to the achievement of gratification — "improving the neighbourhood." It also comes from being established as a valid intermediary with authorities, not in the sense of fame or recognition, but rather in having power. Behind the gratification there is a concrete result.

It is here that the municipality plays a key role. The municipality can develop or destroy interest in influencing local affairs. If a municipal government wishes to facilitate this interest, it must establish mechanisms and channels for popular participation. These structures must grant real power to the people within a legitimate framework which respects the municipality's own power for decision-making as well as that of the citizens. From the people's perspective, it is also possible to destroy interest in affecting local affairs. The limited flexibility of organizations, their rigidity or an overly bureaucratic spirit will not promote the development of an active and empowered citizenship.

Third, it must be remembered that "identities are not just constituted in the polarized class conflicts but also in institutional action contexts — a factory, a hospital, a school — the functioning of which is possible as long as all of its participants, superiors or underlings, regard it as a 'negotiated order'" (Garcia 1995, 175). Thus, from a cultural perspective, the importance of negotiation in the constitution of urban identities is redeemed. Not only are the conflicts between social movements and local governments important, but so are the negotiations between them, and the achievement of joint activities. The notion of citizenship is related to the creation of a "public" sphere, which is not subordinated to the state, nor dissolved in civil society, but rather is redeemed in the tension between both (Garcia 1995, 189).

Finally, in this process of "creating" a citizenry, genuine possibilities for influencing local affairs must be guaranteed. And in a context of decentralization and deconcentration, the central axis of this system must be participation in the municipality.

The Municipality

As we indicated earlier, municipal systems have been reformed in recent years in almost all of Latin America. Mayoral elections, increases in municipal budgets, transfer of power or faculties, and laws which facilitate participation in aspects of local administration are all evidence of this process. This represents substantial progress, but in itself it does not guarantee genuine opportunities for influencing local affairs. For that, there are few truly effective means. In spite of the existence of formal institutions, there is a culture of bureaucracy which frequently immobilizes or impedes — or at the least does not facilitate — the capacity of local people to influence local affairs. The interest, real or created, in participating in the management of local affairs requires a "conduit," formal or informal, which gives it shape and direction, and permits it to flow (Prates Coelho and Diniz 1995, 34). To fulfill this function of conduit, participatory mechanisms must be created where none existed previously. If the existing municipal culture obstructs these channels or impedes these mechanisms, it must be changed. In this system of citizen participation, the flow of information is an essential element (Prates Coelho and Diniz 1995, 17). The municipality should communicate to its citizens not only their duties, but also their rights in community management. At the same time, citizens should go beyond simply manifesting their preferences through voting for one or the other government project, or for one or the other candidate, and make full use of the available channels that promote their influence. This brings us back to creating an interest in participation.

In order to participate effectively in the process of coordinating the demands of differing interests within the city environment, the municipal institution must combine administrative efficiency with a true capacity to govern. This governing capacity, or "good local governance," requires a decentralized state to grant adequate power to the municipality. There are three characteristics which municipalities should have in order to exercise this power. First, they require the capacity to command and direct government, policies, and programmes. Second, they need the capacity to coordinate between different political institutions and interests. Finally, a municipality must have the capacity to implement its own decisions (Prates Coelho and Diniz 1995).

In other words, a municipality must have effective control over the definition of its priorities and strategies. It has to know how to manage the conflicts inherent in the political process. To do so, municipalities must integrate the interests of other levels of government, other government agencies, and other local claimants, and negotiate with them. Ultimately, a municipality also needs the leadership and authority to implement its policies and programmes. In many Latin American countries, this means additional reforms to the laws or codes of municipal administration, and granting them additional powers and resources. It would also be beneficial if municipalities were given greater flexibility in the administration of their duties. One place to start would be in the design of inter- and intra-governmental agreements to implement and administer local programmes and policies.

Metropolitan Areas and Intergovernmental Relations

The resolution of conflicts in cities requires different levels of negotiation and decision. The metropolitan institutional framework is quite complex in the majority of Latin American cities. With the exception of Quito, there is not one effective metropolitan government in the region. In the remainder of the cities, one generally finds a great deal of institutional and geographical fragmentation at the governmental level. The re-invention of city government structure requires a clarification of the roles and responsibilities of the different government agencies that operate within the city sphere (Pírez 1994b). This could manifest itself in the creation of a government authority of the metropolitan area based on the functions that it should fulfill, one that would not damage the autonomy and authority of the municipalities nor the identity of local communities (United Nations 1995, 15). In other cases, this could be an institutional strengthening of central ministries. Without a doubt, not all conflicts that arise within a city can or should be resolved there. Often they require solutions from the central government, in coordination with local government agencies and the municipality.

Notes

1 Caracas 1989: social explosion, "el Caracazo." Buenos Aires 1989: assaults on supermarkets and stores. Santiago del Estero, Argentina 1993: burning of government buildings and houses of politicians and public officials. Curanilahue, Chile 1994: taking of roads in protest of the closure of coal mines. Chiapas 1994: occupation of 12 cities. These are only a few of the social uprisings which have occurred in Latin American cities over the last decade.

2 Structural adjustment measures have significant social costs, at least in the short run. During the period of transition, poorer groups suffer disproportionately due to their vulnerability and lack of economic flexibility. For this reason, compensatory measures have been adopted in order to mitigate the social costs of adjustment. These "safety nets," which embody the so-called "human side of development," generally involve focused social services and various types of project-based social funds. Funds for combatting poverty have been created in 18 countries in the region (CEPAL 1994, 115–16). Although initially of a temporary nature, they are currently considered viable financial intermediaries in a new model for development and the implementation of social policy.

3 Néstor García (1995, 178–80) illustrates this point in describing the complexity of the social work — modernization — in a Bolivian migrants' community in a neighbourhood of Buenos Aires. In a programme "to democratize the access to culture and to promote new practices of political participation that bypassed the existing authoritarianism in the social fabric, a paradoxical dilemma occurred: the promoters with democratizing intentions discovered that it was necessary to negotiate with internal bosses of the neighbourhood to acquire the necessary power to convoke and to insert the program in the local social-cultural structures."

4 Herzer and Pírez (1988) noted that a particular feature of almost all participatory experiences is the close relationship with municipal executives (mayors) as opposed to representative organizations.

5 There are few alternative proposals to the dominant neoliberal focus. José Luís Coraggio proposes a strategy of urban development with a perspective of human development which contemplates a strategic strengthening of the

urban popular economy (Coraggio 1994). Michael Storper (1994, 58) indicates that there are two trajectories for economic development: technology and conventions. He proposes the construction of institutions that promote trust, security and cooperation. These institutions must "be situated in the existing context of the actors, they should not be imposed as formal rules against the will of the actors involved."

6 In speaking of decisions on development, we refer to the visible decisions — policies, programmes as well as the "invisible decisions." We feel that in these invisible decisions — that is, the process through which problems or topics of concern do not enter the legitimate decision-making process — are important clues as to how power and costs are distributed between the agents in a city (Bachrach and Baratz 1969).

7 Public space is the space where the interconnectedness of political decisions and their effects on the use of social and economic resources for development is clearly observed. In this space, representatives or agents from the market, and different sectors of civil society and the state, converge and manifest their interdependence. It is here that the decision-making system resolves social, economic and political problems and conflicts generated by production for development.

References

Bachrach, Peter and Morton S. Baratz. 1969. *Power & Poverty: Theory and Practice.* New York: Oxford University Press.

Borja, Jordi. 1995. "El rostro urbano del socialismo." Document presented to the Conferencia Internacional Socialista, Bolonia, January 28–29.

Brunstein, Fernando. 1991. "Descentralización de servicios urbanos, experiencias cooperativas de saneamiento en el Gran Buenos Aires." *Actas de Coloquio CIUDAGUA Andina.* Quito: Ciudad es Unidas, Federación Mundial Ciudad es Unidas (FMCU).

CEPAL. 1994. *Panorama Social de América Latina.* Santiago: Naciones Unidas, CEPAL.

Coing, Henri. 1989. "Revisitando los servicios urbanos." Document presented to the Seminario sobre Servicios Urbanos, REDES, Sao Paulo, September 4–7.

Coraggio, José Luís. 1994. "A construçao de uma economia popular como horizonte para cidades sem rumo." In Luís César de Queiroz Ribeiro and Orlando Alves Dos Santos Júnior (eds.), *Globalizaçao, fragmentaçao e reforma urbana. O futuro das cidades brasileiras na crise.* Río de Janeiro: Civilizaçap Brasileira, pp. 221–259.

Douzant, Denise and Laura Faxas. 1991. "Equipements urbains et services de remplacement: le cas de Santo Domingo, République Dominicaine." Document presented to the Coloquio Grands Métropoles d'Afrique et d'Amérique Latine: équipements urbains et pratiques culturelles, Toulouse, November 27–29.

García Canclani, Néstor. 1995. *Consumidores y Ciudadanos.* México, DF: Ed. Grijalbo.

Gaete, Hector. 1995. "Invertir en participación ciudadana: Un requisito esencial para fortelecer la gestión de los actores del cambio urbano." Document presented to the Cuarto Seminario de Desarrollo Urbano Los Actores del Cambio Urbano, Universidad del Bío Bío, Departamento de Planificación y Diseño Urbano, Concepción, August 10–11.

Heilbroner, Robert. 1992. *Twenty-first Century Capitalism.* Toronto: Anansi.

Herzer, Hilda. 1992. "Ajuste, medio ambiente e investigación. A propósito de la ciudad de Buenos Aires." In *Habitat y cambio social.* Salvador: FUNDASAL.

Herzer, Hilda and Pedro Pírez. 1988. "Vida política local y construcción de la ciudad en América Latina." *Estudios Sociales Centroamericanos* 52.

Hinkelammert, Franz. 1992. "Nuevo rol del Estado en el desarrollo latinoamericano." In *Nuevo rol del Estado en el desarrollo latinoamericano.* Caracas: Asociación Latinoamericana de organizaciones de Promoción, 191–204.

Infante, Ricardo (ed.). 1993. *Deuda social; desafío de la equidad.* Santiago: PREALC, OIT.

El Mercurio (Santiago). 1995. "Partidos Políticos: El Desencanto de América." August 27.

Minujin, Alberto and Gabriel Kessler. 1995. *La nueva pobreza en la Argentina.* Buenos Aires: Ed. Planeta Argentina.

Montaño, Iraida and Henri Coing. 1991. "Las cooperativas de agua en Argentina. Un cuestionamiento a las formas de gestión tradicionales." In *Actas de Coloquio CIUDAGUA Andina.* Quito: Ciudades Unidas, FMCU.

Pírez, Pedro. 1994a. "Gobernabilidad/gobernanza y pobreza en la ciudad (una película con final abierto)." Document presented to the Subregional Seminar of GURI Pobreza Urbana y Gobernabilidad, Centro de Estudios Sociales y Educación SUR, Santiago, July 4–5.

Pírez, Pedro. 1994b. "Govierno local en capitales provinicales en Argentina: Los casos de Resistencia y La Rioja." In Alfredo Rodriguez and Fabio Velasquez (eds.), *Municipio y servicios públicos: Goviernos locales en ciudades intermedias de América Latina.* Santiago, Chile: Ediciones SUR, pp. 25–50.

Prates Coelho, Magda and Eli Diniz. 1995. "Local Governance and Poverty in Brasil." Document presented to the Regional Seminar GURI, Otavalo, Ecuador, January 17–20.

Rodríguez, Alfredo. 1991. "Cuatro historias de servicios públicos en América Latina y una explicación." Document presented to Seminar Servicios Públicos en Ciudades de América Latina, Universidad de Valencia, Valencia, Spain, April 5–6.

Storper, Michael. 1994. "Desenvolvimento territorial na economia global do aprendizado: o desafio dos países em desenvolvimiento." In Luís César de Queiroz Ribeiro and Orlando Alves Dos Santos Júnior (eds.), *Globalizaçao, fragmentaçao e reforma urbana. O futuro das cidades brasileiras na crise*. Río de Janeiro: Civilizaçap Brasileira, pp. 23–64.

Stren, Richard and Christie Gombay. 1995. "Changes in Urban Governance in South America." Mimeo. Centre for Urban and Community Studies. University of Toronto.

United Nations. 1995. "Metropolitan Governance: Patterns and Leadership." Document presented to United Nations High-Level Interregional Meeting on Metropolitan Governance: Patterns and Leadership, Quito, April 18–20.

Urban Management Programme. 1995. "Documento técnico sobre la ciudad latinoamericana: retos actuales y propuestas." Document presented to the Encuentro Preparatorio de Habitat II, Rio de Janeiro, January 1.

Velásquez, Fabio. 1994. Presentation in seminar-workshop "Decentralization and Social Policy in Latin America," Quito, November.

3 Urban Governance in Brazil

MAGDA PRATES COELHO[1]

I INTRODUCTION

The federal republic of Brazil is divided administratively into states and municipalities, and has a presidential government. It is a highly urbanized country of 146 million inhabitants: 75.5 percent of this total population live in 5,000 municipalities, and 47 percent in 14 cities with more than one million inhabitants. Brazil is also a country where 29 percent of the total population live in poverty. Currently, it is facing one of its greatest historical challenges: to design a new development programme. This new model has to merge two broad goals. First, it must make headway in the fight against abject poverty, a social problem of emergency proportions in Brazil. Second, it needs to introduce reforms and adjustment policies with the dual aim of reducing social and income inequalities and strengthening democratic institutions.

Political and Economic Characteristics of Brazil in the 1990s

From a political perspective, the 1980s may be viewed as a "prosperous decade." After more than 20 years of authoritarianism (1964–86), Brazil returned to a democratic regime and entered the 1990s as an institutionally decentralized state. The Constitution promulgated in 1988 maintained representative democracy, instituted a direct vote, legitimized forms of democratic participation other than elections, and recognized community organizations as legal and legitimate democratic agents. It reinforced municipal finances and cities' political-administrative autonomy within their territorial boundaries.

The constitution now in force could be better defined as a broad political pact among the multiple forces of Brazilian civil society. As the authoritarian regime declined in the early 1980s, it gave way to a higher level of community participation in political life. Civil society emerged greatly strengthened.

From an economic perspective, however, the 1980s would be better viewed as a "lost decade." The international crisis of the 1970s and 1980s,

and the consequent structural adjustment policies implemented by Western governments, had disastrous results for countries on the periphery. In
Brazil, the combination of this geopolitical reorganization and a period of
domestic political and economic transition brought development stagnation. Annual GDP growth rates fell from 8.7 percent in the 1970s to 2.96
percent in 1990. Annual inflation rates increased from about 427 percent
on average in 1988 to 1000 percent in 1990. A crisis in the labour market also produced low annual rates of employment (1.3 percent in the
1980s) and a saturation of the service sector — 57.9 percent of the economically active population (EAP) is employed in the tertiary sector.

Urbanization Trends

Parallel to these political renovations and the economic crisis, the 1980s
introduced new urban characteristics to Brazil. First, the pace of urbanization was consolidated at a much slower rate. When compared with 6.2
percent in the 1950s, 5.4 percent in the 1960s, and 4.9 percent in the
1970s, the current rate of 2.9 percent seems almost insignificant. Along
with this deceleration, one of the most important changes began in the
1970s as the population shifted to metropolitan areas. In 1991, there were
42.7 million people, or 29 percent of the total population, living in the
nine metropolitan regions. Another important phonomenon was the dif-
fusion of urban populations throughout the country and a multiplication
of cities. Brazil's urban network became more dispersed, comprising small,
medium and large cities. The number of cities jumped from 3,991 in
1980 to almost 5,000 in 1990 (Valladares and Coelho 1995a).

II UNDERSTANDING URBAN GOVERNANCE

Urban Governance in the Context of Consolidating Democracy

In Brazil, "governance" is not a commonly used term — not even in analyses of
recent experiments in local governing procedure. In the 1980s, the transition to
democracy and the crisis of the state triggered much debate and brought into
focus the concepts of good and poor governability. Discussions explored various
meanings, often highlighting contrasts between older and newer ideas. While
established formulations stressed non-democratic solutions to governing, more
recent opinions favoured a democratic relationship between the state and society. As this debate progressed, certain ideas were accepted widely in Brazilian

society and emerged in the articulation of a movement seeking to consolidate democracy.

In 1994, a seminar entitled "Governability and Poverty in Brazil"[2] was held in Rio de Janeiro with the support of IUPERJ and the University of Toronto. Urban governance arose as one of the central issues for the Global Urban Research Initiative (GURI) Project. In view of the participants' lack of familiarity with the term "governance," the term "governability" was used in the seminar's title. A great deal of time and energy was devoted to the attempt to reach an understanding of governance, both generally and more specifically in the urban context. One accepted account was that of the World Bank, used in an analysis of the process of change in Brazil in the 1980s. Discussion focused on political aspects of the term, and stressed its democratic dimensions. The emerging view favoured a close relationship between the state and civil society, in a sense quite compatible with the prevalent view of civil society in Brazil.

A general concern with democracy, and how to consolidate it in a context of state crisis, distinguishes the Brazilian version of governance. This is best expressed in the civil society approach that has been developing at the local levels in Brazil, in particular. By the 1980s, a concept of the rights of citizenship presented a contrast to the prevailing process excluding those at the bottom of the socio-economic hierarchy, limiting their access to political decision-making, to adequate income, to the labour market, to quality in health and education services, to urban land and housing, and to a justice system capable of assuring equal protection of the law. The Brazilian understanding of civil society emerged from a discussion of how these restrictions could be lifted. It was raised by the proponents of a consolidated democracy in Brazil — the "democratic actors," in Guillermo O'Donnell's (1988) words.

At the local level in Brazil, the use and meaning of the term "governance" cannot be understood without taking into account the broader process of democratization and the political-administrative decentralization of civil institutions. It is also important to consider the public debate about the relationship between these two elements of reform.[3] As this process advanced, Brazilian society made a positive association between political-administrative decentralization and democracy. At least three basic ideas influenced its emergence.

First, democracy is incompatible with a hierarchical social order and with clientelist and patronage politics. Historically, these kinds of political relationships have encompassed social relations as a whole in Brazil. These conditions were permeated not only by a system of political exclusion, but by a broader "social authoritarianism" (O'Donnell 1988; Dagnino 1994). Second, the possibility of disenchantment with representative democracy places greater value on the principle of participation. It stands as one strategy to legitimate collective actors in the public realm, giving them direct access to decision-making (Souza and Lamounier 1989). Finally, the municipality is the most important point of convergence between collective actors and a democratic system. The proximity of collective actors and public authorities in the municipal sphere can reduce the ordinary citizen's sense of impotence, motivating greater participation and interest in civic issues (Jacobi 1991; Dowbor 1994).

Although a specifically Brazilian definition of urban governance has yet to be articulated, there is now a starting point from which to approach its meaning. In Brazil, urban governance could be considered a governing process characterized by: (a) popular participation in the public sphere based on the rights of citizenship; (b) a modern and democratic relationship between government and civil society; and (c) bureaucratic-administrative efficiency capable of positively associating the technical with the political (Fedozzi 1994).

The Conditions of Urban Governance: Political-Administrative Decentralization

Urban governance, as presented here, implies both a robust civil society, with democratic rules protecting the public realm, and political-administrative decentralization. That is to say, it implies political power being decentralized with respect to relations both between the state and society and between different levels of government. These are the minimum social, legal, and institutional requisites of governance. Researchers and politicians alike now must seek to apply these ideals to the real conditions of a given state and society.

New Social Actors in a Plural Civil Society

Freed from authoritarian rule, Brazilian civil society has emerged as plural and dynamic. The transition period has been one of great vitality in terms of the mobilization of society and citizenry. Of the occupational and community associations currently existing in the country, 65 percent were created since the 1970s. Urban labour unions and employers' associations also experienced notable growth over the same period (Tavares 1988; Santos 1993).

The political party system also changed during this era. In 1979, political party reforms altered the bipartisan system, restoring the multi-party structure that had existed before the 1964 military coup. One noteworthy occurrence was the creation of a new party, the Workers' Party (PT), whose membership is based in urban labour union and social movements.

The revitalization of certain institutions was also achieved at this time, especially those directly involved in organizing urban movements and those defending human rights and the poor. Since the 1970s, several among them have been outstanding. Worth noting in this regard are the Order of Attorneys of Brazil, the Catholic Church through its Pastoral Commissions, and the Brazilian Architects' Institute and its action in the National Urban Reform Movement. Spread out across the country, other social movements have gained notoriety for their role in organizing poor communities and bringing new social identities into focus. These groups have greatly amplified sectoral and ideological demands in the public sphere.

Recent Changes in Civil Society

Since the mid-1980s, the styles of popular participation have changed in several cities. NGOs have increased in visibility throughout the country. They are replacing social movements and filling in the gaps in the government's basic functions and services (Fernandes 1994; Gohn 1994). Countless new partnerships have developed between the public and private sectors, some of them led by NGOs. Examples of such relationships can now be found in the delivery of health, sanitation, food supply, housing, manpower training, small business incentives and youth training, amongst others. Moreover, several studies (Azevedo 1994; Fedozzi 1994; Moura, 1993; Somarriba and Dulci 1995) have observed an increasing willingness among various communities to participate in government initiatives. In spite of the problems faced by popular associations, they now play a major role in formulating policies that affect poor neighbourhoods.

Municipalities and the Constitution in Brazil

Since its independence in 1822, Brazil has had eight constitutional charters. Historically, the constitutional role of municipalities has been characterized by limited autonomy and restricted functional responsibilities. Within that general framework — and through alternating periods of democracy (1891–1930; 1934–37; 1946–65) and authoritarianism (1930–34; 1937–45; 1964–85) — municipalities were accorded varying degrees of autonomy and responsibility by the different constitutional orders. The 1988

Constitution's federalist system has no equal in the country's history. The new role offered to the municipality is dramatically different from any arrangement ever attempted over the past century.

The current constitution maintains both the principle of separation of powers between the executive and legislative branches and the cities' right to elect their governments. Municipal executive power is exercised by the mayor (*Prefeito*), or vice-mayor, assisted by municipal secretaries. Legislative power is exercised by the city council (*Câmara de Vereadores*). The mayor, vice-mayor and council members are elected for four-year mandates, by a direct and secret vote which is mandatory for adults between the ages of 18 and 70. Municipal secretaries are mayoral appointees.

New actors in the urban and national scenarios have played an undoubtedly decisive role in the process of constitutional reform. This culminated, of course, in the promulgation of the 1988 Constitution. They raised progressive demands inspired by the belief in democratic institutional planning as a vital element in reinforcing democratic practice. As a result of the presence of these new social actors on the urban scene and in the national scenario at the end of the 1980s, civil society's demands dealing with citizenship rights and social policies were formally included in the new constitution.

Urban governance has required major institutional innovations. First, it has demanded decentralization of political power and the implementation of participatory democracy. The constitution now ensures that popular sovereignty will be exercised, in addition to the vote, through popular law initiative, plebiscite and referendum. Collective social agents are recognized in the form of nonpartisan associations. At the local level, community organizations ("representative associations") are legitimate representatives of community interests (Caldeira 1992). Governance has also dictated political and administrative decentralization and the creation of organic municipal law. The new constitution gives municipalities the capacity to structure themselves through the elaboration of organic laws. This legislation is elaborated and approved by a city council specifically empowered to establish means of exercising popular sovereignty, to define institutional forms of community participation, and to create municipal boards.

Municipal boards are institutional channels of participation created to assure the presence of "representative associations" in the governing process. This strategy aims to satisfy a constitutional precept (Article 29, XII) related to some areas of government action, especially those involving social policies. A study of the organic laws in the country's 50 largest cities recorded that all

Porto Alegre: the Participatory Budget

Porto Alegre, capital of the state of Rio Grande do Sul, became renowned for its success with the participatory budget during two recent administrations (1989-92 and 1993-96). In the Budget Council and Budget Forum, city priorities are discussed by community representatives who are elected from each of the city's 16 regions. The bureaucratic-administrative structure of city government also has undergone changes to adapt to the new exigencies of popular participation. One of the main innovations was the creation of a Planning Cabinet (*Gaplan*), whose function is to process community demands and transform them into government plans. Another novel approach was introduced by the Community Relations Coordination Committees, which work with other city government bodies and with Gaplan. In Porto Alegre, 64.5 percent of the participants in 1993 were poor people, with incomes of three minimum wages (about US$ 300 a month) or less. Therefore, the major part of government expenditure which was negotiated in the participatory budget has been allocated according to poor people's demands. From 1992 to 1994, resources were concentrated in programmes favouring legalization of property rights and access to land. Community participation has increased from about 1,000 in 1989 to 3,000 in 1992, and to 10,000 in 1993 (Fedozzi 1994; Ribeiro 1995).

except three had created municipal boards. Twenty had founded urban development boards. Six had established housing boards, while two others created sanitation boards. Thirty-five of these cities had also set up environmental boards. The constitution clearly defines health and education as municipal responsibilities, and urban governments have responded accordingly. Of the 50 municipalities surveyed, 45 had boards to deal with health and 40 had bodies to participate in education legislation (Ribeiro 1995).

The participatory budget, one of the most important innovations of the organic laws, was introduced in 18 out of 50 municipalities. Considered the most innovative tool in the decentralization and democratization of power, the participatory budget is created by elected popular representatives. It is a functioning example of transparency in organizing civil priorities and public investments. It favours planning and also discourages the practice of patronage in the apportionment of scarce resources (Moura 1993; Fedozzi 1994; Azevedo 1994). As Maria Somarriba and Octávio Dulci (1995) point out, a participatory budget is a focus for public gatherings as well, and as such it is an effective way of mobilizing different social strata. For example, there is significant participation by representatives of both middle-class and poor neighbourhoods in the regional fora in Belo Horizonte, where community priorities for the participatory budget are discussed.

Under the new constitution, municipalities have greatly increased their autonomy through financial decentralization, especially in comparison to the previous authoritarian regime (1964–85). Municipalities have also gained enormous autonomy in the power to institute and exact taxes on their own constituents. Another great benefit of the new order has been the freedom to augment and organize their own revenue, as well as the power to invest their own funds. Moreover, the new constitution is considered to have reinforced municipal participation in the revenue-sharing system. In addition to their own sources of revenue, from the Urban Building and Land Tax, the Tax on Services, the Tax on Real Estate Transmission (*inter vivos*), and various fees, there are two other major sources of municipal funding: transfers of federal government revenues (FPM), and transfers of state government revenues. Municipalities also rely on negotiated transfers, essentially political in nature. Since the 1988 Constitution, municipal participation in the revenue sharing system has increased progressively. Between 1989 and 1993, it jumped from 17 percent to 22.5 percent, with the greatest gains going to small towns. Indeed, the dependency of these towns on revenue sharing is great — FPM funds represent about 60 percent to 95 percent of their total budget (Netto 1995).

The 1988 Constitution mandated the decentralization of primary education and health policies, areas in which the municipalities already were making their presence actively felt. However, the new constitution was not clear about the distribution of other social issues and responsibilities — such as housing development, basic sanitation, food supply and social work — among the different levels of government. Expanding urban populations and deepening poverty have created pressure on all governments to provide services and implement policies designed to deal with the current rates of population and poverty growth. Notwithstanding those omissions, the 1988 Constitution did accentuate the social function of cities and of urban land ownership which has given the municipalities the leading role in the control of urban development. To reinforce urban development policy, the Constitution instituted the Directive Plan, compulsory for localities with more than 20,000 inhabitants. The executive branch is responsible for its preparation, and popular participation through municipal boards is constitutionally mandated.

A study of 23 Directive Plans in the 50 largest Brazilian cities showed that in the majority of cases the main focus of concern is social justice, especially toward access to land and adequate housing. Some other urban policy tools also were created. The most outstanding of these are the Progressive in Time Urban Building and Property Tax, and the Special Zones of Social Interest, or ZEIS (regions set aside for building housing projects). The Urban Development Fund also deserves attention for channeling resources toward investment in urban infrastructure and the execution of housing programs in the ZEIS. Finally, the tax on created land — building areas which exceed that permitted by the basic use coefficient for untaxed construction — is considered a strategic tool of redistributive policy (Ribeiro 1995).

Recife: the Special Zones of Social Interest Regulation Plan — PREZEIS Law

Recife, the capital of the state of Pernambuco, is located in the country's poorest region, the Northeast. A large city, it has 2.871 million inhabitants, with 1.3 million poor people and, as of 1994, 580 *favelas* (squatter settlements). Legal recognition of the Special Zones of Social Interest (ZEIS), through the Land Use and Occupation Law, took effect in 1993. This was the pioneering experience for this programme in Brazil. With the Prezeis Law in force, 42 *favelas* were defined as ZEIS, coming under the protection of urban standards that provide for their regulation by law and integration into the city's urban structure.

In 1987, the PREZEIS Law was approved, but for a period of five years it was boycotted by the municipal government. In fact, it was not enforced until 1993 when the newly revived urban community movement and the Justice and Peace Commission (a Catholic Church organization) jointly petitioned the Mayor (elected in 1992) for recognition of the ZEIS. Two other institutional channels of community participation were activated in 1993: COMUL (the Land Occupation Urbanization and Legalization Commission) and the PREZEIS Forum. Their main function is to coordinate and oversee the preparation and implementation of ZEIS land occupation-legalization projects (Araujo 1994).

Poor people's access to urban land and housing is a major problem in Brazil, especially in the country's largest cities. Urban growth has been characterized by unfettered real-estate speculation and the inefficacy of the authoritarian regime's urban policy. Beginning in the 1960s, a National Movement for Urban Reform played an important role in preparing the ground for the 1988 Constitution's progressive innovations. While the Movement was almost totally dismantled in most of the largest cities, it is currently being revived. In the city of Recife, this movement has focused on projects dealing with the legalization of low-income property ownership.

Urban Governance and the Effectiveness of Institutional Changes

In Brazil, the constitutional reforms mandating political decentralization are still awaiting effective implementation. Many of the innovations in constitutional precepts and organic laws have yet to be enforced. There are two areas in which additional work needs to be concentrated. First, municipal financial resources must be reinforced, and second, innovations in laws and planning should be implemented.

While it is true that the 1988 Constitutional provisions were designed to overcome the fiscal limitation of municipal autonomy, the outcome is questionable. Expanding municipalities' capacity to generate revenues and to structure resource organization was important, yet there is no clear evidence to support the prevailing view that municipalities have subsequently increased their revenues. This doubt is especially great with regard to the resources coming to municipalities from FPM. Moreover, the new partitioning of tax funds occurred in a context of decline in aggregate public revenue, triggered by the economic crisis and a consequent decline in the tax load (Daim 1995).

There has been some argument over whether large and middle-sized cities' own revenue bases would cover the cost of their new constitutional functions. However, it is important to stress the difficulties faced by cities due to processes outside their sphere of influence. The ISS (Tax on Services) and the IPTU (Urban Building and Property Tax) are cases in point. While municipalities are attempting to modernize the revenue collection system and realize the potential of these two taxes, the changes necessary to do this depend on new federal legislation complementing the constitutional provisions.

The relative inefficacy of legal innovations at the municipal level under the new constitution is illustrated by the situation of municipal boards. Only about 42 percent of all municipal boards created were actually put into effect (Ribeiro 1995). Moreover, it is not uncommon, especially in smaller cities, to find municipal boards being used by members of city councils as a tool of clientelism in their effort to win votes (Caldeira 1992). Furthermore, the mandatory community participation in the elaboration of Directive Plans all have been observed as failures by researchers. Studies of Directive Plans systematically show a significant inefficacy of community representatives. It has also been noted that the improper application of the laws distributing power among municipal committees led to undue advantages for commercial real estate agents (Cavallieri 1994; Diniz 1994; Pontual 1994).

Traditional Local Politics in a Hierarchical Society

Brazilian society is characterized by traditional and hierarchical social relations. These have been based on enormous social and economic inequalities, and on the political and economic elites' traditionally adamant resistance to admitting those at the bottom as collective social actors. Brazilian local politics reflect these social characteristics. Historically, local governments have played a leading role in maintaining the traditional model of government. Municipal politics are notorious for their particularist nature, characterized by the prevalence of patronage and private interest pressures on mayors and city council members (Nunes 1994). Moreover, municipal governments are seen as the place to seek the arbitrary manipulation of executive and legislative power on behalf of private interests. At the municipal level, patronage is prevalent enough that economic groups with local interests act as forces of city degradation and economic stagnation. The situation is grave enough to be considered a real constraint to the modernization of social and political relations. Several studies have revealed that real estate business interests in particular exert considerable pressure on mayors and city council members (Cavallieri 1994; Pontual 1994; Bava 1995).

III CHALLENGES TO URBAN GOVERNANCE

In contemporary Brazil, city governments confront many challenges. Some arise from a lack of effective planning, some from a lack of development programmes which promote improved income distribution, job opportunities, and which make efficient use of funds for investment in social programs. These challenges are manifest, *inter alia*, in high urban poverty rates, in the failure of federal housing, health and education policies, and in the incoherence of the decentralization process. This also is true in the disorganization of primary education and the health sector, which continue to suffer from deficits in their initial resource base.

The accumulation of social problems in the cities has created pressure on municipal governments to provide services and implement social policies. There is ample evidence to support the claims that these problems pose serious impediments to development and good governance. The rate of poverty, the living conditions of the poor, and the state of health service and primary education are all examples of the difficult impediments the new reforms must overcome. These factors demand closer consideration.

Poverty indicators are important markers for gauging economic and social conditions. In 1990, there were 42 million poor people in Brazil. Of these, 16.6 million were considered to be destitute (Rocha 1995). A total of 17.5 million poor and 6.1 million destitute people lived in urban areas, but these figures drop to 12.2 million and 3.4 million respectively in official municipal regions. Over the last decade, the proportion of the poor and destitute who are residents of urban areas has grown in general, and in metropolitan areas in particular.

Another test of economic and social conditions is the situation of housing for the urban poor. In the 1980s, after almost 20 years, the authoritarian regime's housing policies were dissolved. Since then, the absence of federal housing policy has been compensated by clandestine and often violent solutions. A wave of land invasions and the unauthorized settlement of risk areas have spread throughout the country. However, municipal governments are now in charge of the housing problem, and new low-cost housing solutions are being developed. It has been partnership programmes between the public and private sectors which have stimulated projects that benefit the poorer sectors of the population.

Health services are another important social and economic indicator. Several studies have pointed out that enormous cuts in the public health sector's infrastructure have affected poorer people. The proportion of health facilities with in-patient treatment fell from 33 percent in 1980 to 20.5 percent in 1989. At the same time, the number of beds per inhabitant decreased from 4.17 per thousand in 1981 to 3.77 per thousand in 1986. Over this period, private sector participation in the hospital network expanded (Médici, Oliveira and Beltrão 1993, 20), and 78 percent of hospital beds now belong to the private health services.

The state of primary education is similarly disorganized. In Brazil today, educational problems are not related to illiteracy rates or deficits in school supplies, but instead are due to the poor quality of the education being delivered. In the 1980s, there was an increase in the number of schools and the number of students registered in first grade, but this expansion came at the cost of quality. In the education system, growth without quality control has produced seriously high drop-out rates and high levels of grade repetition at the primary level (Gusso 1990; Klein 1994). These facts indicate a situation which is different from the common notion that the cost of keeping children in school and out of the workforce is responsible for high drop-out rates. Instead, poverty appears to be responsible for interrupting a child's education only as a result of the high cost to poor families of maintaining their children in school for a period longer than the regular one. Through grade repetition, the poor quality of public education may be keeping children in school longer and delaying their effective contribution to their family's income.

IV FUTURE RESEARCH FRONTIERS

Urban governance is a novel research theme in Brazil. Currently, the multiple aspects of urban government, local power and political participation, social policies and decentralization, and the role of NGOs are some of the most prominent issues in Brazilian urban research. Discussion of these questions has drawn attention to the concepts of democratic city management, the rights of citizenship, the relationship between the public and the private, and social solidarity. These ideas represent some dimensions of urban governance as understood here, and their discussion can certainly be helpful to its evolution. The following recommendations should be taken into account in order to develop urban governance as a research theme in Brazil.

First, one broad general recommendation can be made. Initially, it is important to invest in theoretical studies, discussing the urban governance concept and approach. Research in the form of case studies, preferably from a comparative perspective, should be a priority. Comparisons of the degrees of success achieved in different urban government experiences would be particularly enlightening. For example, a survey of participatory budgets and sub-governments, social policies, and urban development policy in different municipalities would be particularly useful.

There are three points that can be included as specific recommendations. First, studies should be undertaken in the area of intergovernmental relations, including the process of political and administrative decentralization. Of particular import to research are areas in which local government has exercised its autonomy in the articulation and implementation of social policies. Studies on formal cooperation among municipal governments, such as municipal consortia, are also relevant. Second, studies and research in the sphere of municipal government should be encouraged to examine four factors. The control and development of financial resources must be observed. Of particular interest are the innovative experiments underway in fundraising for social programmes and initiated through partnerships of the private and public sectors. Another is the use of constitutionally mandated revenue bases, like the property tax and taxation of "created" land. The development of local capacities, and the ability of municipal administrations to perform new functions, also needs to be understood.

Second, the process of decentralization should be examined as a device for building power-sharing between the state and citizenry. Studies and research in this area are strongly recommended to pursue several questions. Are municipal boards effective? There must be some effort to understand where the initiative originates, and some analysis of these bodies' origin with regard to their responsibilities. Similarly, a study of the conflicts which occur in municipal boards would be useful. Are there different styles of participation which affect the empowerment of civil society? Research is needed on the styles of organizing interest groups, such as civic associations, neighbourhood associations, community councils, and trade representation groups. How can the process of administration be reformed? It is appropriate to begin by examining the decentralization of the executive branch of municipal government through experiments with sub-governments.

Finally, studies are also recommended on the social role of political parties and the experiences of implementing Directive Plans. Studies on governance must also include research on the direction and effect of social policies and programmes. Already, several recent projects in primary education and health have been carried out at the municipal level, using municipal funds. Specifically, studies and research are needed as follow-up to new experimental partnerships between municipal governments and business, and municipalities and the federal government (like food supply policy). It is important to undertake studies and research specifying the conditions under which the interests of powerful economic groups prevail and the traditional political pattern is enforced.

Notes

1 This is a synthesis of the paper "Urban Governance and Poverty in Brazil," by Magda Prates Coelho and Ely Diniz, presented at the GURI Global Meeting on Urban Governance, Mexico City, October 2–5, 1995.
2 The papers presented in this seminar were collected in the book *Governabilidade e Pobreza no Brazil,* edited by Licia Valladares and Magda Prates Coelho (1995b).
3 Although decentralization has been discussed in the country as an element of fiscal reform, it did not arise as an issue in the discussion of urban governance, at least until the late 1980s. The Brazilian public debate on decentralization is conducted essentially in its political dimension.

References

Araujo, Adelmo. 1994. "Os Prezeis enquanto Instrumento de Regulação Urbanística." *Proposta 62*(setembro): 60–66.
Azevedo, Sergio. 1994. "O Orçamento Participativo e Gestão Popular: Reflexões Preliminares sobre a Experiência de Betim." *Proposta* 62(setembro): 44–49.
Bava,Silvio Caccia. 1995. "Dilemas da gestão municipal democrática." In Licia Valladares and Magda Prates Coelho (eds.), *Governabilidade e Pobreza no Brazil.* Rio de Janeiro: Civilizacão Brazileira, pp. 161–90.
Caldeira, Cesar. 1992. "Entidades Representativas e Poder Local. A Participação Social Institucionalizada." *ARCHÉ* 1(2): 5–35.
Cavallieri, Paulo Fernando.1994. "O plano Director de 1992 da ciudade do Rio de Janeiro: possibilidades e limites da reforma urbana." In Luiz Cesar de Queiroz Ribeiro and Orlando Alves dos Santos Júnior (eds.), *Globaizacão, Frametaçâo e Reforma Urbana. O Futuro das Ciadades Brasilieras na Crise.* Rio de Janeiro: Civilizacão Brazileira, pp. 373–402.
Dagnino, Evelina. 1994. "Os movimentos sociais e a emergência de uma nova noção de cidadani." In Evelina Dagnino (ed.), *Os anos 90. Política e Sociedade no Brasil.* São Paulo: Edta. Brasiliense, pp.103–18.
Daim, Sulamis. 1995. "Dilemas do Estado diante da nova ordem econômica e social." In Licia Valladares and Magda Prates Coelho (eds.), *Governabilidade e Pobreza no Brasil.* Rio de Janeiro: Edta. Civilização Brasileira, pp. 65–106.
Diniz, Urbiratan. 1994. "Plano Diretor em Belém: A Luta pelo Espaço Urbano e por Participação Popular." *Revista Proposta* 2(62): 49–50.
Dowbor, Ladislau. 1994. "Governabilidade e Descentralização." *Revista do Serviço Público* 118(1): 95–119.

Fedozzi, Luciano. 1994. "Poder Local e Governabilidade: O Caso de Porto Alegre." *Proposta* 22/62 (setembro): 23–29.

Fernandes, Rubem Cesar. 1994. *Privadoporém Público. O terceiro seto na América Latina.* Rio de Janeiro: Relume Dumara.

Gohn, Maria da Gloria. 1994. "Organizações Não-Governamentais — ONGs: A Modernidade da Participação." *Cadernos Cidadania-Texto*, número 3. Campinas: UNICAMP, GEMDEC.

Gusso, Divonzir Arthur. ed. 1990. *Educação e Cultura — 1987 — Situação e Poílticas Governamentais.* Brasília: Insituto de Pequisa Econmica Aplicada (IPEA).

Jacobi, Pedro. 1991. "Os Municipios e a Participação: Desafios e Alternativas." *Revista de Administração Municipal (RAM)* 38(198): 32–38.

Klein, Ruben. 1994. "Matemtica da Qualidade de Ensinona Década de 80." *Revista do Rio de Janeiro* 2(3) Semestre 1: 9–20.

Médici, André Cezar, and E.B. Francisco Oliveiro and Kalzó Beltrão. 1993. "Subsídios para a Reforma Constitúcional no Campo da Seguridade Social: Visão Histórica e Perspectivas." *Planejamento e Políticas Públicas* July 9: 1–71.

Moura, Suzana. 1993. "Ideário e Prática da Participação Popular no Governo Local: a experiência de Porto Alegre." In Tania Fischer (ed.), *Poder Local, Governo de Cidadania.* Rio de Janeiro: FGV, pp. 181–90.

Netto, Lino Ferreira. 1995. "A atuação do município no combate à pobreza: possibilidades e limitações." In Licia Valladares and Magda Prates Coelho (eds.), *Governabilidade e Pobreza no Brasil.* Rio de Janeiro: Edta. Civilização Brasileira, pp. 313–36.

Nunes, Edison. 1994. "El Gobierno de las Ciudades de Tamnho Medio en Brasil. Los Casos de Marilia y Piracicaba." In Alfredo Rodrigueza and Fabio Velásquez (eds.), *Municipio y Servicios Publicos: Gobiernos Locales en Ciudades Intermedias de America Latina.* Chile: Ed. SUR, pp. 77–100.

O'Donnell, Guillermo. 1988. "Transições, Continuidade e alguns Paradoxos." In Fabio Wanderley Reis and Guillermo O'Donnell (eds.), *A Democracia no Brasil: Dilemas e Perspectivas.* São Paulo: Ed. Vertice, pp. 41–72.

Pontual, Virginia. 1994. "O último capítulo de uma comédia: a aprovação do plano diretor de Recife." In Luiz Cesar de Queiroz Ribeiro and Orlando Alves dos Santos Júnior (eds.), *Globaizacão, Frametaçâo e Reforma Urbana. O Futuro das Ciadades Brasilieras na Crise.* Rio de Janeiro: Civilizacão Braziliera, pp. 403–26.

Reis, Elisa. 1995. "Governabilidade e Solidariedade." In Licia Valladares and Magda Prates Coelho (eds.), *Governabilidade e Pobreza no Brasil.* Rio de Janeiro: Edta. Civilização Brasileira, pp. 49–64.

Ribeiro, Luiz Cesar de Queiroz. 1995. "A (in)governabilidade da ciudade? Avanços e desafios da reforma urbana." In Licia Valladares and Magda Prates Coelho (eds.), *Governabilidade de Pobreza no Brasil.* Rio de Janeiro: Edta. Civilização Brasileira, pp. 161–90.

Rocha, Suzana. 1995. "Governabilidade e pobreza: o desafio dos números." In Licia Valladares and Magda Prates Coelho (eds.), *Governabilidade e Pobreza no Brazil.* Rio de Janeiro: Civilizacão Brazileira, pp. 221–66.

Santos, Wanderley Guilherme. 1993. *Razões da Desordem.* Rio de Janeiro: Rocco.

Somarriba, Maria das Mercês, and Octávio Dulci. 1995. "Democratização do Poder Local e Seus Dilemas: A Dinâmica Atual da Participação Popular em Belo Horizonte." Paper presented in XIX ANPOCS, October 17–21.

Souza, Amaury and Bolivar Lamounier. 1989. "A Feitura da Nova Constituição: Um Reexame da Cultura Política Brasileira." *Planejamento e Políticas Públicas* 2(dezembro): 17–38.

Tavares, Maria Herminia Almedia de. 1988. "Dificil Caminho: Sindicatos e Política na Construção da Democaria." In Fabio Wanderley Reis and Guilhermo O'Donnell (eds.), *A Democracia no Brasil: Dilemas e Perspectivas.* São Paulo: Vertice, pp. 327–67.

Valladares, Licia and Magda Prates Coelho. 1995a. "Urban Research in Brazil and Venezuela: Towards an Agenda for the 1990s." In Richard Stren (ed.), *Urban Research in the Developing World: Vol. 3, Latin America.* Toronto: Centre for Urban and Community Studies, pp. 45–142.

Valladares, Licia and Magda Coelho (eds.). 1995b. *Governabilidade e Pobreza no Brazil.* Rio de Janeiro: Edta. Civilização Brasileira.

Governance at the Local Level in Mexico, Colombia and Central America

MARTHA SCHTEINGART AND EMILIO DUHAU

I INTRODUCTION

The heterogeneous sub-region comprised of Mexico, Colombia and Central America includes countries that differ greatly in size,[1] in historical, socioeconomic and political development, and in their experience of urbanization.

Urbanization has had an important impact on the societies of this sub-region in recent decades. However, acceleration of the urbanization process began at different times and its rhythm has varied in association with the economic, political and geographic context of each country, and particularly with their process of industrialization. As far as changes in urbanization rates are concerned, Mexico and Colombia changed from basically rural to predominantly urban societies within the last five decades. During the 1980s the Central American countries maintained the trend of the three previous decades toward urbanization, but their levels remain much lower than those of the other two countries.[2]

In 1910 Mexico underwent an agrarian revolution and, beginning in the 1940s, a rapid process of industrialization which mainly benefited the upper- and middle- income classes. At present, it is also the fourth largest oil-producing nation in the world. Since 1929, one political party (first the National Revolutionary Party, renamed in 1946 the Institutional Revolutionary Party, or PRI) has dominated Mexican politics. This situation has been changing in recent years and other parties have won local elections. The Conservative and Liberal parties have ruled Colombia for many years, within a political system where violence, guerilla warfare and drug trafficking have been present. El Salvador is one of the smallest and most densely populated of the Central American countries. The civil war which broke out in 1981 lasted more than 10 years. Increased guerrilla warfare led in 1989 to (a declaration of) a state of siege in the capital, San Salvador, and political violence continued until 1993 when the peace agreement was signed. In contrast, Costa Rica has been, since 1838, one of the most stable and prosperous Central American countries. It has the most even income distribution, the best level of services and fewer discrepancies between urban and rural areas.

II LOCAL GOVERNANCE IN THE SUBREGION

In Latin America, the question of governance first became prominent in the 1980s, linked to the so-called problem of transition from authoritarian to more democratic regimes. Nevertheless, that transition, as well as the importance of governance, expressed both in political discourse and practice, has varied within the different countries according to their political context and the general advances made.

Although the notion of governance is important to consider at the local level, the concept has been included only rarely in studies of local government or urban development. Therefore, we have tried to reconstruct the notion at the urban level in Mexico, Colombia and Central America.

Local governance will be addressed first by discussing the relationship between municipal and other levels of government. Governance will then be discussed in terms of the relationship between municipal government and local society (which includes citizen participation). Finally, some consideration will be paid to governance in the local context of the countries concerned. In addition, in order to talk about governance, we need to include the issue of poverty in our analysis and the policies that have been implemented to combat it. How can "good governance" exist and democratic values be supported in a society whose institutions of political democracy have failed to show tangible achievements in the material living conditions of a large proportion of the population?

The Relationship Between the Municipal and Other Levels of Government

In almost all the national cases considered for this chapter, one important common factor has been the high degree of centralism that prevails. Nevertheless, the historical evolution of the relationship between central and local governments has been different in the cases of Mexico, Colombia and the countries of Central America.

The Mexican political regime has been defined as "federal," but underlying this designation is an institutional network that strongly differs from what one might expect. The history of the formation of the Mexican state is one which favoured centrality at the cost of severely hindering the development of municipal power. Since 1983, constitutional reforms, effected within the framework of State Reform, have sought to give the municipalities a new identity. However, these reforms have not profoundly modified the centralist dynamic to the extent of restoring the municipalities' initial importance (Merino Huerta 1994). Nonetheless, as a consequence of the reforms, municipal governments have redefined their relations with both state and federal governments, and with local society.

In Mexico, municipal autonomy was guaranteed to some degree by the Constitution of 1917 and by the provisions of Article 115, which referred to the "free municipality." This autonomy, however, was not respected by state and federal governments. In 1983 a constitutional reform to Article 115 was proposed, with the intention of making that autonomy a reality. The most important provisions that were amended relate to financial issues. However, the situation is such that, "municipalities are expected to raise revenues without having an adequate capacity to do so (e.g., from collecting property taxes and from the fees for the provision of public services) and, virtually all municipalities depend for approximately 80 percent of their budget on transfers from higher levels of government" (Rodriguez and Ward 1992, 65–6).

Unlike Mexico, Colombia is a unitary republic. From 1863 until very recently, radical liberal reformist intentions had not been fulfilled, and attempts to institute the popular election of mayors had failed. While this type of election has a rather long history in the majority of Latin American countries, it was only incorporated into Colombian law in 1986.

The new Colombian Constitution, approved in 1991, confers the status of territorial entity on the department, the district, and indigenous territories, which gives them political and administrative autonomy and includes the popular election of governors. The political reform of municipal life also became especially important within the modernization project. It included measures which tended to redistribute power by strengthening municipal budgets and laying the groundwork for citizen participation. Nevertheless, an inconsistency has been noted between the transfer of funds and the magnitude of responsibilities delegated to localities, as well as the volume and cost of social demands to be satisfied (Gaitán and Moreno 1992).

Some analysts believe that there is still too much control from the centre in Colombia, and that the reassignment of responsibilities to departments and municipalities contrasts with their insufficient development as institutions and their limited technical and administrative capacities. The new institutions, though favouring the building of democracy, have barely begun to develop their transforming potential. They are also hindered by the deficiencies of the central state, the excluding character of the regime and the passivity of civil society (Gaitán and Moreno 1992).

Central American countries are similarly challenged. In El Salvador, the centralism of the political system and the contradictions between different levels of government are notable. As in Mexico, where more and more voices demand increased decentralization and municipal autonomy from the central and state governments, Salvadoran political leaders seem fundamentally concerned with modernizing the municipal government structures and training local administrative personnel.

In 1983, in the midst of the civil war, a new municipal code granting important powers to municipal governments was approved in El Salvador. However, the war as well as political, economic and administrative weaknesses prevented this legislative intention from being carried out. It was only with the signing of the peace agreement in 1993 and the debate on decentralization that this situation began to change (Lungo 1994).

Costa Rica is the most democratic nation in Central America, but also the most centralized. Centralization of services began in the 1950s. Municipalities lost control over basic urban services and the limitation of municipal responsibilities was accompanied by significant budget reductions. In the past few years, however, a process of decentralization and recovery of autonomy has been initiated. The municipal councils, supported by the principal actors in the cities (including, for example, chambers of commerce and grass-roots organizations), have stated their demands for decentralization amid great obstacles imposed by the centralized agencies and ministries. In this way, municipal councils are revising their relationship with central government, in an attempt to progress from a position of subordination to one of negotiation and equitable coordination (Méndez Acosta 1994).

This process is exemplfied in a number of instances. For example, the municipal council has elaborated the Master Plan for Costa Rica's capital city, San José. In addition, legal measures have been imposed by municipal councils on the Ministry of Housing, since it developed land without municipal authorization. Similarly, opposition has formed to street and transit regulations imposed by the Ministry of Public Works and Transportation without the approval of San José municipal authorities (Méndez Acosta 1994).

In general, the redistribution of responsibilities between central and local governments — attributed, in part, to the necessity of relieving the central government of its fiscal duties in order to share the burden of the current financial crisis — conflicts with the limited resources and administrative capacity of municipalities. This situation is leading to frustration of popular expectations, to increasing social conflicts and to difficulties in the exercise of "good governance" at the local level.

Municipal Government, Local Society and Participation

When analyzing the relationship between local society and municipal government in Mexico, researchers have focused mainly on electoral issues. However, even when municipal authorities are elected democratically, government actions will not necessarily be democratic. Notwithstanding who governs, the main issue is whether the municipal government is capable of reflecting differing social interests. In other words, the institutional design of the municipal government should allow for the representation of diverse social interests. While this tolerance remains somewhat unproven, the constitutional changes we have already mentioned — the redefinition of the relations between local entities, other levels of government, and local society — bestow upon municipal government the character of an institution in transition with an increasingly relevant role in regional development.

Mexico has suffered from a "representation crisis" which is partly due to a lack of political opportunities, as evidenced by the fact that the crisis has persisted despite the existence of democratic elections for municipal governments. This crisis is apparent in the fact that first, the constitution and the federal and state electoral laws only recognize political parties, as opposed to local governments, as legitimate actors of local politics. Secondly, the formation of municipal governments, in practice, does not conform to legal precepts. Since 1983, the federal constitution has established the formation of municipalities under rules of proportionality, but state electoral laws distort these rules, thus converting the proportionally representative councillors into party councillors. The needs and proposals of those social organizations not tied to parties are left on the sidelines of the main debate (Guillén 1994a).

There is a significant gap between what laws establish with regard to social participation and the entities and channels that actually exist for that purpose. In practice, local governments often establish mechanisms for participation beyond those provided by law. Moreover, different sectors of local society create parallel or alternate mechanisms to those established by the governments, while municipal government structures are sometimes subject to intrusions by federal programmes (Negrete Mata 1994).

The democratic performance of municipal governments is also limited by presidentialism, an expression of centralism on a local level. Councillors are aware that their position within the government structure is marginal, and demands from local society are oriented directly toward the municipal presidency and, to a lesser degree, toward non-elected civil servants (Guillén 1994a).

There is no provision within the structure of municipal government for the implementation of urban policies which take into account its relation with the local population. If the general framework of citizens' rights in Mexico indeed offers the legal basis for social protest, there are no fora for the discussion of these policies. Social protest must be carried out externally, through rallies and demonstrations, and the intervention of social actors in the policy-making process is not allowed for in legislation. Only in the final stages of the process is it possible to find out whether municipal policies are accepted by society, and therefore whether there is a consensus. Usually, urban policy is created by a very limited group, headed by the mayor, a process which reproduces traditional authoritarian models. Although many municipalities have transformed their administrative technology, parameters of efficiency, personnel qualifications and so on, authoritarian procedures have not been modified (Guillén 1994b). This situation increases the possibility of conflict, as well as difficulties in the exercise of governance. One novel characteristic of governance on a local level is the growing tendency on the part of the citizens to use mass media, especially radio, as a substitute channel for directing their demands to municipal government (Guillén 1994a).

We may conclude that the municipality seems to be an increasingly important institution within Mexico's regional development. We may also conclude that municipalities are under pressure to effect instrumental and political modernization while they also continue to be the inheritors of traditional practices, organization and political culture. This conflicting dual nature surely makes this transformation a more difficult process. Case studies from different municipalities have shown that conflicts and protests from local groups have increased significantly. For the most part, they represent a reaction to abuses and negligence on the part of the authorities, a rejection of governmental actions, and the defence of citizens' fundamental rights (Merino 1995).

Within the perspective of governance that we are trying to develop here, it is important to clarify that in Colombia, besides the direct and popular election of municipal authorities, other institutions contribute to broadening the effects of the reforms. These include community administrative committees for all municipalities in the country, and committees on building in the capital district, whose members are now elected by popular vote. Users of public services now participate in the negotiation and fiscalization of state enterprises that provide the services. A popular legislative initiative for the presentation of ordinances which according to citizens should be carried out by Assemblies and Councils, has also been proposed. In spite of all the progress made, ideological and political pluralism are still in their early stages. This is true even though the constitutional reform has, in a way, influenced the decline of bipartisanship, thus strengthening other social actors. In the larger cities and department capitals, "civic candidatures" outside traditional parties have become more and more common (Ungar 1994).

Colombian municipal reform has evolved within a context of social polarization, armed confrontations and the fragmentation of political power. It has also had to contend with the presence of drug traffickers in widespread areas of the country, and their use of mayoral elections to increase their influence over, or become part of, the political class. Nevertheless, this process has shown that the municipality, in addition to being a source of conflict, is also an arena for rediscovering democracy and reconstructing policies. It is the setting of daily needs and the area where the relations between government and civil society are closest, and where the negotiation of public affairs can produce the most visible results (Gaitán and Moreno 1992).

In El Salvador, several changes which further democratization of the political system have resulted from the peace agreement. These are creating greater possibilities for social participation through modifications to the electoral system, to the administration of justice, and to the political party system. As in the case of Mexico, however, agencies of local government have not been transformed in practice. A vigorous debate is taking place in El Salvador on the issue of urban democracy, especially in the San Salvador Metropolitan Area. Nevertheless, as in the other cases discussed here, it is widely accepted that demands for social participation surpass the capacity of the existing political framework. This suggests that continuing calls for political reform could encourage further steps toward a true democratization at all government levels.

New social agreements, new legislation and modifications to constitutional order in this subregion, especially since the beginning of the 1980s, have proven to be insufficient to convert traditional institutions into modern, more democratic municipal governments where good governance could be the rule. The examples of Mexico, Colombia, El Salvador and Costa Rica show very clearly that demands for political participation exceed the capacity of the general political framework of those countries. They also demonstrate the exclusionary nature of the political regimes, sometimes the traditional passivity of civil society, and the lack of plurality resulting from their electoral systems. Greater pluralism at the local level, and the increased decision-making capacity of the municipalities on the orientation of public expenditure, are demanded.

Governance and Poverty

Poverty was recognized as a phenomenon which existed in Mexico, Colombia and Central America long before the change to a new paradigm in the development model which occurred during the 1980s. It worsened during the crisis of that decade and, within the framework of a more even distribution of resources, is an important variable in democratic governance.

With regard to governance, the issue of poverty has also acquired new meaning through the new social policies designed to fight it. Accordingly, good governance must incorporate institutional fora and mediators for negotiating conflicts and demands, and the moderation of open social conflict. Nevertheless, when we attempt to apply that concept to the case of Mexico, it is necessary to keep in mind the fact that legitimacy of public authority is in doubt. More precisely, effective official responses to people's demands are not common within the current legal constructs and the universalist forms of communication between the authorities and the citizen. Therefore, the absence of open social conflict in Mexico is explained by a combination of mechanisms, such as co-optation, clientelism, corporatist representation, through which the government relates to society and broadly negotiates objectives and situations.

Incorporating the idea of the preservation of order into the idea of governance, the relationship between poverty and governance tends to be interpreted as "where there is poverty, there are obstacles to governance." Nevertheless, in some cases and under certain conditions, poverty may be an element which contributes to reproducing a specific form of governance. From this perspective, the official party (PRI) in Mexico has used poverty to maintain its own stability and continuity, and poverty has been used to benefit that preservation of order.

Within the group of countries included in this chapter, it is difficult to prove that any government's response to urban poverty expresses a common understanding of the evolution of social spending and the design of new social policies. Generally speaking, social policies designed in response to the effects of the economic crisis and structural adjustment policies, either assume what might be considered a compensatory character or aim to support the "popular" economy. However, Mexico is the only country within the sub-region where the relation between the state and the poor seems to have been explicitly incorporated into the design of new social programmes. This is demonstrated in the National Solidarity Programme (PRONASOL) (see box on p. 66).

The evolution of poverty is most commonly measured by two methods: Unsatisfied Basic Needs (UBN) and Poverty Line (PL). If we were to employ the first indicator alone, and consider only the satisfaction of the poor's basic needs, we would conclude that poverty declined in sometimes spectacular proportions in Mexico, Colombia and Central America during the 1980s and 1990s. However, if we use the PL method on its own, and thought only of the number of people living at or below a recognized "poverty line" of subsistence, we would find that poverty levels have increased or remained the same over the same period of time. These diverging tendencies are reflected in a decrease in the income of the majority of the population and a simultaneous increase in basic facilities and services (tap water, education, health). This is in keeping with the orientation of the policies designed to fight poverty, which have promoted the expansion of basic services and facilities and only marginally incorporated instruments and programmes to increase the income of families in poverty.[3]

III CONCLUSIONS

While there are instances of progress in Mexico, Colombia and Central America in the gradual evolution towards democratic governance, that process is still in its initial stages. It is important to further state reform at all levels of administration, but especially at the local level, and to enhance the capacity of the population to participate in the design of policies and solutions for their own communities.

The PRONASOL Programme in Mexico

During the presidential administration of Salinas de Gortari (1988-94), a vast government mechanism, through PRONASOL, was established in Mexico. Its aim has been not only to tackle the problems of poverty but also, and fundamentally, to provide the grounds for new forms of interaction between the state and the poor. For that reason, PRONASOL has been presented as the greatest recent innovation in social policy.

Most of PRONASOL's sub-programmes intended to combat poverty are investments in local infrastructure, facilities and services, or they provide small, individualized and temporary support (scholarships, for example). However, these programmes really do not affect the poverty indicators that express income levels; and it is obvious that the decline of these indicators has not abated over the last few years. We can also state that the effects of this programme are contradictory. Poor people participated at a local community level, but this has not meant that they are involved, in any way, in the definition of the general orientation of the programme, much less of broader social policies.

The decline of traditional political party regimes and old forms of representative democracy point to a need for new modalities and channels of popular representation. What kind of actors could promote the transformation of municipal structures to produce democratic local governance? Possible candidates include the parties, with their limitations, but also the newer social actors like non-governmental and grass-roots organizations. New election procedures and structures at the local level would also help to assure a more pluralistic representation of local society in local governments. Of course, these reforms must come from the communities, as well as from supporting actors at the local and central levels.

The transnational dimension should also be included when dealing with governance. In some countries of the sub-region, where the impact of migratory processes has been more intense, political parties have learned to shift the logic of national political struggles from the strictly national arena to one which also encompasses the migrant community in some parts of the US (such as New York and Los Angeles). This means moving the discussion of urban governance and its related issues beyond the national context.

The process of "globalization" affects the majority of the population in the region. Far from being the result of agreements or negotiations among the principal national actors, globalization is a consequence of the conditions imposed through the more distant, ultra-national "rules of the game." Urban governance has a place in the discussions which determine this "game," discussions which take place among the international organizations, and the financial and power centres which operate at a world level. As the recent Mexican crisis has shown, a contradictory perspective at the global level casts a shadow of doubt over the possibility of achieving real advancements in the construction of democratic governance within the national and local arenas of the countries covered.

Notes

1 For example, in 1985, while Mexico reached 79 million inhabitants, the population of Central American countries varied between approximately 8 million for Guatemala and 2 million for Panama.

2 In 1985, 69.5 percent of the Colombian population and 68.4 percent of the Mexican population lived in cities, while in most Central American countries urban population represented less than 50 percent of the total.

3 The Poverty Line (PL) method indicates that poverty levels have increased or remained the same in the sub-region; during the 1980s and 1990s, poor families represented the absolute majority of the population. For example, in Colombia the proportion of poor families rose from 56.3 percent in 1978 to 56.6 percent in 1992, and in Mexico from 48 percent in 1981 to 58 percent in 1992 (Boltvinik 1994; Fresneda 1994).

References

Boltvinik, Julio. 1994. "Estrategias de lucha contra la pobreza en América Latina, promovidas por tres organismos internacionales. Bases conceptuales y de medición." Paper presented at the International Seminar on Governance and Poverty at the Local Level, Mexico City, July 7–9.

Fresneda, Oscar. 1994. "Pobreza y política social en Colombia." Paper presented at the International Seminar on Governance and Poverty at the Local Level, Mexico City, July 7–9.

Gaitán Pilar and Carlos Moreno. 1992. *Poder local. Realidad y utopía de la descentralización en Colombia.* Institute of Political Studies, National University, Bogotá: Tercer Mundo Publishers.

Guillén Tonatiuh. 1994a. "Ayuntamientos, sociedad local y democracia." Paper presented at the International Seminar on Governance and Poverty at the Local Level, Mexico City, July 7–9.

Guillén Tonatiuh. 1994b. "Ayuntamientos en transición. Nuevas políticas, conflictos y actores sociales en los municipios fronterizos." Tijuana, Mexico: El Colegio de la Frontera Norte (mimeo).

Lungo, Mario, 1994. "Pobreza, gobernabilidad y desafíos de la democratización. El gobierno de las ciudades salvadoreñas en los noventa." Paper presented at the International Seminar on Governance and Poverty at the Local Level, Mexico City, July 7–9.

Méndez Acosta, Hubert. 1994. "Pobreza urbana y gestión municipal." Paper presented at the International Seminar on Governance and Poverty at the Local Level, Mexico City, July 7–9.

Merino Huerta, Mauricio, 1994. "Algunas tendencias en la evolución del gobierno local en México." Paper presented at the International Seminar on Governance and Poverty at the Local Level, Mexico City, July 7–9.

Merino Huerta, Mauricio, 1995. "¿Conclusiones? Obstáculos y promesas de la democracia municipal." In Mauricio Merino Huerta (ed.), *En busca de la Democracia Municipal*. (La Participación Ciudadana en el Gobierno Local Mexicano). Mexico City: El Colegio de México.

Negrete Mata, José, 1994. "Participación ciudadana y gobiernos municipales en la frontera." Tijuana, Mexico: El Colegio de la Frontera Norte (mimeo).

Rodriguez Victoria and Peter Ward. 1992. *Policymaking, Politics and Urban Governance in Chihuahua*. US-Mexican Studies Program, Policy Report no. 3. Austin, TX: University of Texas at Austin.

Ungar, Elizabeth. 1994. "Gobernabilidad democrática y participación ciudadana en Colombia." Paper presented at the International Seminar on Governance and Poverty at the Local Level, Mexico City, July 7–9.

Section III

Asia

5 Urban Governance in Southeast Asia Implications for Sustainable Human Settlements

EMMA PORIO

I INTRODUCTION

Urban growth and economic liberalization in Southeast Asia have been accompanied by increasing decentralization and democratization of state-civil society relations. These changes, in turn, have redefined the inter-relationships between urban governance and poverty alleviation. These developments suggest that the governance of cities has become a crucial factor in the creation of sustainable human settlements in the 21st century.

The cities in this region face great challenges in "urban governance" — that is, the relationship between state/city governments and groups in civil society (McCarney, Halfani and Rodriguez 1995) such as NGOs, CBOs and progressive groups from the business sector. In terms of economic growth, Southeast Asia is the fastest growing region in the world today (Asian Development Bank [ADB] 1994). This rapid growth has generated social tensions springing from environmental degradation, congestion, and the escalation of land prices. For the poor it has also meant decreased access to housing, and increasing structural unemployment, poverty and inequality. The state has responded to these conditions through poverty alleviation initiatives — state policies and programmes designed to reduce the economic and political vulnerabilities of the poor. However, these initiatives have not achieved their goals. Thus, the state must forge new relationships with the different sectors of civil society which respond more effectively to the challenges of urban governance and which will create sustainable cities for the future.

The first part of this chapter outlines the broad socio-demographic and economic changes occurring in Southeast Asian cities, while the second part discusses the characteristics, patterns and significance of urban governance in this region. The discussion concludes with an examination of the challenges of urban governance in the changing political and economic climate of Southeast Asia.

II SOCIO-DEMOGRAPHIC, ECONOMIC AND POLITICAL TRENDS

The four countries covered in this chapter — Indonesia, the Philippines, Thailand and Vietnam — have a total population of 367 million, with 117 million (32 percent) living in urban areas. Both Indonesia and Thailand have reduced their population growth rate drastically, from a high of over 3 percent in the 1970s to below 2 percent in the 1990s. In contrast, the Philippines continue to maintain a high 2.3 percent population growth rate. The urban populations, as a percentage of total population in these countries, range from a low of 20 percent in Vietnam, to a medium 30 to 31 percent in Indonesia and Thailand, and a high of 50 percent in the Philippines.

High urban growth rates have intensified problems of subsistence, housing, basic services, crime and violence. This is especially true for the urban poor. With its highly concentrated urban population, Bangkok reflects these conditions. During the boom years of the 1980s, the population growth rate of metropolitan Bangkok grew as high as 11 percent (Mekvechai 1994, 8). On the average, urban growth rates in Indonesia, Thailand and the Philippines have hovered around 5 to 6 percent for the past 10 years. Thus, high urban growth rates challenge the successful governance of the cities in this region.

Rapid economic growth and expansion have greatly influenced urban development and politics in Southeast Asia. During the last five to six years, the Asia-Pacific region as a whole registered very high economic growth rates compared to other parts of the world (ADB 1994). With the exception of the Philippines whose economy grew at about 3 percent per year, Indonesia, Vietnam and Thailand all consistently registered annual economic growth rates of 6 to 12 percent. As these economies undergo rapid growth, major urban centres in the region are also confronted with new problems and responsibilities. Attracted by the growth and promise of jobs, migrants have continued to flock to the cities. This, in turn, further strains the cities' already inadequate infrastructure and basic services.

The collapse of socialist regimes and their integration with global markets has encouraged the assertion of democracic tendencies in the region and accordant shifts in developmental paradigms and strategies. The states in the region have embarked on major reforms, namely decentralization, greater privatization of state-led sectors of the economy, an increased role for the private sector, and recognition of the critical roles played by NGOs and CBOs in national and urban development. These reforms, in turn, have spawned a number of state policies and programmes which transformed the relationship between the state and polity and between national and local state structures in particular. These changes promise the emergence of a civil society willing to engage, and form partnerships with, state bureaucracies in a new urban political and developmental alliance.

III URBAN GOVERNANCE IN SOUTHEAST ASIA: PATTERNS AND TRENDS

Owing to the rapid growth of the economies and urban populations in the region, a new framework and strategy for effective urban governance in Southeast Asia is needed. Increasing urbanization of these societies demands a new paradigm to guide the formulation of new strategies and create sustainable human settlements into the next century. This model is defined by transformed state structures, markets and communities, whose inter-relationships are marked by a need for collaboration and compromise in a new urban social order.

Rapid urbanization and economic growth have resulted in discernible shifts in the concentration of poverty. In the previous decades, poverty was largely defined as a rural phenomenon because the majority of the population lived in the countryside. With 20 to 50 percent of the population now living in urban areas, poverty is increasingly recognized as a major concern among governments and local development councils in Southeast Asian cities.

The following section highlights the key characteristics of urban governance in the four countries and its implications for the Habitat II agenda. These patterns and trends are viewed within the history and evolution of each country's political system. These new understandings will delineate the fundamental structure underlying state-civil society relations which ultimately shape the nature of governance in their metropolitan and urban centres.

Vietnam

The integration of the Vietnamese economy with capitalist markets has transformed the relationship of state and society, and the relationship of city governments to their constituencies. In the planned subsidy system (1975–85), the Vietnamese state was hierarchical and centralized in the capital city of Hanoi and other major urban centres like Ho Chi Minh City and Haiphong. To balance this central dominance, people's committees and mass organizations were set up, so "voices from below" could be integrated into the political decision-making processes of the state bureaucracies. However, in reality, these bodies functioned largely to implement the political goals and programmes of central political authorities. Under the subsidy system, people expected the state to undertake the major political and economic decisions and to take care of their needs as well (Thai Thi 1994).

In 1986, state/party officials unveiled the new political framework of "a free market economy with a socialist orientation under the leadership of the state," popularly called *doi moi*, or renovation. Two years later, it installed a new model of state-civil society relations: the "state in collaboration with the people" (Thai Thi 1994). Thus, the government and the party decentralized its decision-making process and implemented development programmes through people's organizations in collaboration with district officials. Increasingly, the state has also privatized sectors of the economy, forged joint ventures with foreign capital, and allowed private entrepreneurship.

The broad political and economic reforms have changed the relationship of the state to its citizenry. It has led to the recasting of mass organizations and other community-based organizations. With the liberalization of the economy, mass organizations are pressured to take on more representative roles in order to sustain people's interest.

Prior to the "economic renovation" in 1989, social differentiation within Vietnamese society was characteristic of a small, privileged, and elite group of state/party officials while the rest of the population was poor. With economic liberalization, state subsidies in some sectors have either diminished or completely stopped. Meanwhile, the emergence of private enterprise without the central institutional framework — state policies and regulations, social norms or ethics — has led to some getting very rich quickly, while a large number have remained poor or become poorer. Coupled with inflation, a large gap has emerged between the rich and the poor.

Doi moi, then, initiated radical changes in the state's relationships to the different sectors of the economy and civil society. As state policies are still anchored on a centrally planned economy, the surge of entrepreneurial activities is causing social tensions in the cities. In response, new policies and new sets of relationships have to be formulated and implemented by local authorities. Understanding these forces will reveal the bases of relationships between mass organizations, state bureaucracies, the party and business groups.

The current reforms to the Vietnamese economy and political environment offer opportunities for initiating new policies and programmes to support sustainable human settlements. The challenge lies in transforming centrally oriented and hierarchically organized urban structures to respond more positively to private and community-based initiatives for human settlements and livelihood.

Indonesia

Highly centralized and authoritarian, the Indonesian state has shown no signs of opening up since the installation of Suharto's New Order Era 25 years ago. The first 15 years of this regime were marked by an overriding concern for political stability and economic growth and a low tolerance for criticism and dissent. Supporting this political climate, a strong military has performed a *dwifungsi* or dual role (security and developmental) in Indonesian politics and state administration. This also coincided with the boom in oil revenues during the 1970s, which financed the Indonesian state's heavy investments in social and physical infrastructure.

This arrangement changed in the 1980s. By then, oil revenues had declined and the state had to recognize the role of the private sector in shaping state policies. In turn, the leadership also "civilianized" the military-dominated state and politics by considering the role of the business sector and NGOs in economic and social development. This led to a growth of NGOs/CBOs in advocacy and community development.

In general, local/city officials are directly accountable to the central state. However, political stability has allowed more autonomy for city councils to formulate their own budgets. Nevertheless, their development plans largely continue to mirror the national plan. The growing political maturity of segments of civil society has also led to an increasing demand for greater political participation and better urban services. The dwindling resources of the state and the trend towards privatization has led some officials to look at NGOs as helpers in local resource mobilization. Although still vulnerable to government control, NGOs provide potential avenues for influencing the state to be open to participatory politics. Currently, "KADIN," or the Chamber of Commerce and Industry, constitutes an effective lobby group for economic policies, while social development NGOs are influential in environment-related issues.

Thailand

Since the establishment of a constitutional monarchy in 1932, the Thai political system has experienced 45 authoritarian regimes, interrupted by short, fragile bureaucratic systems. The Thai economy has enjoyed consistent high economic growth rates (7 to 12 percent) since the early 1980s. While this has broadened the income opportunities of urban dwellers, the boom has also inflated real-estate prices and led to widespread eviction and displacement of the urban poor. However, it has continued to enjoy the stability, continuity and influence of an elite bureaucratic class. This fact accounts for the legitimacy and influence of state bureaucrats in shaping urban policies. With the exception of Bangkok officials, most city executives are appointed by the Ministry of Interior. Thus, most city officials feel accountable to central authorities rather than to their own constituencies.

Thai officials are pressured to implement programmes and, as such, they seem to be more responsive to their constituencies compared to their Philippine counterparts. Moreover, Thai NGOs and Urban Poor Organizations (UPOs) seem to be better able to discern what they can gain from pressuring and lobbying state bureaucracies. For example, they have pioneered an innovative strategy for land-sharing schemes between residents and developers.

The Philippines

The end of authoritarian rule under the Marcos regime and its dismantling by "People Power" in 1986 has spawned a vibrant civil society. Currently, the central government has devolved most of the responsibility for planning and for the provision of basic services to local governments. The passing of the 1991 Local Government Code provided the blueprint for a comprehensive decentralization programme. These broad political reforms have carved out key roles for NGOs and for people's organizations in shaping urban development and politics. The landmark legislation, contained in the Urban Development and Housing Act of 1992, was mainly a result of NGO/UPO advocacy and mobilization.

While Philippine cities now have a vibrant civil society, the state and class structures are still heavily biased towards the elite. Thus, despite the installation of participation and empowerment ideology in state laws and policies, much remains to be implemented. The rigidity of bureaucratic structures and processes have also pushed NGOs to employ more sophisticated strategies of "demand-making." The 1990s, particularly, have ushered a shift in NGO/UPO orientation and strategies. At the same time that some NGOs have continued their political advocacy for the poor, they have also started to facilitate the delivery of basic services and to assist in the organization of UPOs. Nonetheless, Filipino popular urban movements have also retained their character and function as vehicles for developed demand-making assaults on the state (Karaos 1994). Despite the persistence of this ability, the strategy only seems to reinforce the high level of indifference to the problems of the urban poor among state officials, bureaucrats and business groups.[1]

The NGO movement has a basically middle-class character, and its success in social mobilization is anchored on this attribute. Thus, the NGO agenda for social reform does not seem to be integrally linked to broader economic strategies in the capital nor to labour markets, which have more redistributive potential than poverty-alleviation programmes (Porio 1995).

The state and its bureaucracy suffer from their own limitations. Their lack of accountability and weakness can be traced to the lack of legitimacy and prestige of the civil service in the Philippines compared to those in the other three countries. Career civil service commands high pay and status in Indonesia, Thailand and Vietnam. Thus, urban state bureaucracies and their managers in Bangkok are far more influential than bureaucrats in the Philippines in making decisions on land-sharing schemes and are better able to persuade landowners of a particular scheme.

A Summary

All four countries are undergoing rapid economic, political and demographic changes which have given rise to particular transitions and transformations in state structures and civil society. These changes stem, in fact, from globalization trends which are found to be particularly dynamic in the Asia-Pacific Rim countries. With economic growth, there has been increasing pressure from civil society for political and social liberalization, in order to ensure that the benefits of growth spread to broader sectors of the population, especially the urban poor.

The increasing democratization in the region has also led to pressures for greater accountability of state officials and bureaucracts to their constituencies. In Indonesia, urban development plans and programmes used to be a source of mystery and misunderstanding because they were hardly ever revealed to the public. During the last 10 years or so, the Indonesian state has launched an aggressive campaign outlining the roles of the state, the military and the citizenry in the pursuit of development goals. In the

Philippines, the local development councils have NGO representatives and are beginning to consult their constituencies on city development plans and programmes. Community organizing and mobilization by NGOs/CBOs has meant their increased participation in developmental issues and programmes. In Vietnam, even the state's model of centralized democracy is becoming more liberal by giving more developmental roles to popular organizations and by opening up channels of information on urban development programmes and housing/land regulations. In Thailand, mobilization by the urban poor has grown in response to increasing demand for infrastructure and higher numbers of evictions as a result of economic growth. Thai NGOs and CBOs continue to pressure and engage in dialogue with state bureaucrats in the search for creative solutions.

The varying patterns of urban governance among the four Asian countries are related to three variables: state/bureaucratic strength; the accountability of local/city officials; and the relationship of groups in civil society to the government. These, in turn, affect the capabilities of nation-states and city governments to respond to the needs of the population. This remains especially important for the urban poor in their struggle for access to jobs and sources of income, housing and other basic services.

IV GOVERNANCE PATTERNS IN SOUTHEAST ASIA: IMPLICATIONS FOR THE HABITAT II AGENDA

The abovementioned patterns of urban governance indicate a promising context for pursuing policies and programmes supportive of the Global Plans of Action (GPA) developed for the Habitat II meetings. With the fast pace of economic growth in this region, the challenge of creating mechanisms for building humane cities is centrally anchored on the political relationships between state and civil society. The process calls for progressive business groups, state and local bureaucracies, and NGOs/CBOs to craft creative partnerships in order to address the basic needs of urban dwellers. NGOs have criticized current economic systems for generating inequalities in access to jobs and other basic needs. Without diminishing the value of these critiques, there is merit in calling attention to the need for NGOs/CBOs to initiate creative avenues for the negotiation and renegotiation of the role of the market in social development. The state as an enabling actor must forge relationships with NGOs/CBOs and progressive business groups towards policies and programmes which infuse profit-driven enterprises with human developmental values.

To advance the goals of Habitat II, the contradictions inherent in urban governance must be faced. One particularly prominent need is a solution to the tension between well-entrenched state structures that nurture hierarchical relationships, and civil societies which embrace an ideology of egalitarianism and equity. At the same time, urban governance must begin to create "negotiated" participatory structures and processes. These will progress from the recognition of the differential capacities of various players and communities, and will lead to the identification of strategic partnerships that involve maximizing the distinctive competencies of each player (Porio 1995). Accordingly, the so-called disadvantaged groups will begin to realize that the tradition of state intervention and "dole-out" programmes have bred incapacitating structures and processes. This sets the stage for the realization that governance rests in collectivities governed by an ideology of negotiated goals and directions.

This spirit of "negotiated participation" must form the foundation of sustainable and humane settlements in the 21st century. Beyond the provision of shelter and other basic needs to sustain life in the cities, urban governance must create mechanisms to support institutional partnerships with NGOs/CBOs. These channels must be pursued as a strategy for capacity-building and as a vision of people-centred and sustainable development. More concretely, the gains achieved by groups in civil society — participation, consensus-building, collegiality — have to be balanced with the state's concern for technical efficiency and output-driven systems.

Linking the issue of governance of cities to the creation of sustainable human settlements in the 21st century will allow us to think beyond housing, food security, and the other basic needs of city dwellers. This will facilitate a vision of urban development which includes, and thus moves beyond the minimum provisions to, the urban poor. It pushes for collaboration and calculated compromises among civil society groups, including progressive sectors of the business community and the state. As such, urban governance offers the chance to create a new urban social order based on humane and progressive values.

Challenges and Prospects

More than ever, the challenges of urban governance in Southeast Asia have assumed centre stage because of the rapid economic growth of this region. As a key centre of integration in the increasingly globalized economy, the focal concerns of Habitat II become central to the governance issues of

Southeast Asia. The increasing polarization of social classes, the increased pressure upon city governments, and the dynamic character of civil societies in this region present enormous challenges and opportunities for both the state and groups in civil society. To make cities livable and sustainable in the coming century, these groups need to forge more creative and effective linkages between policy interventions, market forces and community responses facilitated by NGOs/UPOs.

There are two strategies available to meet these challenges. First, state support for beneficial policies and programmes must be broadened. The impacts of specific poverty alleviation programmes are negligible. But the social development advocacy of civic associations, development-oriented NGOs and people's organizations have centred on progressive social reforms. The current middle-class character of social development movements also points to the need to include elites and business groups in the process of urban development in addition to NGOs/CBOs/UPOs. The experience of Indonesia and Thailand has shown that the reduction of poverty involved the invitation of broader state policies and programmes which increased the role of the lower-income classes in manufacturing jobs, and encouraged higher salary levels, more value-added industries and greater agricultural diversification.

The challenge, then, for civil society in its efforts to engage state bureaucracies is to push for broader political and economic reforms which have a greater distributive potential. Possible outcomes include more effective taxation systems, policy supports for the creation of more jobs, and solid income bases within diversifying national economies and globalized markets. This policy advocacy is necessary because the poor must have decent housing and access to services to participate effectively in the growth of the economy as productive actors and income-earners. Similarly, creative policy, structural supports to industries and human resource development, are needed to broaden access to jobs among the poor. The remaining test is in how institutional partnerships between groups in civil society and the state will be forged, and how broad interest in creating quality and sustainability in urban life — through decent shelter, jobs and livelihood — will be maintained.

The second strategy is to solidify the state's role as moderator and facilitator in this larger process. The modes of sustaining urban settlements have been changing over the past 15 years and the role of the state must be redefined. Owing to dwindling state resources, recognition of the capabilities of the private sector, and of people and communities, state institutions and bureaucracies must continue to create collectivities informed by strategic partnerships with the private sector and community organizations. Only these efforts will respond effectively to the increasing demands for housing, services, and economic opportunity in urban areas.

Future Research Frontiers

The challenge for research in urban governance lies in the examination of the intersecting agendas of key actors and the ways in which these are expressed in the practice of negotiated participatory politics. In doing so, there is potential to identify areas of strategic partnership which address the following tensions and intersections in the field of urban governance: the developmental goals and humane values pursued by civil society groups as they advocate for the urban poor; the seeming inability of state structures and bureaucracies to respond to these concerns while they provide policy supports to the broad economy; and the profit-seeking demands of businesses and markets within the globalized economy.

Note

1   A survey of Asian business conducted by the Far Eastern Economic Review showed that Filipino business groups felt that they did not owe anything to society while their counterparts in Indonesia and Thailand were less inclined to think so.

References

Asian Development Bank. 1994. *Asian Development Outlook 1993.* Manila: Oxford University Press for the Bank.

Dharmapatni, Indira. "Urban Governance and Poverty Alleviation in Indonesia." Bandung: Institute of Technology.

Karaos, Anna Marie. 1994. *Urban Governance and Poverty Alleviation in the Philippines.* Manila: Institute of Church and Social Issues, Ateneo de Manila University.

McCarney, Patricia, Mohamed Halfani and Alfredo Rodriguez. 1995. "Towards an Understanding of Governance: The Emergence of an Idea and Its Implications for Urban Research in Developing Countries." In Richard Stren with Judith Kjellberg Bell (eds.), *Urban Research in the Developing World: Vol. 4, Perspectives on the City.* Toronto: Centre for Urban and Community Studies, University of Toronto, pp. 91–142.

Mekvechai, Banasopit. 1994. "Patterns of Urban Development, Planning, and Government in Thailand." Bangkok: Faculty of Architecture, Chulalongkorn University.

Porio, Emma. 1995. "Urban Governance and Poverty Alleviation in Southeast Asia." Paper presented at the GURI Global Meetings, El Colegio de México, October 2–6.

Thai Thi, Ngoc Du. 1994. "Urban Governance and Poverty Alleviation in South Vietnam." Ho Chi Minh City: Department of Women's Studies, Open University.

6

Urban Governance in Bangladesh and Pakistan

NAZRUL ISLAM AND MUHAMMAD MOHABBAT KHAN

I COUNTRY PROFILE

For over 23 years between 1947 and 1971 Bangladesh and Pakistan formed a single country, but in December 1971 they became two independent sovereign states. Bangladesh is a small country with only 142,000 square kilometres of territory. Pakistan is much larger, with an area of 803,300 square kilometres — five and a half times the size of Bangladesh. However, the two countries are nearly equal in population size, each with around 120 million people.

Bangladesh and Pakistan are both low-income countries. Bangladesh with about US$ 220 per capita GNP is the poorer of the two. Pakistan's GNP per capita is around US$ 400. The economy of Bangladesh is still predominantly agrarian, while that of Pakistan is comparatively more industrial and service-oriented.

Both countries have a common British colonial history of nearly 200 years, followed by four decades of intermittent dictatorship and democracy. Parliamentary democracies have existed in both Bangladesh and Pakistan since the early 1990s, the former in a unitary structure and the latter in a federal setting. Pakistan is an officially declared Islamic Republic, while Islam is the official religion in Bangladesh but with a significant minority population. Both countries have been experiencing constant political disturbances arising out of strong differences between the party in power and those in the opposition. Frequent strikes and violent demonstrations are common features in major urban areas, affecting both the economy and law and order.

II URBANIZATION TRENDS AND PROBLEMS OF GOVERNANCE

Bangladesh and Pakistan still have low levels of urbanization. Bangladesh, with only 20 percent of the population living in urban areas (in 1991) is the less urbanized of the two; Pakistan has nearly 32 percent of its present population in urban areas (Table 6.1). However, the absolute size of urban populations in the two countries is already quite substantial, with over 22 million in Bangladesh and over 39 million in Pakistan. Both countries are experiencing rapid growth of their urban populations, with the annual rate of growth around 5.5 percent in Bangladesh during 1970–90, and around 4.5 percent in Pakistan for the same period.

In both countries large cities are growing more rapidly than the national average. This trend has led to the transformation of metropolitan cities into mega-cities, the major examples being Karachi in Pakistan and Dhaka in Bangladesh. There is an increasing incidence of violence in these mega-cities, which has created a situation of crisis from which easy escape is not foreseen. Endemic poverty, resource constraints, environmental deterioration and poor management have made the task of effective service delivery a difficult proposition for urban bodies in Bangladesh and Pakistan. Moreover, local governments in both Bangladesh and Pakistan have been weakened considerably over the years due to the interference of successive central governments in their affairs. Interestingly, both democratic and authoritarian governments have shown an inclination to dominate local government bodies in order to attain partisan political objectives. Elections to local bodies are manipulated in favour of contestants who are supporters of the central government and, in the process, the representative character of these local institutions become compromised. In Pakistan, democratic governments suspended elected local government bodies in order to extend their direct control to the nooks and crannies of the country. Of course, this greatly narrows the scope of popular participation at the local level (Zaidi 1994). Consequently, urban bodies in Pakistan and Bangladesh have not been able to cope with the many responsibilities bestowed upon them.

III THE IMPORTANCE OF URBAN GOVERNANCE AND ACTORS
IN THE LOCAL ARENA

The critical importance of governance, in light of the discussion above, can hardly be overemphasized. Though there are disagreements about the meaning and components of governance, no one denies its pivotal role as an explanatory construct for understanding the relationship between the civil society, the state and institutions operating within them. Despite the problems faced by mega-cities, large cities and even small towns, they are still major contributors to the national economies of both Pakistan and Bangladesh. The role of cities is also important socially and politically.

TABLE 6.1: Urban and Total Population in Bangladesh and Pakistan

	Bangladesh		Pakistan	
	Urban Pop'n (000s)	Urban Pop'n as % of Total	Urban Pop'n (000s)	Urban Pop'n as % of Total
1980	9,968[a]	11.3[a]	23,946[a]	18.1[a]
1990/91*	22,455[b]	20.15[b]	39,250[a]	32.0[a]
2000	34,544[a]	22.9[a]	61,477[a]	37.9[a]

SOURCE: [a] Yeung (1994, 22); [b] BBS (1994, 48).
* For Pakistan, the year is 1990; for Bangladesh, the year is 1991 (actual census year).

These factors make the issue of urban governance vitally important. Governance needs to be examined from the perspectives of accountability, transparency and the participation of the various actors involved.

There are multiple actors involved in the urban arena, including agencies of the central government, the local government itself, the private sector, NGOs and CBOs. However, there is an increasing realization on the part of the government that it can no longer play the role of provider of urban services to all the citizens. This is in spite of the fact that 34 Ministries and 21 Divisions in Bangladesh, and over 100 agencies in some cities in Pakistan, are involved in one way or another with the administration and management of urban areas.

These central government units are performing functions in such areas as resource mobilization, urban administration, physical development, planning, land use control, environmental management, poverty alleviation, housing, water and sanitation. Second, local government authorities — side by side with central government agencies — provide services in such areas as waste disposal, primary health care and education, and provision and maintenance of roads. Third, increasing private sector participation, both formal and informal, in urban areas is becoming more visible. Formal private-sector participation has mostly been in such sectors as health, education, housing, industrial production, business and commerce. The involvement of private organizations in these areas has not only led to employment creation but has also improved the quality of services.

However, such services have not come cheap. Only the rich and the upper middle class have benefitted from the enhancement of the role of the private sector in both Bangladesh and Pakistan. There is also a noticeable surge of the private informal sector in the two countries. Nevertheless, the role of the informal sector in the national economy has not been properly appreciated by the national governments. The informal sector is involved in land, housing, construction, trade, services, transportation and employment creation. The entrepreneurial role of this sector is yet to be fully harnessed.

The role of CBOs and NGOs in understanding this urban scene is essential. CBOs, in the form of neighbourhood associations, have not grown to the extent that was expected, so their role in urban governance is still limited. The situation of Pakistan in this regard is marginally better than that of Bangladesh. Similarly, NGOs are not fulfilling their potential in urban areas. While NGO involvement in urban affairs has been on the increase in recent years, it is not yet as extensive as it is in rural areas.

IV KEY ISSUES IN URBAN GOVERNANCE IN BANGLADESH AND PAKISTAN

Urban governance can be viewed in relation to various issues in the urban context. These include poverty, resource mobilization, land, housing, infrastructure, social services, environment, economy, gender, violence, urban planning and others. This chapter considers only five of the above issues: urban poverty, resource mobilization, urban land, urban planning and urban environment.

Urban Poverty

Urban poverty is a stark reality and it exists in Pakistan and Bangladesh in a massive way. Although the statistics on poverty from various sources differ significantly, even in the late 1980s and early 1990s it is obvious that more than 36 percent of the urban population in Bangladesh and Pakistan was living below the absolute poverty line (Table 6.2). At that time, the urban population living in poverty was more than 12 million in each country. The absolute number of the poor in urban (as well as in rural) areas continues to rise, and to rise at more than the average rate of urban (or rural) population growth. These growing numbers remain one of the starkest development challenges in both Bangladesh and Pakistan.

TABLE 6.2: Percentage of Urban Population below Absolute Poverty Line

	1977–78	1988–90
Bangladesh	68.4	36.9
Pakistan	32.0	38.0

SOURCES: Khundker et al. (1994, Table 4); UN-ESCAP (1993, Table 4.1, p. 4.4).

The Government of Bangladesh has committed itself to face this challenge of poverty. In its Fourth Five Year Plan (1990–95), poverty alleviation was accepted as one of the three major objectives and budgetary allocations were made accordingly. However, the thrust of the poverty alleviation programme was in the rural sector. This is true particularly for the public sector programmes and the NGO-supported programmes. Consequently, the urban sector was left with little more than the formal private sector and the informal sector for government assistance.

Both these economic sectors have recorded rapid growth during the 1980s, and the trend continues in the 1990s. Both formal and informal sectors have done well in the large urban agglomerations, thanks to economies of scale and public policies encouraging the concentration of export-oriented garment manufacturing industries. Thus, more than a million new jobs (of which over 90 percent were for the poor) were created in the garment industries in the Dhaka Metropolitan Area alone. In turn, the informal sector responded rapidly to the growth of this formal sector, providing low-cost housing and other services to the industrial workers. It also has provided employment to a huge number of individuals in the transport sector and in small-scale trades and services. Although most of the informal sector participants are still below the poverty line, a significant proportion have moved above the line.

While poverty alleviation through extended access to credit has achieved remarkable success in rural Bangladesh, similar programmes have not been a significant feature of urban areas. Since the early 1990s, some urban NGOs began to provide credit to poor households in Dhaka following the Grameen Bank model. The coverage is still rather limited, but the results are encouraging. An important support role is played by international and bilateral donor agencies in these activities.

In recent years, the national governments in both Bangladesh and Pakistan have started some programmes to improve the physical living conditions of the urban poor, in slums and squatter settlements. This has helped to raise the value of such areas and indirectly to alleviate poverty to some extent. The *Katchi Abadi* programme in Pakistan and the Slum Improvement Project (SIP) supported by UNICEF in Bangladesh are examples of such programmes. In Bangladesh, the national government implements the project through local governments and urban authorities.

The time has not yet arrived when elected city governments or local municipalities are in a position to design their own poverty-alleviation programmes. Until now, they generally have been inducted in the national programmes which also may be externally inspired and funded. For example, in the nearly 10 million dollar SIP program running between 1985 and 1995, UNICEF's contribution was close to 90 percent. UNICEF has agreed to continue its support to slum improvement in a somewhat revised approach known as the Urban Basic Services Delivery Programme which begins in 1996. Similarly, the Asian Development Bank and the World Bank are also participating in urban poverty alleviation programmes. In the final analysis, however, it should be realized that unless the urban (and also the national) economy becomes stronger, alleviation of poverty will remain a difficult challenge. The local urban government authorities and national NGOs must also play a more vigorous role in the reduction of poverty in urban areas. On a more traditional front, the political parties also should play a more positive role and demonstrate their commitment to such initiatives (CUS 1990; Task Force on Urbanization 1991; Khundker et al. 1994).

Resource Mobilization

Resource mobilization is extremely important for urban governance in countries like Bangladesh and Pakistan. As a resource-poor country, Bangladesh's attempts to locate and harness resources for municipal governments have not been successful. Resource mobilization needs to be accorded top priority, not only for efficient and effective service delivery but also for survival of local governments, whether urban or rural.

It has been estimated that grants or transfers of resources from the government account for an average of one-third of the total revenue of urban governments in Bangladesh (Chowdhury 1994). The contribution of the national (and provincial) government in Pakistan is somewhat less (approximately one-fifth) in the case of urban local government (Khan 1994). Two things need to be noted here. First, there are no positive fiscal incentives built into the present system of grants. National governments in both countries have never made any attempt to analyze or evaluate the implications of grant-funded projects on the general and fiscal viability of local government bodies. Second, government agencies have shown more interest in creating and retaining special development authorities rather than strengthening urban representative institutions like municipalities. These authorities received funds to meet their investment demand, and as such municipalities lost their prominence and potency. However, the disbursement of public funds to special development bodies — which could have been given to local governments as grants — failed to transform these organizations into financially viable bodies.

But the role and responsibilities of representative institutions in local government, like municipalities and municipal corporations, in local resource mobilization cannot be changed by blaming only government policies. Local resource mobilization is highly ineffectual. The poor availability of resources for local governments can be attributed to a number of factors.

First, taxes have never been collected properly. In fact, none of the urban governments since independence has managed to collect all taxes fully. Poor tax collection is the result of a host of factors, such as low level and poor coverage of services, the tendency of the well-to-do to cheat on taxes, and the improper assessment and non-punishment of tax defaulters. In addition to these factors, politicians who seek office at the local level often promise, if elected, to freeze property taxes in order to increase their chances of election. This seriously affects the capacity of the concerned cities to mobilize resources. In reality this occurred in Dhaka during the mayoral elections of 1994. Second, the lack of trained and motivated officials has contributed to an under-valuation of properties in many cities. Finally, there also have been allegations of corrupt practices on the part of officials and employees of urban bodies in assessing and fixing the tax rates.

Neither the central governments nor the local governments of Bangladesh and Pakistan have been able to generate adequate resources for running their cities efficiently. At the same time, the private sector, NGOs and the citizens have not shown the capacity to enhance the resource base of their cities for adequate provision of necessary services. As a result, the running of basic urban services and the improvement of infrastructure is gradually but increasingly becoming dependent on donor agencies. This dependence imposes some obvious limitations on the autonomy of these local governments.

Urban Land

The importance of the urban land issue can hardly be over-emphasized. The distribution of land ownership in urban areas is extremely skewed and unequal. Less than 30 percent of the households in the city own more than 80 percent of its land, while the vast majority (70 percent) who constitute the poor have access (mostly non-owned) to only about 20 percent of the residential land (Islam 1985–86). At the same time, access by the urban poor to other types of land is rather limited. Inequality in land ownership is also a feature of small towns.

In the case of some of the large cities in Pakistan, the government owns a significant portion of the land. For example 80 percent of the land in the Karachi metropolitan area is publicly owned (Shivaramakrishnan and Green 1986, 210). However, the government has inadequate control over its land, and this has given the poor some access to urban land, if only by squatting or land grabbing. Good examples of this are the huge informal settlements of Orangi in Karachi, or Agargaon in Dhaka.

For urban land, no distinct management system exists. Instead, it is a part of a society's total land management system. Although a number of agencies — ministries, departments, directorates, development bodies, private developers and urban local governments (ULGs) — are involved in the management of urban land, it is the Ministry of Land which plays a pivotal role with respect to land throughout Bangladesh. In this country, ULGs have to face most of the urban problems even though these bodies are consistently short of resources, lack proper orientation and capacity. They suffer chronically from lack of jurisdictional authority over many of the important urban management and development subjects, particularly those relating to the use of land.

The preponderance of government agencies in almost all important urban matters has created insurmountable obstacles for the development of local representative institutions. The formal private sector organizations have so far been unable to provide a viable alternative to the government in the area of urban land. In fact, the urban poor have not benefitted at all from the private sector's entrance into the urban land market. Finally, CBOs and NGOs have yet to make their mark in arranging land and shelter for the urban poor. Consequently, it is the informal sector which provides land, in the form of private slums, to house the poor.

In Pakistan, CBOs and NGOs have been more effective in providing access to land for the urban poor, as illustrated in the case of Orangi in Karachi. Sometimes, even the government has behaved like an NGO by assisting the poor to get their right to urban land originally owned by the government — as in Hyderabad (Hasan 1990).

A number of land management policy options can be mentioned which, if taken in the right spirit and acted upon accordingly, may lead to an effective system of urban governance. First, it is imperative that the role and capacity of ULGs be enhanced and their jurisdictions enlarged. This would necessitate transferring many functions of the government to ULGs. Second, those planning and development agencies which are involved in the area of urban land should be placed directly under the jurisdiction and control of the ULGs. Finally, appropriate mechanisms need to be devised and a congenial environment created to enable increased participation of the majority of the urban inhabitants in the planning and management of urban land in both Bangladesh and Pakistan.

Urban Planning

Urban planning in the large metropolitan areas of both Bangladesh and Pakistan is the responsibility of urban development authorities. These specialized bodies were established either by the promulgation of acts or the framing of statutes in major cities. The first of such bodies in Bangladesh was created for Dhaka through a special act known as the Town Improvement Act, 1953. The Dhaka Improvement Trust (DIT) was established in 1956 under this Act. The Trust was later renamed the Rajdhani Unnyan Kartripakkha (better known as RAJUK) or the Capital Development Authority, in 1987. The second such authority, the Chittagong Development Authority, was established in 1960, followed by the Khulna Development Authority in 1961 and the Rajshahi Town Development Authority in 1976. Each of these authorities, as in the case Dhaka, was established under a special ordinance. These authorities have been entrusted with considerable power, to draw up and implement urban development plans. They are thoroughly techno-bureaucratic organizations directed by the Ministry of Housing and Public Works, and run by official functionaries without any popular participation.

At present, there are around 120 municipal towns in Bangladesh without a planning and urban development authority like those set up by the four large city corporations. By ordinance, these municipalities have a mandate to propose and implement plans, but none of them has any planning department or even an official urban planner. However, the national-level organization, the Urban Development Directorate (UDD), is sometimes called upon to prepare master plans for such municipalities. The preparation of master plans for municipalities and nearly 400 other small towns began after the *upazilas* were chosen as the appropriate level of administrative decentralization in 1982. All the 460 *upazila* towns (nearly 400 of which were non-municipal) were to have master plans prepared by the UDD itself or by consultants working under its supervision. Thus 392 *upazila* town plans were prepared by 1990 and in addition *zila* (or district) town plans were also prepared. Subsequently, the Local Government Engineering Bureau (LGEB), later Department (LGED), under the Ministry of Local Government, was given responsibility of overseeing the preparation of such *upazila* and *zila* plans. This created some uneasiness in the relationship between the two (UDD and LGED) central government agencies.

Ultimately, however, virtually none of these so-called master plans was implemented. Instead, the municipal towns went ahead with their informal and ad hoc "planning" and development work. The direct participation of the citizens in the urban planning and development process is generally limited to occasional written complaints and demands made to the municipal authority about local problems and needs. Elected ward commissioners also represent the neighborhoods or communities in the municipal council. In spite of this limited inclusion, the 21 municipalities which have the Slum Improvement Programme, supported by UNICEF, have experienced some form of participatory local area development.

As in Bangladesh, the urban development authorities in Pakistan have wide-ranging powers to regulate and plan urban development. Their jurisdiction covers most building and planning controls. More specifically, the responsibilities of such bodies include the preparation of master plans/structure plans, and implementation of these through their housing infrastructure schemes and through their approval of additional private sector designs (Khan 1994). Over the years, these authorities have provided services such as housing, water, sewerage and road networks, and *Katchi Abadi* improvement. Multi-sector urban development programmes have also been taken up from time to time by some of the bodies, with donors providing financial support.

The *Katchi Abadi* programme is a nation-wide activity begun in the early 1970s to improve and regularize squatter settlements in urban areas in Pakistan. The programme sought to provide infrastructure to all squatter settlements which had developed on government land. It also sought to "regularize" these sites, in order to legalize the land occupation and adjust the site plan so that access roads could come into the settlements. The programme hoped that significant community participation could be mobilized and that costs could be recovered. However, the *Katchi Abadi* programme has had very limited success, as no more than 10 percent of all squatter settlements have benefitted from its implementation (Hasan 1990). Nevertheless, the principle of involving the community in the improvement of their own settlement is laudable.

Urban development in general, and urban planning in particular, have been affected adversely by the simultaneous presence of a number of factors, variables and conditions occurring in both Bangladesh and Pakistan.

First, too many agencies have been involved in urban development. Complications have arisen from government ministries as well as numerous other organizations which operate at both the national and local levels. This situation has resulted in overlapping jurisdictions and a lack of coordination. For instance, urban development activities in the Dhaka Metropolitan Area have suffered in the absence of coordinated decision-making, planning, implementation and maintenance of services. Second, among other things, municipalities were created to undertake planning and management of urban areas but, in almost all cases, municipalities and municipal corporations have not been able to perform such functions. Administrative, financial and technical capabilities of these bodies have remained rather weak. As a result, municipalities have been unable to play a decisive role in guiding and controlling growth of urban areas in spite of the availability of requisite laws and regulations.

Third, urban development policies have been formulated to maintain and promote the interests of individuals belonging to privileged classes and groups. In line with such policies, a major portion of the development authorities' activities has concentrated on providing developed plots of land to middle- and upper-income people at below-market rates. Consequently, in Bangladesh, the poorer section of the population has been denied its share of the land. There, the government has provided serviced land at subsidized prices to higher-and middle-income groups, and only to a small extent to the lower-income groups. Accordingly, municipalities have participated in the Slum Improvement Programme with LGED and

UNICEF. However, the situation in Pakistan is a little different. The development authorities have shown considerable innovation and experimentation in the development of various housing solutions for the poor — like the *Katchi Abadi* improvement programme, and the construction of labour colonies.

Fourth, political leaders at the helm of the government institutions have been lukewarm in their general commitment to urban development and planning. This has not furthered the cause of balanced city development. Fifth, efficiency, equity and citizen welfare have not figured at all as considerations in urban planning. Sixth, urban development planning has suffered in most instances because there have been no effective linkages or meaningful integration between central planning and local level requirements. And finally, in both Bangladesh and Pakistan, urban planners have failed to identify the critical nature of land issues in urban development as well as in macro urban issues relating to the economy, society and the environment.

Urban Environment

Urban areas in Pakistan and Bangladesh, like those in other developing countries, suffer from a number of environmental problems. A rapid increase in urban population and slow economic growth have caused overcrowding, shortages of housing, and an uncontrolled growth of slum and squatter settlements. This has caused a general deterioration in the physical condition of cities. An increase in the number of vehicles and industrial growth have aggravated air and water pollution in most of the large cities. Waste management is another serious problem common to all major cities. In Bangladesh, floods also cause enormous problems for urban areas, and some of the cities are vulnerable to erosion of the river banks as well.

In recent years, the response to rapidly growing environmental problems in Bangladesh has been quite significant. The government has been able to formulate a National Environment Policy (NEP) which includes the participation of a reasonably large number of professionals. A massive Flood Action Plan (FAP) has been prepared with the help of professionals and ordinary citizens at various stages, though the actual degree of participation in the planning process by people to be affected by implementation of FAP is questioned by many. Even the justification of FAP itself has been debated, particularly by NGOs. The issue was even raised at several international forums including the European Parliament, to convince donors to influence national-level decision-makers. However, at more local levels and with issues like the environmental improvement of slums, the concept of citizen participation has been quite effectively incorporated. This is the case in several cities in Bangladesh and in the *Katchi Abadis* underway in Pakistan.

Tackling environmental problems effectively and managing them properly requires understanding of a number of basic determinants. First, no amount of effort will reduce environmental problems to any significant degree without poverty alleviation, which must include increased food production and stabilization of population growth. Second, the political system must ensure direct, effective and meaningful participation of the citizens of the country in the political process. Finally, the economic system must be premised on ensuring equity as well as growth, otherwise the sustainability of the system itself will be at stake.

V FUTURE ISSUES AND RESEARCH IN URBAN GOVERNANCE
IN BANGLADESH AND PAKISTAN

In both Bangladesh and Pakistan, urban governance issues and their determinants need to be understood in the context of economic underdevelopment and massive poverty. After years of development efforts with heavy and constant doses of foreign aid, a very large section of the population in these countries still lives in abject poverty and suffers from malnutrition, illiteracy and poor hygiene.

Besides economic underdevelopment and poverty, the two countries also suffer from political unrest which results in considerable social insecurity. The large cities in particular are faced with problems of political and ethnic violence. In some cases, law and order is breaking down, and under such circumstances the governance of urban areas becomes very difficult. The state and civil society lose opportunities to interact properly and positively. Even state agencies in the same city fail to coordinate amongst themselves. Tussles between state and local governments continue as well. In this process, critical issues like access of the poor to housing, health, education, infrastructural services and credit get bypassed and overshadowed by political events, and the environment continues to deteriorate. Thus, the successful management of major cities in Bangladesh and Pakistan requires these countries to face the challenges of national political problems as well as local urban issues.

Local urban governance issues which require immediate attention and deserve analysis through research are the following:

- *Governance and urban poverty.* The relationship between poverty and governance remains to be analyzed in the exclusive context of the sub-region. The consideration of the poor in urban development planning, their empowerment and participation are some of the issues to be examined.
- *Reform of the local government system.* The role of local governments and their possible reform need to be examined from the perspective of the governance context. Why is the autonomy of local governments in Bangladesh and Pakistan under threat from the central government? How do local government systems respond to the emerging civil society organizations? What can be done to ensure active participation of the poor in urban local government bodies?
- *Governance and service delivery.* The role of various actors in urban governance needs to be researched with regard to delivery of urban services, including waste management. What actions can be initiated to improve service delivery by local urban governments? What kind of role can the private sector play in urban service delivery?
- *Governance and economic development.* In the context of an open market economy, what is the role of the local government with respect to the national government, the private sector, and NGOs? How can they cooperate towards achieving more rapid economic growth, while at the same time protecting the interest of the majority of the population — particularly the poor?
- *Governance and violence.* Violence, crime and the condition of law and order have worsened in the large cities in Bangladesh and Pakistan. The role of the community, NGOs, political parties, local government and police needs to be examined from the perspective of governance if urban violence is to be addressed.

References

BBS (Bangladesh Bureau of Statistics). 1994. *Bangladesh Population Census 1991. Volume 1, Analytical Report.* Dhaka: Bangladesh Bureau of Statistics.

Chowdhury, Amirul Islam. 1994. "Resource Mobilization and Urban Governance in Bangladesh." Paper presented at the Sub-Regional Workshop on Urban Governance in the Development: Bangladesh and Pakistan, Dhaka, June 16–17.

CUS (Centre for Urban Studies). 1990. *The Urban Poor in Bangladesh: Comprehensive Summary Volume.* Dhaka: Centre for Urban Studies, University of Dhaka.

Hasan, Arif. 1990. "Community Groups and Non-government Organizations in the Urban Field in Pakistan." *Environment and Urbanization* 2(1): 74–86.

Islam, Nazrul. 1985–86. "The Poor's Access to Residential Space in an Unfairly Structured City, Dhaka." *Oriental Geographer* 29/30: 37–46.

Khan, Atta Ullah. 1994. "Urban Governance in Pakistan with Relation to Urban Planning and Development." Paper presented at the Sub-Regional Workshop on Urban Governance in Bangladesh and Pakistan, Dhaka, June 16–17.

Khundker, Nasreen, W. Mahmud, B. Sen and M.U. Ahmed. 1994. "Urban Poverty in Bangladesh: Trends, Determinants and Policy Issues." *Asian Development Review* 12(1): 1–32.

Shivaramkrishnan, K.C. and Leslie Green. 1986. *Metropolitan Management: The Asian Experience.* Washington, DC: The World Bank.

Task Force on Urbanization. 1991. *Report of the Task Forces on Bangladesh Development Strategies for the 1990s: Vol. 3, Social Implications of Urbanization.* Dhaka: University Press.

UN-ESCAP. 1993. *State of Urbanization in Asia and the Pacific.* New York: United Nations.

Yeung, Yue-man. 1994. "Urban Research in Asia: Problems, Priorities and Prospects." In Richard Stren (ed.), *Urban Research in the Developing World: Vol. 1, Asia.* Toronto: Centre for Urban and Community Studies, University of Toronto, pp. 17–45.

Zaidi, Syed Akbar. 1994. "Governance and Urban Local Government in Pakistan: Expecting too Much from too Little?" Paper presented at the Sub-Regional Workshop on Urban Governance in the Developing World: Bangladesh and Pakistan, Dhaka, June 16–17.

7 Urban Governance in China: The Zhuhai Experience

WANG YUKUN

China's economic reform has succeeded in expanding the country's economy at an annual rate of at least 10.5 percent for the past 15 years. Inevitably, a nation of 1.2 billion with such a high economic growth will show its enormous purchasing potential and investment strength. This, in turn, will make China one of the leading economic forces in the Asia-Pacific region and worldwide. International capital is continuing to rush into China: international investment reached US$ 11 billion in 1992, 150 percent above that of the previous year, and in 1993 it grew to US$ 25.8 billion. If one considers total investments through contractual obligations, that figure rises to US$ 111 billion.

Substantial Changes in China's Economy

As long as the market generates spectacular growth in the Chinese economy these trends will persist. The potency of market forces in China can be explained briefly. First, there has been a deregulation in pricing. Previously, nearly all prices were determined by nationally integrated plans, but now only 6 percent of products are priced under the restrictions of economic planning. The law of supply and demand has returned as a market regulator.

Second, market demand is burgeoning. The percentage of private earnings in China's GNP has climbed nearly 20 percent, from 53 percent in 1978 to 73 percent in the early 1990s. The expansion of effective market demands has enabled further growth of the national economy.

Third, the financial system has deepened. Accumulated household financial assets (HFA) have reached over 2000 billion yuan. The percentage of HFA as a proportion of the GNP has grown from 10 percent in 1978 to 64 percent in 1993 (CSYB 1994), which is markedly higher than in typical developing countries. In fact, it is closing in on that of the developed market economies in the West. Chinese households have become the major force in financial investment.

Fourth, capital has become increasingly liquid. By the end of 1993, the number of share-holder companies had reached 13,000 in China, with 122 of them being listed domestically and six listed on overseas markets. The capitalization of domestic listed companies amounts to 133 billion yuan, and there are 45 funds with varying financial portfolios. Twenty-three of these funds are listed on the market at a value of 4.2 billion yuan. There are also 30 commodity exchanges in the country, with 300 brokerage firms dealing in commodity futures.

Fifth, there is a greater dependence on foreign trade. The total value of China's international trade now amounts to 30 percent of its GNP, which amounts to a relatively heavy dependency on overseas trading. The expansion of the overseas market will only further stimulate China's economy.

II URBAN CHANGES AND THE CHALLENGES TO URBAN GOVERNANCE
IN CHINA

To understand the new approaches to urban issues the old system of urban development under the traditionally planned system must be considered. In the early years after the founding of new China, the central decision-makers were confronted with very narrow alternatives. Decades of war had subjected the Chinese people to the agony of hunger and poverty. The most urgent problem was supplying the people with basic food and clothing. In that regard, the Cold War and the international economic embargo posed a serious threat to the survival of the new regime.

While the legitimacy of the new-born regime depended on the Chinese government's ability to supply basic necessities to the people, it was also understood that China must quickly industrialize to realize national independence and prosperity. Thus, Chinese social development policies were formulated to ensure the basic needs of the people, emphasizing equal distribution, and giving priority to heavy industry. Just like the former Soviet Union, China regarded the development of heavy industry as the only way to achieve industrialization under the circumstances. This strategy enabled China to realize a high level of industrialization with a rather low per capita income. The manufacturing sector as a percentage of the GNP reached 35 percent in 1979, 1.7 times higher than most low income countries (where the rate averages 13 percent), and far higher than that of the middle income countries (25 percent) and countries with industrialized market economies.[1]

The strategy of giving priority to heavy industry and a closed self-servicing industrial structure has had a direct impact on urban development. The tertiary sector and some public facilities were regarded as non-productive and their development was restricted. To change the structure of these policies, China has had to address three main problems: capital accumulation, labour allocation and control over consumption.

Pricing policy had played a leading role in capital accumulation for centrally controlled industrialization. The main feature of the traditional pricing policy was a reliance on farmers for the capital accumulation required for industrialization. Implementation of this pricing policy began with grain in 1954, as China began to establish a unified purchasing and marketing system for basic agricultural products. The unified purchasing and marketing system was a rather complete system, designed to accumulate capital for national industrialization, to ensure the supply of agricultural products, and to stabilize the general price levels. After 30 years of use, the unified purchasing and marketing system has made historical contributions to China's industrialization program. It is estimated that it contributed 800 billion yuan to industrialization, based on the price differentials between industrial and agricultural products.

The use of agriculture to subsidize the growth of industry had some unavoidable consequences for a country with a huge population and limited arable land. The main variable stabilizing this arrangement was the allocation of labour, and towards this end China adopted a unique policy. In urban areas, technology and capital-intensive industries were encouraged, while labour-intensive undertakings were concentrated in rural areas. Through this policy the state had been able to contain the surplus of rural labour in rural areas while also ensuring the development of heavy industry in cities.

The functioning of this policy was guaranteed by systems which enforced strict control over the registration of urban residences, food rationing, and employment guaranteed through the state. Under China's traditional planned system, key market factors like labour, land and capital did not have much impact on the formation and development of cities. Even the commodity market remained largely insignificant since commodities were only circulated through planned channels.

Opportunities and Challenges of Reform

While effecting fundamental changes to China's economy, market reforms have also brought about opportunities in, and challenges to, urban development.

First, fundamental changes have taken place in the motivation for urban development. The reforms have liberated urban development from its original orbit and the central decision-makers' preference for heavy industries which dominated everything else. Since the reforms began, the development of various commodity and service markets has become the motivating force behind urban development.

Second, drastic changes have occurred in urban employment structures and channels. Previously, all employment opportunities were controlled by a centralized national economic plan. Market development today creates work opportunities and has created a non-planned labour force from a floating population. The employment rate of the non-registered "floating" population in cities has increased considerably. Rough estimates for 1990 show that this population accounted for around 20 percent of total urban employment. However, the rate varies widely in different cities. The floating population represents 300 percent of the registered population in Shenzhen and 45 percent in Guangzhou (Li at al. 1991, 67, 97–98). This population constitutes an important new force in urban development.

Third, the sources of capital for urban development have totally changed. In the past, the only source of financing for urban development was a centrally allocated budget. However, urban economic reforms have featured decentralization and have favoured consumers in the initial distribution and re-distribution. The accumulation of household financial assets has laid a solid foundation for urban development in the future. The acquisition of private capital will enable urban development to cater more towards the inspirations of consumers and investors rather than being swayed by arbitrary preferences.

Fourth, the main actor in urban affairs has shifted from the central government to urban local governments. Previously, the city was only a spatial unit for production, the city government was only a branch of a centrally controlled administration, and the mayor was just a cog in the big machine. Today, the municipality is no longer a passive object but a vigorous subject with independent decision-making powers. A mayor is no longer a cog, but a positively charged entrepreneur full of pioneering spirit. City governments have now gained their own independent resources, and hence the capacity to control the living environment of their citizens and enterprises.

Nonetheless, the adoption of a market system has also posed serious challenges to urban development. These challenges differ in form but the background of their emergence is surprisingly similar. For example, industries continue to be concentrated in big cities and continue to operate at very low levels of efficiency. Comparative advantages are supported by those industrial sectors with a more competitive function. This trend seems to be stimulated by the comparative advantages of some industries and appears to be a problem generated by the market system. However, in reality, it is the result of the failure of basic market forces — like the labour opportunity cost, the price of land, and the preferences of investors and consumers — to become significant factors in the adjustment phase of the reforms. Soaring urban housing prices are often blamed on the wanton levying of fees and surcharges by developers and local government, while the economic rationale of housing price increases has become obscure. The higher cost of urban housing actually represents the labour opportunity cost in large cities. All these issues reveal the continuing distortion of urban economies towards heavy industry. Consequently, it may be concluded that urban planning faces difficult strains emerging from both the traditional system and the process of rapid change.

With decentralization, the central government cut away its budget for financing urban infrastructure, which made the shortage of public facilities generated by previous development strategies even worse in the new market economy. Financing for urban construction remains a beguiling problem in the new environment. The trend toward in-kind financing in many municipalities may be a short-term solution to a chaotic financial mess. However, it is a quite distorted approach and cannot be considered sustainable. Currently, local urban governments have gained their independent status in development management, but they have failed to find adequate financial resources to sustain this new authority. In response to the transformation of urban areas through economic reform, market development, and social and technical innovation, a new concept has emerged. Urban governance offers a new model for examining these processes.

III URBAN GOVERNANCE

Concept and Focus

There is no equivalent to urban governance in the Chinese literature.[2] The closest concept in Chinese translates as urban management, which includes urban planning, financing and legislation. Management itself is a well-developed science and may be analysed from many perspectives—by looking at the manager or the managed, at a whole process or a distinct aspect of the process. The same is true of urban governance. The remainder of this chapter attempts to explain several features of urban governance as it has developed during China's process of reform.

The Zhuhai Approach

A group of leading cities has emerged with China's economic reforms, and Zhuhai is one of the most impressive. Fifteen years ago, Zhuhai was little more than an unknown border village with one street and several thousand people. Its major businesses were fishing and agriculture. When it was chosen as a special economic zone in 1979, it had barely 6.8 square kilometres of developed land. Today Zhuhai is a medium-sized city with a population of 520,000 and 41 square kilometres of built-up area. Among all Chinese cities in 1994, Zhuhai was first in per capita terms in deposits, first in roadway and green space area, second in private earnings, second in gross industrial and agricultural products, and fourth in living space. The gross product growth rate has stayed over 30 percent for the last 15 years. All of these achievements in Zhuhai are related to the city's thorough inquiries into urban governance and have resulted in a higher capacity for urban development.

Urban capacity refers to the ability of a municipality to turn its preferences and objectives into reality. It reflects the interrelationship between urban development objectives and the capacity to realize them. A case study of governance in the city of Zhuhai provides evidence for this discussion.

The Capacity to set up Development Objectives Overstepping Available Resources

Despite initial problems. the city of Zhuhai is meeting the challenges of urban growth. Today, Zhuhai has established a new concept of urban development to meet the needs of the globalized economy. As a starting point, there are large ports, well-developed industries and broad infrastructure services. Zhuhai is carrying out an urban master plan, oriented towards the future and making urban modernization concordant with the natural environment.

China has needed an authorized urban master plan for a long time. There are three reasons for a plan like that to exist. First, the current development strategy lacks far-reaching meaning. People usually pay too much attention to short-term reality. Second, the methodologies employed are not yet market-oriented. The price of land, its appreciation, and effective supply and demand attract little attention. Third, there are many imperfections in the existing system of management.

Zhuhai has advantages in all three of these areas. Their strategic plan looks 60 years ahead. An understanding of effective demand and differential rent has also been incorporated into their master plan. Finally, there is a unified management system which supervises all urban development projects with one authoritative voice.

Extractive Capacity

The ability to mobilize financial resources through land development and modern financial tools is known as extractive ability. The more impressive the municipal development strategy and master plan, the more influential the municipality is in terms of fundraising, the more investment that city will extract, and the more of its development objectives it will achieve. There must be a qualified governing body to protect municipal development objectives, especially during the transition period where interest groups conflict with each other. In addition to the force liberated by the new urban concept, there are other dimensions to Zhuhai's extractive capacity. The "Five Unification" policy in land management shows this government initiative. Debt financing, equity transaction and other market vehicles are also effectively employed by the Zhuhai government.

Implementation Capacity

Implementation capacity is the ability to implement given tasks through the effective organization of institutions. Zhuhai rules out all the difficulties with the One Governor System (OGS). The power of Zhuhai's OGS is absolute, with the mayor being also the Party secretary. The same is the case with the head of any bureau, district, institution and state enterprise. The OGS creates a firm base for the Party's leadership, and automatically makes the chief administrative officer subject to Party supervision. Actually, an OGS-type system is the regular case in enterprise management. An enterprise has to keep its authority focused at one level in order to survive in an arena of tough competition. This principle has its heritage in Chinese history but brings about new trials in China's current political system.

The OGS lies at the core of Zhuhai's high administrative efficiency. Zhuhai's strong "implementation capacity" is directly related to the OGS and the competency of the Mayor.

Steering Capacity

The ability to guide urban socio-economic developement is known as steering capacity. How can a municipality strengthen its large-scale steering capacity in a market economy? Zhuhai seems to have made some headway in this direction. Since the Zhuhai special economic zone was established, the more market-oriented the economy has become, and the stronger has become the municipality's steering capacity. The nature of, and approaches to, this strategic planning have changed. Referential economic planning has replaced the strict national economic plan, and forward-looking urban planning, innovative land management, and appropriate local policies have begun to function as the main instruments of government regulation.

Legislative Capacity: Creating Legislation on the Principle of Successful Experience

Urban legislative capacity refers to the municipality's ability to legally regulate urban activities to work towards achieving maximum benefits for the citizens. It is a sign of progress that an element of legitimacy has been installed in Zhuhai's urban government. A responsible municipality in any system must govern the city according to law. However, in the primary stage of achieving this legitimacy, Zhuhai's urban governance depended a great deal on the personalities of its governors.

IV CONCLUSIONS

The transition from a planned economy to a market economy remains one of the world's most difficult problems. Zhuhai's experience in this sense is a contribution to modern development thinking. The factors behind this city's success are chiefly transition management and strong government. Things would not have worked without these two conditions.

What are Zhuhai's distinct features? First, Zhuhai was only a small fishing village a decade ago. It was like a piece of clean paper on which a most beautiful picture might be drawn. In one sense, this was a great advantage.

Even if a large inland city did set long-term goals, the complexity of their existing situation may still hold back the achievement of such goals. Second, Zhuhai was one of the first special economic zones in China and consequently it has enjoyed preferential policies for some time. Third, there is a mayor with more than ten years of experience, a fact which allows him to think about development objectives from a longer-term perspective. A mayor with three to five years' experience may think about the future but will not bother to struggle for objectives that might not be realized for another 60 to 100 years. This foresight remains another distinct feature of Zhuhai's experience.

But some limitations and challenges remain. This chapter focuses on development management rather than on governance. The formal structure of governance has not been explained. It is certainly true that China is a well-organized society and the majority of services it provides are effectively delivered by the formal sector. However, along with market development there is an emerging role for civil society which will create a place for popular participation in the future. Some attention should be given to this new development. There are also other significant issues to be addressed, such as the structures of public participation, the role and function of NGOs, the role and structure of social security, housing, transportation, medical care, and justice amongst others. Cities are among the most important supporting bases of modern civilization. The significance of the study of urban governance cannot be over emphasized. It is a cause that will require the efforts of several generations to accomplish.

Notes

1   The rate in developing countries is different from that in developed countries. The low industrial rate in developing countries represents a higher rate in the agricultural sector, while the low industrial rate in developed countries represents a higher proportion of service sector enterprises (Zhou et al. 1987, 13).

2   "Governance" is not yet a well defined term. Linguists take the term as the act or manner of governing or exercising control or authority over the actions of subjects: a system of regulations. It can also refer to how people are ruled, and how the affairs of a state are administered and regulated; a nation's system of politics and how this functions in relation to its public administration and law. Other definitions of governance, like that of the World Bank, focus more on the management of development, suggesting

that governance is the manner in which power is exercised in the management of economic and social resources for development.

References

CSYB (China Statistics Year Book). 1994. China Statistics Press.

Li, Mengabai, et al. 1991. *Effects of Floating Population on Big Cities.* Economic Daily Press.

Zhou, Qiren, et al. 1987. *New Stage of National Economic Growth and Rural Development.* Zhejiang People's Press.

8 Governing Cities in India, Nepal and Sri Lanka: The Challenge of Poverty and Globalization

OM PRAKASH MATHUR

The standing and competitiveness of a country will largely be determined by how the development and growth of its cities are managed (International Conference on Cities and the New Global Economy 1994).

I INTRODUCTION

Interest in urban governance, and more specifically the governance of cities, has grown at an extraordinarily rapid pace in recent years. Who should manage and govern cities, and how and with what kinds of instruments should the cities be governed, are important issues in many developing economies. But, unlike earlier discussions, the debate is not confined to what municipal and other governmental institutions should do to manage cities. Nor is it restricted to the mechanisms for improved provision and delivery of urban services, long seen as the sole index of "good government."

Rather, embracing a wider canvas, the present discussion on governance is concerned with the broader questions about the capacity of urban areas to deal with changes that are taking place both within cities and, externally, in the global economy. Indeed, the capacity of city-related and city-wide institutions to deal with the demands and pressures that are being generated in cities as a result of these changes has become a major issue. Do these institutions have the capacity to deal with the growing pressures of poverty and deprivation? Can cities effectively respond to the challenge of the opening of national economies, into what Kenichi Ohmae (1991) calls a "borderless world?" The new state of world affairs involves the globalization of economic activities and a freer mobility of capital, labour, technology and other factors of production. Can existing institutions take on this challenge? What kind of an environment — rules, regulations, procedures and systems through which cities are governed — should be in place for cities to contribute effectively to and, in turn, benefit from, the process of economic liberalization?

An important aspect of these discussions relates to changes that have taken place in the concept of governance itself. What is governance? Is it synonymous with "good government" or is it distinct from government? Is it a *mechanism*, as alleged in the classical theories, needed to make certain social goods available — providing water supply, conservancy services, primary health and street lighting to people residing in cities? Or, is it a *process* designed and planned to involve people in decision-making? To what extent do present-day cities conform to the new norms of governance?

For low-income economies such as India, Nepal and Sri Lanka, which are urbanizing at moderate-to-rapid rates and undergoing major structural and policy shifts, the issue of governance is particularly significant. There is some doubt whether institutions in these countries have what they need to manage urbanization. No one is certain whether these structures can provide basic services and infrastructure productively for their fast-growing urban populations, or if they can effectively deal with poverty which has accompanied the process of urban population growth.

During the past few years, India, Nepal and Sri Lanka have embarked on programmes of economic liberalization, involving the de-licensing of industries and trade, the deregulation of foreign investment, and a host of other measures. Questions are beginning to be asked about how cities in these countries will be able to meet the incremental infrastructure demands that may be generated by the process of economic liberalization. What do these policies mean for institutions such as the municipal authorities, special-purpose parastatal agencies, and other layers of administration and bureaucracy which have historically been at the centre of city affairs? What kind of an adjustment will be required for the city-related and city-wide regulations and systems to enable urban areas to meet the challenge of the opening of the world's economies?

For reasons that are now widely established, initiatives have been taken worldwide to strengthen the process of democratic decentralization and to revitalize local government institutions. India, Nepal and Sri Lanka are no exceptions. These initiatives include the Constitution (Seventy-Fourth) Amendment Act, 1992 on Municipalities (India), the Municipalities Act, 1991 (Nepal), and the Thirteenth Amendment to the Constitution, 1987, followed by the Provincial Council Act No.42 of 1987 (Sri Lanka). A central question is how these initiatives impact on the governance of cities. Will the constitutional and legislative changes that have been carried out in India, Nepal and Sri Lanka be able to improve the governance of cities, ensuring and promoting wider participation and greater accountability?

Will these do away with the arbitrary nature and ad hoc approaches that have long characterized centre-local and state-local functional and fiscal relationships, and improve the functioning of city-wide institutions?

II WHO GOVERNS CITIES? AN OVERVIEW OF THE EXISTING INSTITUTIONAL STRUCTURES

Who governs and manages cities in India, Nepal and Sri Lanka? What is the role of "government," particularly municipal government, in the management of cities? What role do the private sector and the non-governmental institutions play in the affairs of cities? This section gives a brief description of the composition, functions, responsibilities, and fiscal powers of urban governmental institutions, and in particular the municipal governments, parastatal agencies, and NGOs.

Municipal Governments: Composition, Functions and Powers

Municipal governments are at the very centre of the affairs of cities in India, Nepal and Sri Lanka. Owing historically to the Lord Ripon resolution of 1882 in India, Ordinance No. 17 of 1865 in Sri Lanka, and the establishment in the early 1920s of sanitation offices and wards in Nepal, municipal institutions have over the years come to acquire a pivotal position in the management and governance of cities, and to play a paramount role in the management of the urban economy. The extent to which they manage cities, however, differs enormously between countries and between cities within the same country. In some, their role might even be regarded as peripheral at best.

In general, there are three distinguishing features of municipal governments. First, municipal governments in India, Nepal and Sri Lanka are, by law, democratic in character and based on full adult franchise. Thus, the municipalities in these countries have directly elected councils, boards and corporations. Another important point relates to the powers of the elected council, including those of the mayor or council chairperson. In India, for instance, the elected council chairpersons in smaller municipalities share powers of decision-making and administration with the councils and the various standing committees. This is the essence of local democracy. However, the management pattern in the case of large cities is based on the principle of separation of power between the elected body, the standing committees, and a bureaucracy which is usually headed by a municipal commissioner. The elected body deliberates on policies and approves the budget, but the municipal commissioner exercises executive powers.

A second consideration is that the municipal institutions are typically responsible for the provision of basic public goods falling into four broad categories: public health, public safety, public work and public order. They also perform important regulatory functions relating to public health (for example, they check the sale of flesh of diseased animals, and the cutting of fruit); public safety (control of the use of premises for dangerous trades); public works (relating to urban planning and building codes); and public order (control over the use of public places). Conceptually, municipal functions include those goods and services whose benefits are localized and for which there is a differential scale of preference. Other services, whose benefits spill over to other jurisdictions, rest with the higher levels of government. In practice, the division of functions between the municipalities and higher levels of government is rarely neat or airtight — joint occupancy of functions is the rule rather than the exception. Moreover, their responsibilities have expanded in recent years.

A third feature worth noting is the fiscal domain of municipalities in India, Nepal and Sri Lanka, which includes property taxes. The property tax typically includes a tax for general purposes, a water and drainage tax, a lighting tax and a scavenging tax. It also includes taxes on carriages and carts, animals and advertisements, as well as duties on transfers of properties, and *octroi* in selected states. Several states in India permit municipalities to impose taxes on cinemas, theatres, circuses, carnivals and other shows. The main municipal taxes in Nepal consist of a house tax, a rent tax, a business tax, a vehicle tax, parking fees, service charges and *octroi* duties. In Sri Lanka, the primary source of municipal income is property tax. Other sources of revenue include fees for services, licensing charges, and borrowings and grants under permit from the central government.

The Role of Parastatals

The management of cities in India, Nepal and Sri Lanka is not an exclusive responsibility of municipal governments. Parastatals and special purpose boards and corporations have developed crucial stakes in city growth and management over the years. A product of the 1960s and 1970s, these parastatals are interdisciplinary bodies, responsible for planning, coordinating, implementing, funding and supervising urban development works. Many of them have made major inroads into what was traditionally the municipal domain, particularly in the sphere of water supply and drainage, and slum clearance and improvement. Most states in India have state-level water supply and sewerage boards, slum improvement boards, housing boards and city-based development authorities. Nepal has a country-wide water supply corporation, a housing development finance agency, a solid waste management and resource mobilization centre, and other boards dealing with bus services, town development and housing finance. Similarly, in Sri Lanka, the production and delivery of services which are connected with the areas of responsibilities of urban local authorities rest with the National Water Supply and Drainage Board, the Road Development Authority, the Central Environmental Authority and the Central Electricity Board.

These parastatals are essentially concerned with developmental and capital works, and it is these functions that distinguish them from municipal bodies whose principal domain lies in the operation and maintenance of services. In fact, as several studies indicate, the developmental role of parastatal agencies provides the primary rationale for their establishment. It is argued that the creation of new assets (capital works) is a discrete function, distinct from the one required for the upkeep, maintenance and operation of existing stock and assets. Also, the technologies required for the creation of new stock are very different.

The Private Sector and Urban Services

The role of the private sector is substantial in the provision of such services as transport and health. The share of the private sector in intracity transportation, for instance, varies from a low of 22 percent to a high of 94 percent in several Indian cities. Even in a service like water supply, which is a "natural monopoly" and a stated public responsibility, the non-governmental organisations and private agencies play a noticeable role. According to the 42nd round of the National Sample Survey, 28.5 percent of water supply in India is provided by non-governmental sources.

Mention should be made here of the role of voluntary groups — the term being used here to include neighbourhood-based community organizations (often referred to as CBOs), NGOs, and different forms of civic and consumer fora in city management and city affairs. It should be noted that the active participation of voluntary groups in the cities of India, Nepal, and Sri Lanka is a comparatively recent development, and is commonly characterized by three features:

- The predominant focus of such groups on the problems and development needs of disadvantaged groups, especially the urban poor, women and children;
- An increasing professionalization of voluntary groups' activities;
- A shift away from a "welfare" to a "development" focus in their activities.

A review of the literature shows that voluntary groups are primarily engaged in three types of activities:

- *Participation in government development projects.* In terms of reach and coverage, incorporating community participation in government-sponsored development projects is probably the most widespread form of participation in urban governance. Important examples of this are the Hyderabad Urban Community Project in India and the Million Houses Initiative in Sri Lanka.
- *Delivery of urban services.* The EXNORA group in Madras (India) presents an interesting example of voluntary groups in delivering specific services; it has introduced a system of garbage collection by retaining the informal rag-pickers and by enabling them to receive salaries from the resident groups. The main advantage of this activity is not just service delivery, but also a more meaningful participation of stakeholders in the process of urban development.
- *Consultation on public policies and issues.* In the past, much of the attention of voluntary groups was on creating models, innovations and experiments, but not so much in influencing the process of formulating and implementing public policies. The voluntary groups today recognize the limits of their efforts in working with isolated communities, and are beginning to exert pressure on policy-making exercises.

This is, at best, a partial overview of the institutional network that is concerned with and involved in the management of cities. The question as to who does what and which agencies and institutions deliver services, or regulate activities, or organize communities has not been systematically examined in the literature. It continues to be, as noted by Douglas Yates, "an intractable jigsaw puzzle because of the inherent fragmentation of urban service delivery and the historical fragmentation of urban policy-making process" (Yates 1977, 6). Although stated in the context of the US, this aptly describes the situation in South Asia.

III HOW EFFECTIVELY ARE CITIES GOVERNED? AN ASSESSMENT

How effectively urban institutions have been able to govern cities and grapple with their problems is one question that lies at the centre of the issue of governance. More broadly, the issue encompasses the functioning of municipal governments — indeed, the entire *process* of governing urban areas. An attempt is made here to select evidence on four aspects of the functioning of city-wide institutions: the delivery of services, financial management, the regulatory framework, and the representative and participatory character of municipal institutions.

Delivery of Services

The basic function of municipal governments is service delivery, and it is a distinctive function. Studies on service delivery demonstrate that the municipal and other institutions in the three countries examined here are not able to provide adequate and equitable access to basic shelter, infrastructure and services. Anywhere between 11 and 30 percent of India's urban population is dependent on questionable sources of water supply, and another 57 percent lack any form of sanitation. Cities of over 100,000 in population are reported to have capacities to collect and treat only about 60 percent of solid waste. Smaller cities have virtually no arrangement for the collection and treatment of different kinds of wastes. Towns in Nepal are faced with serious urban services deficits. In 1987–88, while 83 percent of the urban population had water supply services, and 70 percent had electricity, only 47 percent had sanitation, 18 percent had solid waste disposal, and virtually zero percent had any form of stormwater drainage. It is crucial to note that large-scale exclusion of the urban population from such services is the most visible aspect of the poor performance of urban institutions in these countries.

Finances and their Management

Municipal and other city-wide institutions in all three countries are financially weak and unviable, and are not able to generate enough resources to meet their expenditure responsibilities. The revenues of municipalities in India account for only about 2.9 percent of the combined revenues raised by the centre, states and municipalities. Only a few municipal administrations are able to put into practice the principle of user charges for recovering the cost of the services that they offer. In practice this has meant large-scale subsidization of civic services which, in turn, has increased the dependence of city administrations on higher levels of government. As a result of inappropriate financial management systems, many cities are reported to have amassed large internal and external debts.

Municipal governments in these countries continue to rely on an extremely narrow, relatively inelastic and non-buoyant tax base for their financial resources, and are consequently forced to employ high rates of taxation. It is estimated that only about 15 to 25 percent of properties are in the property tax net of the cities on the Indian sub-continent. The balance stand exempted because their rental values are below the threshold or because they fall in the tax-exempt categories. Many taxes — particularly those imposed on non-motorized transport, animals and vessels — are obsolete, having lost their economic relevance over time. Others which have a large potential — like taxes on advertisements, professions, entertainment and licence fees — are beset with the non-revision of tax rates and enforcement procedures. The weak financial position of municipal institutions and the inefficient manner in which the finances are managed constitutes a major impediment to the effective governance of cities in all three countries.

The Regulatory Framework

Most of the municipal governments in the three countries use regulations, procedures and systems that are exceedingly cumbersome, time-consuming and costly. Although specific studies on the cost of municipal laws and regulations are few and sporadic, it is estimated that the cost of every transaction — be it a building permit or a licence for operating a kiosk or a shop — is at least 35 to 40 percent of the benefits of the proposed activity to the citizen making the request. As Alain Bertaud has noted, "The additional time and cost involved in getting the legal permits is so costly that they [individuals] often prefer to relinquish the benefits attached to the formal process, particularly access to housing finance . . ." (see Lee 1994).

Participation in Governance

A crucial aspect of governance relates to the representative character of municipal institutions. Although the municipal governments in India, Nepal and Sri Lanka are democratic in character and based on a full adult franchise, the systems of participation are weakly developed and provide little articulation of interests of different population groups. An estimated 50 percent of municipal bodies in India are under supersession at any given point of time, and are run by administrators. In the opinion of experts, the state governments in India have used their powers of suspending or dissolving the municipal bodies too liberally, based mostly on political considerations but occasionally sometimes on technical-administrative grounds.

While forming an important complement to the network of municipal institutions, the parastatal agencies in India, Nepal and Sri Lanka have not made any significant impact on the governance of cities. Indeed, these agencies have been able neither to improve the delivery of services nor to help reduce the demand on scarce public resources. K.C. Sivaramakrishnan's observations with regard to the functioning of parastatals are worth noting:

> In reality these special purpose bodies have also been as prone to indiscipline, and inefficiency and financial problems as the municipalities which they sought to replace. The special purpose bodies do not come under any significant public control and are usually an extension of the State bureaucracies. The absence of public participation and lack of public accountability are also cited as reasons for resisting attempts of cost recovery and the continuation of subsidies, hidden or overt (Sivaramakrishman 1992).

Judged by the criteria applied in this section, it is evident that the existing system of governance is grossly deficient. The institutional framework is unable to meet the demand for services. Moreover, it is financially weak and unviable, and it is far from being representative or participatory. Historical efforts to make the urban governmental system cohesive have not helped to bridge the fragmentation that characterizes the urban institutional network in the countries of this study.

IV THE CHALLENGE OF URBAN GROWTH, POVERTY AND GLOBALIZATION

Propelled by internal and external events, cities in developing countries are undergoing changes that are unprecedented in history. Significantly, the changes are as much demographic as economic and social in character. This section attempts to present those changes which constitute a direct challenge to the governance of cities.

Urbanization and Urban Growth

Urbanization, in the sense of more and more people living in urban areas, is by far the most important social change that has taken place in the Indian subcontinent in recent times. From a base of approximately 147.4 million in 1970, the number of urban dwellers rose to 328.2 million, signalling an increase of 122.7 percent over the two decades 1970–90. During the same two decades, India's urban population doubled, increasing from 109.1 million to 217.6 million, and that of Nepal rose from 462,000 to 1.68 million. No census was held in 1991 in Sri Lanka, but the urban population is estimated to have risen from 2.74 million in 1971 to about 3.68 million in 1991.

One outcome of this process of urban growth will be the emergence in these countries of very large cities. In 1971, the number of cities with over one million population in India was nine and their share in the urban population was 25.5 percent. By 1991, the number had increased to 23, their combined population to 70.7 million, and their share of the total urban population to 32.5 percent.

The impending urban growth in these countries is of even greater importance. According to the United Nations, by the year 2020 India will have close to 648 million people in urban areas, accounting for roughly 47 percent of its total population. Of Nepal's total population, 26 percent or 8.9 million people will be urban. Approximately 9.1 million out of a total population of 23.6 million in Sri Lanka will be urban dwellers. This scale of urbanization and the expanding size of cities are basic facts with which urban institutions and municipal governments must come to terms. The efficient and effective management of urban areas and the removal of constraints to the expansion of basic services and infrastructure form the core of the current policy concerns in these countries.

The process of urban growth in India, Nepal and Sri Lanka is accompanied by significant changes to the structure and character of cities. It is not the formal economic activities but the informal ones that have expanded with urbanization, growing at a phenomenally high rate in all three countries. In Sri Lanka, for instance, employment in the informal sector accounts for approximately one-half of all employment, with the self-employed accounting for nearly 58 percent of this segment. The employment structure in Indian cities has likewise undergone similar shifts. According to Nurul Amin, employment in small firms accounts for anywhere between 40 percent and 70 percent in the four major cities of

India. Thus, one may argue that cities in these countries have undergone dramatic changes in the nature and structure of employment, and it is these changes which carry different implications for municipal governments and urban institutions. Dealing with cities which have very large informal components must mean developing more flexible responses, procedures and policies than those that happen to be on the statute books today.

Poverty

The existence of large-scale urban poverty presents to the governments of India, Nepal and Sri Lanka perhaps their biggest and most formidable challenge. Estimates indicate that close to two-fifths of the total urban population in India falls below the poverty line. Nearly 50 percent of Nepal's urban population is stated to be living in abject poverty. In Sri Lanka which is otherwise characterized by high quality of life indices, the nutritional levels of approximately 54 percent of urban households were found to be inadequate, and 24 percent "at risk." Similarly, 3.2 percent of the total number of urban households were categorized as extremely poor.

Poverty reduction and alleviation policies in India, Nepal and Sri Lanka have generally been the concern of national governments. Local and city-level governments have played little direct role in the formulation or design of such policies and programmes. Recent assessments have, however, shown the ineffectiveness of top-down conventional strategies of poverty alleviation. Either the strategies have proven to be irrelevant or they have encountered problems of delivery and proper utilization. It has since been recognized that poverty problems are highly location-specific, and are best tackled at community levels, by using community-centred approaches, and making use of community resources for the delivery of basic social and economic services. The questions of what should be done to promote and internalize community-level approaches, and how to enable communities to organize themselves, are directly facing city governments in these countries as they attempt to address growing poverty.

Globalization

During the past few years, major reforms have been introduced in the industrial, trade and fiscal policies of countries in the Indian subcontinent. All industrial licensing in India, apart from industries relating to security, strategic and environmental concerns, has been abolished in all cities of less than one million people. Complementary measures have been taken in the fiscal and financial sectors and in overall macroeconomic management. Various kinds of fiscal incentives and subsidies have either been reduced or withdrawn, and the expectation is that the process of financial reforms that has now begun will lead to integrated international financial markets.

Concerted efforts have been made by Nepal since the early 1980s to attract direct investment in order to help bridge the resource gap and to meet domestic technology needs. Generally, the incentive structure available to foreign investors has been on a par with that of domestic producers. In addition, the repatriation of profits and dividends is now permitted under the Industrial Enterprises Act of 1981. In Sri Lanka, major initiatives in trade liberalization and domestic deregulation were introduced in 1977. On the trade policy front, most quantitative restrictions on imports were replaced by a simplified system of tariffs. The dual exchange rate was unified at a rate which represented a currency devaluation of about 50 percent. Controls on foreign exchange transactions and repatriation of profits were eased and an industrial free trade zone was created. Recent years have seen further deregulation of the Sri Lankan economy.

These changes in economic policies and procedures in India, Nepal and Sri Lanka are aimed at stepping up economic growth, improving market efficiency and competitiveness, and integrating their economies with the global commodity markets. Such changes have important implications for the different sectors, especially the urban sector and cities where most of the new investments, both domestic and foreign, are expected to be made.

The impact of these policy shifts on urban areas cannot be estimated, and remains in the realm of speculation. At best, it is possible to argue that the import substitution policies of the past several decades, the reliance on domestic as opposed to international markets, the provision of urban services and infrastructure at subsidized rates, the licensing practices, and countless official regulations all tended to favour concentration of activities in capital cities and large market areas. Export orientation could change the pace and pattern of urbanization and may lead to different types of growth in different city locations. Similarly, de-licensing could mean dispersal of economic activities and consequently a more balanced spatial distribution of population.

However, the economic impacts of policy shifts in India are beginning to be known, with some signs of an increase in the country's share in global trade and marketing. Evidence of this is available from the data on foreign direct investments which have risen rapidly since the opening up of the economy. The implications for *governance* of the opening up of economies, however, can only be assessed in general terms. For instance, it is broadly understood that future economic growth in these countries is contingent on the efficient functioning of cities. Similarly, it is understood that the process of economic liberalization, which is expected to be reinforced with the second cycle of reforms, will have major ramifications for cities and their network of urban institutions and financial systems. It is also understood that economic liberalization will entail competition between cities, and may involve higher levels of investment in land, housing, infrastructure such as transportation, energy and communications, and essential services. These may be traditional local functions but globalization has modified the type of environment appropriate to them, and the rate of economic and technological change that affects investments.

A crucial task will be to adjust the existing frameworks to meet the changing requirements of the national and international economies. Land, housing, infrastructure and services, and the efficiency with which these can be delivered, will remain crucial variables in urban development and vital issues in urban governance. The accountability of urban institutions and their new roles in handling these factors will be decisive in meeting the challenges of urbanization, poverty and globalization in the coming century.

V THE CONSTITUTION (SEVENTY-FOURTH) AMENDMENT ACT 1992
ON MUNICIPALITIES (INDIA)

The issue of governance is inextricably linked with constitutional and legislative provisions. As pointed out earlier, municipalities in India, Nepal and Sri Lanka derive their powers either from central government legislation, or from state legislation, or both. The constitutions of these countries recognize municipalities as units of self-government but do not endow them with any powers.

Mention should be made of a major amendment made in 1992 to the Constitution of India, intended to strengthen the process of democratic decentralization and local institutions. Certain features have a direct bearing on the governance of cities:

- The amendment visualizes municipalities as fully representative institutions. Municipalities cannot remain under supersession after dissolution for an indefinite period; while state governments still have the powers to dissolve municipalities, reconstitution is required within a period of six months from the date of dissolution.

- Municipal governments are no longer viewed as civic bodies responsible for the provision of a few merit goods or public goods. Rather, the amendment sees them as vitally important for such tasks as "planning for economic and social development," and "poverty alleviation." Endowing the municipalities with functions of economic development and poverty alleviation constitutes a major departure in the government's position about their role.

- The amendment aims to minimize the arbitrary nature and ad hoc approaches in state-municipal fiscal relations, and provides for a greater flexibility in fiscal management. In state-municipal fiscal relations, the amendment provides for the setting up of finance commissions at the state level, with responsibilities for determining the principles governing: (a) the distribution between state and municipalities of the net proceeds of the taxes, duties, tolls and levies collected by the state, which may be divided between them; and the allocation between the municipalities at all levels of their respective share of such proceeds; (b) the determination of the taxes, duties, tolls and fees which may be assigned to, or appropriated by, the municipalities; (c) the grants-in-aid to the municipalities from the Consolidated Fund of the state. The state finance commissions are also empowered to make recommendations on the measures needed to improve the financial position of the municipalities.

The Constitution (Seventy-Fourth) Amendment is a milestone development, aimed at strengthening democratic decentralization and bringing order to state-municipal functional and fiscal relations. It is also an opportunity for countries such as India to involve people, particularly disadvantaged groups, in the process of decision-making.

VI CONCLUDING REMARKS

The general importance of urban governance in developing countries has increased enormously in recent years, especially in countries on the threshold of rapid urbanization and urban population growth. The explanation for its increasing importance, as this chapter points out, lies in a number of factors, such as the broadening of the concept and meaning of governance in the particular context of cities; rapid urbanization; the breakdown of the mandates of existing urban institutions; the concentration of poor people in cities; and the opening up of economies.

Cities are economically crucial for most countries. Urbanization is the natural outcome of economic development and a necessary requirement for the rational use of resources. The opening up of economies is expected to enhance the economic importance of cities. It is also contingent upon the ability of cities to meet the complex demands that it may place upon them for integration with the world economy.

Governing cities in light of these tasks and challenges requires a three fold agenda:

- *Designing an institutional framework that can meet the growing needs of land, infrastructure and services.* It is of crucial importance to indicate the respective roles of the government and the market. Over the years, sufficient evidence has accumulated to demonstrate that the government alone cannot fulfil this responsibility; more important, it need not necessarily do so. The earlier practice of ignoring the potential of the market needs to be shed for two reasons: the private sector has demonstrated a potential role in spheres such as land, shelter, infrastructure and services; and there now exists a widespread view that the government need not directly engage in land development and the production of infrastructure and services. New ideas suggest that the government should play an enabling role and focus on removing the impediments to the involvement of other stakeholders.

- *Choosing the right kind of financial instruments and mechanisms which are crucial for building up the financial viability of city governments.* This is an important ingredient for effective governance. The important aspects of this include the reduction of reliance on public funds; an appropriate pricing of publicly provided goods and services, and implementation of the principle of cost recovery from the users/beneficiaries; and a forging of partnerships with the private sector in the spheres of land development, urban infrastructure and the provision of services. Any governance strategy which is based on the premise of a large-scale commitment of public funds is unlikely to be acceptable. Moreover, any strategy that does not provide for cost recovery is not likely to be sustainable.

- *Adjustment in existing legislative and regulatory instruments for effective governance of cities.* Most of the instruments available to city governments have outlived their utility, and have no place in a forward-moving economy. The point to stress is that there is no way in which the problems of land, shelter, infrastructure and services, and economic growth can be solved unless legislation such as the Urban Land (Ceiling and Regulation) Act and the state-wide Rent Control Acts are repealed, and city-wide regulations are made simple, inexpensive and transparent.

Urban governance in India, Nepal and Sri Lanka is at a crossroads. Long considered to be an exclusive responsibility of the government and state-owned and state-led institutions, it is now being viewed as a collaborative effort of all stakeholders in the cities' futures. Among the stakeholders, the governments at national, state and local levels will have an important role to play, but so will industrial and business enterprises, as well as the communities themselves.

Finally, the need to undertake systematic research on issues of governance must be stressed. Virtually nothing is known about the process of governing urban areas. Even less is known of what distinguishes the governance of larger cities from that of smaller ones. A few key questions to guide the urban research agenda of developing nations include: What is the process of governing urban areas? What kinds of relationships exist among the different stakeholders? What institutional reforms are needed in order to be able to govern cities of the 21st century?

References

International Conference on Cities and the New Global Economy. 1994. *Brochure*. Melbourne, November 20–23.

Lee, Michael. 1994. *The Cost of the Second Best: The Price of Land Regulation in Asia*. London: Development Planning Unit, University of London.

Ohmae, Kenichi. 1991. *The Borderless World*. New York: Harper Collins.

Sivaramakrishnan, K.C. 1992. *Urban Governance in India*. New Delhi: Centre for Policy Research.

Yates, Douglas. 1977. *The Ungovernable City: The Politics of Urban Problems and Policy Making*. Cambridge, MA: MIT Press.

Section IV

Africa

9

Building Democratic Local Urban Governance in Southern Africa: A Review of Key Trends

MARK SWILLING

I INTRODUCTION

An exploration of the meaning and modalities of local urban governance in Southern Africa in the mid-1990s comes at an opportune moment in this region's history. Across Southern Africa fundamental transformations at the political, socio-economic, spatial and sub-continental levels are rapidly changing the very complex set of vertical and horizontal relations that compose *local urban governance*. Southern Africa in the 1990s is a remarkable sub-continent due to the extent to which all its countries are going through decisive strategic — indeed even paradigmatic —shifts in their respective modes of governance.

After reviewing the emerging literature on governance (see Swilling 1996 [forthcoming]), the following formulation has been used as a basis for the case studies in this chapter: *democratic local urban governance in our towns and cities will develop if accountable and democratically managed local governments are developed that, in partnership with well managed formations in civil society who are committed to the principles of trust and reciprocity in the promotion and defense of citizen interests, have the capacity to formulate and implement policies that deal effectively and efficiently with urban development problems.*[1]

South Africa[2]

Urban Development

South Africa's population of 38 million people in 1990 is expected to double over the next three decades. The Urban Foundation has estimated that the population will be 46.5 million by the year 2000, and 59.7 million by 2010. The black population alone is expected to increase by 130 percent between 1980 and 2010, from 21.1 million to 48.5 million (Coetzee and De Coning 1992).

It has been calculated that 65 percent of the population was function-
ally urbanized by 1989. The 3.4 percent growth rate in the urban population between 1980 and 1985 is expected to level off now at 3.09 percent.
The main contributing factors are rural-urban migration and natural population increase, with the latter now the dominant rather than secondary
cause of urban population growth rates (Coetzee and De Coning 1992,
14). It is expected that 69 percent of the black population will be living in
urban areas by the year 2000.

South Africa has five major metropolitan agglomerations: the Pretoria-
Witwatersrand-Vaal (PWV) region (which has been renamed Gauteng
and is now one of the nine Provinces), Greater Cape Town, the Durban
Functional Region (DFR), Port Elizabeth-Uitenhage and East London-
Mdantsane. By the year 2010, 75 percent of the population are expected
to be living in these five metropoles which, in turn, will be responsible for
75 percent of the GDP. Gauteng, as the primary metropole, will have a
population reaching 12 million people by 2010 and it will be responsible
for the production of up to 50 percent of GDP by this time. There are
indications, however, that Gauteng's economic performance is weakening
relative to other centres such as the DFR.

With a national budget of approximately 160 billion Rand (US$ 50 bil-
lion), 91 percent is allocated to operating and recurrent costs. This leaves
at most only R16 billion (US$ 5 billion) for capital investment. After
noting the level of urbanization and the spatial concentrations of the
population, it is not that surprising that the government has identified
investment in urban infrastructure as the most important developmental priority. In a policy framework entitled the Municipal Infrastructure
Investment Framework, it has been calculated that approximately 4 million people (15 percent) have access to only untreated and unreticulated
water, and that approximately 8 million (30 percent) have access to only
minimal sanitation (i.e. shared toilet facilities or unimproved pit latrines).
The same study indicates that about 17 million people (65 percent) do
not have access to electricity, and that about 8 million people have neither formal road access to their residence nor stormwater runoff. It has
been calculated that it will cost: R44.7 billion to bring these service levels up to "basic level" (i.e. communal taps, pit latrine, graded roads,
street lights), R62.7 billion to bring levels up to "intermediate level"
(one tap per yard, water-borne sanitation, graded minor and tarred major
roads, and 15–3-amp electricity point to each housing unit), and R89 billion to achieve full service levels (i.e., house connections for water, full

water-borne sanitation, paved roads and piped stormwater, and a 60-amp electricity connection).

Urban Government

The transformation of South Africa's local government system has taken place in a way that is probably unique from an international comparative perspective. Out of all the political systems that have gone through a non-revolutionary transition from authoritarianism to democracy, South Africa is the only one where this transition occurred *simultaneously* at a national and sub-national level. Between 1992 and 1994, Local Negotiation Forums were established in each town and city within a statutory framework that defined their composition and role. The local forums were then mandated to negotiate locally appropriate solutions consistent with the principles of non-racialism, democracy, one tax base, accountability and so on. The first phase was to establish appointed Transitional Local Councils. The first elections for these bodies took place in November 1994. The second phase will last until the National Constitutional Assembly has finalized a new national constitution which is to occur by 1998.

Local Urban Governance

Like many other countries in Asia, Africa and Latin America, South Africa is acknowledged as one of those developing countries that has highly developed networks of institutions, organizations and associations within civil society that organize collectively to defend and promote their interests and values. (According to the Development Resource Centre, South Africa has no less than 54,000 NGOs of one kind or another.) This is not the place to provide a detailed account and analysis of these networks. However, it is possible to identify four very broad categories within which there are, in turn, a wide range of organizational forms, namely CBOs,[3] NGOs, business associations, and quasi-NGO/parastatals. These are all very active in urban areas.

The remarkable bottom-up transformation of local government according to non-racial and democratic principles occurred in a way that brought CBOs, NGOs and organized businesses directly into the policy process. In other words, unlike the other countries analyzed in this chapter, local urban governance in South Africa revolves around the negotiated reconstitution and re-institutionalization of local government structures in each specific context.

Namibia[4]

Urban Development

Although Namibia is largely a poor rural society with a total population of 1.6 million, the share of the nation's population living in urban areas increased from 25 percent to 33 percent between 1981 and 1991. During this period, the urban population grew by 5.8 percent per annum nationally and 3.89 percent per annum in Windhoek for the same period. These urban population growth rates are considerably higher than the annual population growth rates of 3.1 percent. The total population is expected to double over the next 17 years.

Government spending on social services has increased, although the Government remains dependent on a very narrow tax base. Given that donor aid is declining, economic growth is the only hope for increasing government revenue to sustain the financing of extended social services. Unfortunately, GNP per capita dropped by 15 percent between 1980 and 1992. For the decade 1980–1990, GDP increased by less than 1 percent. During the four years since independence, growth has averaged just below 2 percent.

Urban Government

Namibia inherited a divided local government system with autonomous, fully developed local governments in the former white areas, and highly dependent local government bodies in communal towns, villages and townships. The basic new legislative framework for local government is detailed in the Local Authorities Act and the Regional Councils Act, both of 1992. The Ministry of Regional and Local Government and Housing is responsible for the management of this framework.

Since independence, private investment in urban development has been heavily concentrated in the capital city, Windhoek. This means that local governments outside Windhoek are suffering from dwindling revenue bases and increased financial dependence on central government at a time of increased demands for urban services. Capital allocations from the central government for urban infrastructure, however, are dwindling. This is forcing many local governments to increase the costs to the consumer of water and electricity and they are trying to raise additional revenue by speculating on the sale of serviced land. These measures effectively marginalize the urbanizing poor to informal settlements on the urban peripheries — a process that ensures the ongoing replication of pre-independence urban forms and functions.

The newly created Regional Councils and Local Governments that have been established in accordance with the 1992 legislation are only just beginning to operate as viable governing bodies. Virtually all suffer from a lack of qualified personnel and many officials from the pre-independence era have resisted affirmative action. Newly elected politicians with little or no experience in the business of government are slowly beginning to come to terms with their roles and the constraints they face in meeting the urban challenges in their respective areas. The real problems, however, derive from an inappropriate allocation of functions and powers along the vertical axis.

Local Urban Governance

As far as accountability is concerned, Namibia's robust quasi-federal constitution, multi-party system, relatively strong judiciary and regular elections makes it one of the few fairly substantial constitutional democracies in Africa. As was already pointed out, however, the regional and local levels of this state system are still in their early stages of development. Namibia also has a fairly well developed non-governmental sector that is actively involved in policy formulation and capacity building. Nevertheless, this is manifested largely at a national level because this is the locus of policy-making — centralized systems concentrated in a capital primary city tend to have this effect. The relative weakness and newness of Local Governments as loci of urban development policies that NGOs and CBOs can relate to means that governance at the local level is still embryonic. As one NGO activist put it, even in Windhoek "we never go into the municipal offices for anything."

Conclusion

In conclusion, it is possible to argue that local urban governance in Namibia is relatively weak. Poor urban management policies, centralized policy-making, the underdeveloped nature of sub-national government, the legacy of strict urban regulation and the nature of inter-governmental fiscal relations combine to undermine the salience of locally constituted urban dynamics in the shaping of urban development policies and processes. The emergence of NGO and CBO lobbies at a policy-making level are indicative of trends that are beginning to counter state domination of urban policy. However, until they develop strategies for empowering local governments to attain greater control over urban policy and urban development resources, and until urban civil society is focused on local governance, it will not be possible to build democratic forms of local urban governance in Namibia.

Mozambique

Urban Development

In a United Nations report entitled *The Emergency Situation in Mozambique: Priority Requirements for the period 1988–89,* it was pointed out that Mozambique had 1.1 million displaced persons, 2.2 million people affected by severe shortages of food and essential items, 2.6 million people affected by commercial food shortages and about 700,000 people living as refugees in neighbouring countries. Mozambican researchers now operate on the assumption that the population is 16 million and that one third of the population is displaced by war, drought and economic collapse (Swilling 1994, 287). Although it was assumed in 1980 that there was a 13 percent urbanization rate, the impact of the displacement of 5 million people and fundamental societal dislocation had placed perhaps half the population either within the urban areas or directly dependent on the urban economies as massive numbers of people moved towards urban settlements and as the rural economies collapsed.

The structural adjustment programme that Mozambique adopted and implemented in the 1990s is fundamentally reshaping the urban economies. During 1992, growth rates were negative at -0.8 percent. However, growth rocketed to 19 percent in 1993 after the war formally ended and the drought was broken. This dropped to 5.2 percent in 1994 with a predicted growth rate of 6 percent for 1995 (Mozambique 1995, 8). The introduction of new fiscal policies resulted in the reduction of the budget deficit. Inflation is being brought under control, exports have been rising and imports have also risen.

While these economic indicators seem to support the objectives of the SAP, poverty indicators tell a different story. Up to one third of the urban population are poverty stricken. Although slightly better off than their rural counterparts, the following national indicators reflect the condition of the urban poor: a life-expectancy level of 47 years, a mortality rate of 150 out of 1,000 births, an adult literacy rate of 33 percent and a daily calorie supply of 77 percent of the total requirement. All these indicators are worse than the average for countries in Sub-Saharan Africa (Mozambique 1995, 10).

Urban Government

Urban governance in Mozambique must be seen in the context of the Portuguese colonial administrative heritage, despite the fact that almost 20 years have elapsed since independence. Important changes were proposed in the first three years of the independence era. However, the immediate priority that the confrontation with the Rhodesian regime and later the apartheid system came to represent, reduced the chances of success for these early experiences. Later on, the spread of permanent conflict and the emergency situation led to a void in policy formulation. This ended only with the adoption of a new set of constitutional guidelines for local government when a new multi-party Constitution was adopted in 1990. It is significant that it was only in September 1994 that it was possible to adopt a new law on local government both for urban and for rural areas incorporating the principles set up in the Constitution.

The Mozambican local government system has evolved through three phases: the colonial phase of racially segregated local government, the post-independence phase of racially integrated politically centralized and administratively deconcentrated local government, and the third phase of politically decentralized local government that has yet to be implemented. It is still too early to predict what the substance of this third phase will turn out to be. In theory, it could result in high levels of decentralized policy-making around local issues. However, Mozambique's political culture, very serious capacity weaknesses and inadequate local tax bases could combine to undermine the purported intentions of constitutional and institutional decentralization.

Local Urban Governance

The evolution of local urban governance in Mozambique is intimately tied up with the process of state formation that followed the collapse of the Portuguese colonial state in 1975 and the subsequent transformation of Frelimo from a Liberation Movement into a State-Party. Two dynamics

intersected. Firstly, Frelimo's self-conscious Marxist-Leninist political ideology was always premised on a tension between a real commitment to
popular participation at a grassroots level and the *dirigiste* imperatives of a
"people's war." These dual strands of populism and *dirigisme* were able to
coexist until independence, and for a short period after independence. It
was state control, however, which was asserted as Frelimo became the
State-Party.

The second dynamic, then, related to the fact that, unlike political
transition in South Africa and, to some extent, Zimbabwe, the settler
classes did not accept independence and political democratization.
Instead, they quite simply left en masse and in the process sabotaged the
state machinery they had run and took with them the knowledge and
skills that were needed to run the administration. In short, unlike Zimbabwe, Namibia and South Africa, the liberation movement did not take
over a functioning state system. Instead, a new state system needed to be
created from remnants of the old order mixed together with the only functioning nationally organized institution available, namely Frelimo itself.
The result was the transformation of Frelimo from a liberation movement
with a strong popular base in many parts of the country into a state system responsible for governing a country. This had major implications for
state-society relations.

As part of the deepening of its organizational strength and effectiveness
at the grassroots level, Frelimo established "party committees" in local
communities. These organizational forms buttressed a revolutionary ideology that was focussed on removing the colonial state, defending liberated zones and providing rudimentary services. After independence, two
things changed. Firstly, the ideology of resistance and revolution changed
to an ideology that emphasized unity, work and discipline. Secondly, the
party committees were transformed into the Dynamizing Groups that
were referred to in the previous section. The point, however, is that these
Dynamizing Groups were effectively created by the "Frelimo-as-State."

With structural adjustment, economic liberalization, political democratization and even peace, civil society is going through a remarkable
transformation. A wide range of non-state economic actors have emerged.
The bulk of them have emerged out of the newly established urban markets, the privatized services and the informal sector. A growing blackmar-
ket and organized crime sector is enmeshed with these new economic sectors. The formal private sector is relatively small, and the developmental
NGO sector is even smaller. The recovery of Mozambique's civil society,

therefore, is being shaped by a new set of for-profit informal and formal sector economic actors rather than by social movements and communities. If this continues and so-called "gangster capitalism" continues to grow, many in Mozambique are pessimistic about the building of a sustainable foundation for development.

Conclusion

Considering Mozambique's urbanization pattterns, it is apparent that the withdrawal of the state from its post-independence economic role has fundamentally transformed the conditions for local urban governance. With liberalization and democratization has come the construction of a new constitution that puts in place the formal mechanisms of democratic accountability. This achievement, however, is dangerously threatened by the fact that, unlike in South Africa and Zimbabwe, there is still a very weak set of governing capacities across the state system.

Zimbabwe

Urban Development

Zimbabwe had a population of 10.4 million in 1992, growing at 3.2 percent per annum. Given the 1982 census definition of urban settlements as those containing 2,500 people or more, then 27.3 percent of the population (or 2.84 million people) was urbanized in 1992. The United Nations estimated that Zimbabwe's population will be 54.1 percent urbanized by 2025 (Mlalazi 1994).

Whereas the first two national development plans — the Transitional National Development Plan (1983–86) and the First National Development Plan (1986–1990) — were focused on rural development, it was only in the Second National Development Plan (1991–95) that public investment in urban areas was regarded as a significant priority. Despite this, by the mid-1990s, it is difficult to argue that Zimbabwe had a coherent urban development policy with its own identity and goals. Whereas urban policy in the Transitional National Development Plan was "to minimise the rate of rural-to-urban migration," this in reality resulted in what Mlalazi (1994) called "rural urbanization" — urbanization outside the main cities in the smaller towns. By the late 1980s/early 1990s, the growth-point approach was challenged and it began to be replaced by the notion that public investment should build on existing centres, rather than attempting to create new ones. This was one of the spatial consequences of increasingly severe fiscal constraints resulting from the recession confronting the Zimbabwean economy. Equally important, however, the use of planned regional development to rectify spatial imbalances was replaced by the notion that urban economies must compete for investment, people and resources. For Mlalazi, this change, together with structural adjustment measures to reduce public spending on social infrastructure, could lead to the gradual return of an economy dominated by Harare as the primary city (Mlalazi 1994, 13).

Urban Government

At the time of Independence, the Zimbabwean Government's two main priorities with respect to local government were the racially divided systems of local governance and access to land. There was no real understanding of urban governance in the first five years of independence in central government policy thinking. Most of the policy and institutional work on changing local governance in Zimbabwe was focussed on the transformation of rural local government.[5]

Urban Councils in Zimbabwe have enjoyed a high level of policy and implementation autonomy with respect to their existing urban infrastructure. However, the participatory development planning system forced them to become highly dependent on provincial and national governments for extra finances for new development. This planning system effectively defined local governments as implementors of the national development plan. Urban Councils were not subject to pressures to implement national policies, however, because urban investment was not seen as priority. Instead, the councils were subject to pressures that came from the absence of urban development policies.

With structural adjustment and the new policy significance of urban development, Urban Councils are expected to increase their autonomy with respect to managing urban development. However, this increase will likely come without the requisite resources for new development from higher levels of government. This situation will worsen as decentralization takes effect, and things like local clinics and other public services previously run by national departments on a deconcentrated basis at the local level get transferred to Urban Councils. This, in turn, may lead from a fiscal crisis — as development needs fail to be met by Urban Councils — to a capacity crisis as operating budgets get pruned down to finance newly acquired responsibilities that will initially be regarded by politicians as priorities. If all this leads to a serious failure in the urban local government system, then this may, in turn, result in a reversion to provincial or national control of local service provision and development. In the final analysis, Des Gaspar's warnings may prove correct when he argued that the implementation of decentralization policies without proper attention to the local context may result in exactly the opposite to what was intended by those who promoted these policies in the first place (Gaspar 1991).

Local Urban Governance

Soon after independence in 1980, the governing party — the Zimbabwe African National Union (ZANU-PF) — mounted a political consolidation strategy. It had three elements: (i) the creation of a one-party system by absorbing the only other significant liberation party (ZAPU) into ZANU; (ii) the systematic control of the state administration by ZANU via political appointments and affirmative action; and (iii) the subordination via incorporation of all major socio-political forces outside the state into ZANU's sphere of political hegemony. When translated into developmental policy, the result was a form of developmental populism. It emphasized the complete unity of purpose of the people around the state-party policies and therefore the absence of differentiations along class, regional, ethnic or gender lines that could be the basis for alternative policies.

Although a significant group of developmental NGOs did play a role in Zimbabwe's development process since independence, they had a limited policy influence in relation to Government and were not connected to significant community-based social movements.[6]

Conclusion

In conclusion, Zimbabwe's urban policy-makers, urban governments and urban civil society stakeholders face formidable challenges as the urban population increases and urbanization rates remain high. Meeting urban development needs within a structural adjustment framework will open severe tensions between urban needs, urban governing capacities and the fiscal requirements of the growing cities and towns. This, in turn, will create a new urban political dynamic that could either manifest itself in terms of development-oriented partnership-based local modes of urban governance, or it could become an urban-based conflict between the urban poor and its petit-bourgeois allies on the one hand, and powerful party-state forces on the other who may want to defend the old political regime and its anti-local biases. Either way, it will soon become apparent that Zimbabwe's future will be determined in its urban areas, not its rural areas as has been the case to date.

Towards Democratic Local Urban Governance in Southern Africa

As argued at the outset of this chapter, the problem of local urban governance lies at the point of intersection between changing governance systems in general (liberalization, democratization, bureaucratic reform) and the impact of changes in the development process (markets, fiscal policies, structural adjustment, public investment, budgeting, macro-economic management and so on). As urbanization levels increase, the governance and management of urban development processes becomes increasingly important for the governance and development of the country as a whole. As towns and cities get bigger and their economies more important for the GDP and environmental resource utilization, so too does the level, spatial framework and governing capacity of governmental and non-governmental organisations. In other words, urbanization not only has socio-economic and spatial implications, it also has implications for governance.

As Southern African societies rapidly approach the point where the majority of their citizens live in urban areas, they will be forced to acknowledge the importance of urban development. Unfortunately, there is as yet no evidence of a coherent urban development policy framework that can be the basis for sustained development programmes and projects aimed at resolving the key urban problems in the region's towns and cities. There are great statements of policy intention in some countries, and a few successful urban development programmes in others, but an integrated urban development policy and programme has yet to emerge. This is probably the single greatest legacy of the colonial order. This was an order that made racially based spatial planning the primary basis of development and governance. The only way this underlying spatial order can be dismantled is via a combination of public investment, creative planning, interventions in the land market and economic development strategies that are labour- and community-based. Without this, the inefficiencies, cultural divisions and political consequences of a divided urban spatial order will continue.

Liberalization and democratization, economic restructuring and rising levels of urbanization have in combination fundamentally redefined the problem of urban governance across Southern Africa. Liberalization opens up space for local action; while democratization reduces the dominance of the central state by *inter alia* creating and strengthening sub-national government; and economic restructuring has led to the increased autonomy of local economies that must now fend for themselves or sink under the pressures of a globalizing world economy. Similarly, urbanization is relocating the population into a hierarchy of urban centres that must now find ways of meeting socio-economic needs without too much assistance from national governments. If urban governments are inappropriately structured without resources to meet these challenges, the results across the Southern African sub-continent could be disastrous.

Widely divergent responses to the new significance of urban government are evident across Southern Africa. There is the introduction of a completely new constitutional and statutory framework in Mozambique using the traditional approach of agreeing at the central level on a model, and imposing it uniformly across all localities through legislation. This differs substantially from the South African approach where a uniform national approach was imposed by legislation, but this approach was not about a single *model*, but rather a uniform *process* that local stakeholders must participate in to reach agreement on a model that is suitable to the local conditions. Whereas urban government was reconstituted in Mozambique and South Africa as part of the overall reconstitution of the state system as a whole, the same does not apply to the cases of Namibia and Zimbabwe where pre-existing post-independence state systems have been retained. As far as Zimbabwe is concerned, the problem is not being seen as a constitutional or institutional one, but rather one about the new roles urban government must play and how they will find the fiscal resources and institutional/human capacity to perform these new roles. In Namibia, much of the focus is on capacity and legal constraints rather than on the redefinition of roles.

What is common across the sub-continent, however, is the search for institutionalized participatory modes of governance in response to the generally accepted incapacity of urban governments to meet the urban challenges on their own. In other words, probably more so than at any other level of government, urban governments are searching for modes of governance that will meet the new governing needs emerging in rapidly urbanizing societies in a context where these urban governments do not have the combined fiscal, institutional and human capacity to meet these needs on their own. This has major implications for the democracy and development debate. If this argument is correct, then development will depend on a deepening and extension of democratic space for heightened levels of popular participation in governance. However, if this space is repressed both formally and informally by state and/or party-political actions, then urban governments will be left stranded to face the urban challenges on their own.

Local governance in Southern African cities will be shaped by the socio-economic dynamics of urban development, and the political dynamics of democratization. There is significant evidence that the trends referred to are already stimulating and creating the space for emerging networks and coalitions within civil society that can and want to participate in organized modes of local urban governance. However, the relative strengths, coherence and interactions with urban governments differ from country to country.

Although South Africa is often cited as having a highly organized civil society that has already been defined as playing an integral role in the Mandela Government's *Reconstruction and Development Programme*, it has been argued in this chapter that this is by no means a problem-free ful-fillment of the logic of liberation. Instead, the consolidation of the politi-cal power-bases of the new urban political elites will probably lead to decreased participation in policy-making at the local level as the space for reciprocity is narrowed, if not closed down altogether. However, due to the high levels of urbanization and industrialization in South Africa, trust, across basic cleavages, about the rules of political interaction and reci-procity remains very high. This, plus the institutionalization of a multi-party elected urban government system and the perpetuation of governing incapacities within urban governments, could well translate into a partic-ipatory mode of governance as new formations within civil society are reconstituted outside the direct controls of the political party machines that have gained control of the urban governments.

Namibia's centralized policy-making system militates against the consol-idation of local urban governance as civil society formations organize them-selves around national coalitions to influence policy-making at this level. However, this could change if decision-making and resource allocation responsibilities are decentralized to empower urban governments to meet the challenges of rising levels of urbanization. Participatory modes of gover-nance at the local urban level, however, will require the space for reciproci-ty to be underpinned by genuine local accountability. Given the strength of the dominant political party and its control over most aspects of political life, there is some concern that this space will not be allowed to open out sufficiently to facilitate the consolidation of civil society formations with a local urban focus. This, in turn, could mean relatively weak forms of accountability of urban governments to local urban communities.

The development of democratic and participatory modes of local urban governance in Zimbabwe is still, at this stage, hampered by a tradition of limited accountability of politicians due to party controls and the power of officials in the policy-making process, but also by the relatively under-developed state of civil society formations. This has meant limited reciprocity despite the participatory planning experiments and relatively low levels of trust across ethnic cleavages in particular. However, as many writers suggest, the changing political economy of urban development, the newly recognized significance of urban development policy and the moves to make the bigger urban governments more directly accountable via directly elected executive mayors, are all beginning to have an impact on civil society in ways that could stimulate new forms of organization and association. Local economic development strategies, in particular, will require not only new roles for urban governments but new relationships between them and the community and the private sectors.

Finally, it is probably too early really to judge how local urban governance is going to emerge in Mozambique. The ending of the war, the still-to-be established urban governments, and the consolidation of newly emerging civil society formations still need to solidify into a functioning set of urban relationships before it is possible to make projections about the future.

In short, local urban governance is being shaped in different ways and is going in different directions in each of the countries studied. However, the common denominator is that, as urban governments develop to the point where they come to take on the urban challenges directly, they will find themselves needing allies in the community and private sectors to mobilize the necessary resources for sustained urban development. How they do this will directly affect the quality and durability of local urban governance. If they fail, civil society formations may well emerge to take up urban development problems, but as direct challengers to urban governments, rather than as development partners.

Conclusion

There is little doubt that our knowledge base with regard to urban development, urban government and local urban governance in Southern

Africa is inadequate. However, to hold back until everything can be fully substantiated by research will also retard the process of conceptual discussion needed to clarify the research questions. In the meantime, urban research and policy networks should strive to deepen their subcontinental linkages with a view to raising the necessary resources to build up databases of best practices and innovation, structured conversations to increase mutual learning, collaborative policy formulation that can be used to lobby for policy change, and direct interventions in institutional change processes in order to build capacity and redefine vision and role. If this begins to happen on a sub-continental basis, then maybe a shared vision of an indigenous Southern African approach to local urban governance will begin to emerge. This chapter is merely a primer aimed at stimulating discussion about what this could possibly mean in practice.

Notes

1   We are aware that, although we have used some of Hyden's concepts, this definition is much less state-centric than his definition of governance because his definition is focused on the management of "regime structures" only, and not on the wider set of relations that mesh together at the local level in urban areas to create each city's and town's unique patterns of governance. The notion of regime in a Southern African context is much too restrictive to be used profitably. For a less state-centric approach that is similar to the one used here, see McCarney, Halfani and Rodriguez (1995).

2   Karen Johnson of INLOGOV helped with the formulation of the first draft of the final parts of the South African section of this chapter.

3   CBOs — community-based organizations — refer to a very wide range of organizational forms that exist in South Africa, including civic associations, cultural and religious groups, women's organizations, self-help welfare associations, among others.

4   This section draws heavily on a paper commissioned for the GURI project, by Rosy Namoya-Jacobs and James Hokans (1994), as well as on a paper commissioned for the previous phase of the GURI project, by B. Frayne and K. Gowaseb (1992).

5   For an overview, see Hammar (1994) and the various articles in Helmsing et al. (1991).

6   See de Graaf and Willmore (1987) for a useful review of certain trends.

References

Coetzee, S.F. and C. De Coning. 1992, "An Agenda for Urban Research: South Africa in the 1990s." Paper contributed to the Workshop on an Urban Research Agenda for Southern Africa, Johannesburg, University of the Witwatersrand, June.

de Graaf, D. and B. Willmore (eds.).1987. *The Importance of People*. Hlekweni FRSC, Zimbabwe.

Frayne, B. and K. Gowaseb. 1992. "Urban Research in the Developing World: Towards an Agenda for the 1990s." Paper contributed to the Workshop on an Urban Research Agenda for Southern Africa, Johannesburg, University of the Witwatersrand, June.

Gasper, Des. 1991. "Decentralisation of Planning and Administration in Zimbabwe: International Perspectives and 1980s Experiences." In A.H.J. Helmsing et al. (eds.), *Limits to Decentralisation in Zimbabwe: Essays on the Decentralisation of Government and Planning in the 1980s*. The Hague: Institute of Social Studies.

Hammar, A. 1994. "Amalgamation of Rural and District Councils in Zimbabwe: Institutional Strategies for Policy, Planning and Implementation." Paper presented to the Workshop on Metropolitan and Local Government Issues in Zimbabwe and South Africa, Harare, Holiday Inn, March 24.

Helmsing, A.H.J., N.D. Mutizwa-Mangiza, D. Gasper, C.M. Brand, K.H. Wekwete (eds.), 1991. *Limits to Decentralisation in Zimbabwe: Essays on the Decentralisation of Government and Planning in the 1980s*. The Hague: Institute of Social Studies.

Hyden, G. 1983. *No Shortcuts to Progress: African Development Management in Perspective*. Berkeley and Los Angeles: University of California Press.

_____. 1992. "Governance and the Study of Politics." In G. Hyden and M. Bratton (eds.), *Governance and Politics in Africa*. Boulder, Colorado: Lynne Rienner.

Mozambique, Ministry of Planning and Finance. 1995. "The Poverty Reduction Strategy for Mozambique," unpublished mimeo, March.

Mlalazi, A. 1992. "Urban Planning, Development and Research in Zimbabwe." Paper contributed to the Workshop on an Urban Reseach Agenda for Southern Africa, Johannesburg, University of the Witwatersrand, June.

_____. 1994. "Reflections on Some Aspects of Urban Development and Policy in Zimbabwe." Paper presented to the Workshop on Metropolitan and Local Government Issues in Zimbabwe and South Africa, Harare, Holiday Inn, March 24.

McCarney, P., M. Halfani and A. Rodriguez. 1995. "Towards an Understanding of Governance: The Emergence of an Idea and Its Implications for Urban Research in Developing Countries." In R. Stren with J. Kjellberg Bell (eds.), *Urban Research in the Developing World, Vol 4: Perspectives on the City.* Toronto: Centre for Urban and Community Studies, University of Toronto, pp. 91–141.

Namoya-Jacobs, R. and J. Hokans. 1994. "Urban Governance in Namibia." Paper presented to the Workshop on Urban Governance in Southern Africa, Johannesburg, University of the Witwatersrand, October 25.

Swilling, M. 1994. "Towards an Urban Research Agenda in Southern Africa in the 1990s." In R. Stren (ed.), *Urban Research in the Developing World: Vol. 2, Africa.* Toronto: Centre for Urban and Community Studies, University of Toronto, pp. 283–374.

_____. 1996. "Building Democratic Local Governance in Southern Africa: A Review of Key Trends." In M. Swilling (ed.), *Governance and Development in Africa Cities.* Johannesburg: University of the Witswatersrand Press (forthcoming).

10 Crisis of Urban Governance: Morocco, Algeria, Tunisia and Egypt[1]

MOSTAFA KHAROUFI

I INTRODUCTION

During the last two decades, North Africa's cities have been the focus of a crisis. Political problems have been manifested not only in a wave of relatively spontaneous forms like strikes, but especially in subliminal forms such as religious movements. In the cases of Algeria and Egypt, this latter form of popular opposition has been expressed through violence. As the urban population of these countries has doubled in one generation, the needs of millions of citizens — in terms of employment, housing and social services — have continued to go unsatisfied, while the process of urban integration has become more and more combative. It is this strife which is most often seen in the news media. Having experienced more than 50 years of exponential urban growth, and an increasing rural exodus, the result of agricultural decline, North Africa's cities are experiencing the acute limitations of imposed urban policy.

Today, in the case of Algeria and to a lesser extent that of Egypt, it is difficult not to draw a direct relation between the state of virtual civil war and the situation of crisis which now characterizes urban centres. Certain neighbourhoods in Algeria's larger cities are now practically devoid of economic activity, the consequence of inefficient supply channels and distribution systems which fail to meet current consumption. All that can be seen of governance in these areas are the repressive instruments of the state. Moreover, the rioting which has marked urban centres during the last two decades in Morocco (1981, 1984 and 1990), in Algeria (1988), in Tunisia (1978, 1980 and 1984) and in Egypt (1977 and 1986) is no longer confined to large cities — Casablanca, Algiers, Tunis or Cairo — but has also reached into small and medium-sized cities. Urbanization has increased the frequency and the reach of these protests. The rapid expansion and organization of urban societies, manifested by the emergence of social movements (see Liauzu 1989), has revealed more than ever the incapacity of the state, often confounded by its own chaotic expansion, to find successful solutions.

Hasty conclusions notwithstanding, these urban conflicts cannot, in recent years, be solely attributed to cuts in state-subsidised emergency goods. Currently, no inquiry has succeeded in demonstrating that it is only the poor who are rising up against the establishment. Indeed, these convulsions nearly always occur amid times of relative political and social calm. Police and military surveillance of urban demonstrations is now the only response the established powers are offering. Far from attempting some global action which aims to attack the cities' problems at their source, we observe instead a concerted effort to quarter off the routes which surround populous urban sites in order to facilitate police and military operations.

Today, urban political events reveal the nature of relations between urban populations and government powers. The latter seem to lack any view of governance capable of promoting democratic principles.[2] To understand better the characteristics of this crisis, a number of factors must be considered: (1) the mode of urban production, (2) the current models of city governance, and (3) their roles in the origin of grave instances of dysfunction. It is, after all, an understanding of cities as places of conflict management which is likely to provide insight into the current situation of the North African city. The will of the new citizens of North Africa's cities reflects the contradiction between aspiring toward "modernity" and a nostalgic return to the past.

II SPECIFIC TRAITS OF A POORLY PLANNED URBANIZATION

In Morocco, Algeria, Tunisia and Egypt, the urban population is growing at a steady rate. This fact is in direct conflict with poorly balanced urban infrastructure and geographic constraints.

In Morocco, the number of cities has practically doubled (from 128 in 1960–66 to 240 at the time of the 1982 census) and urban growth is high, averaging 4.28 percent per year. In the coastal axis (Casablanca-Rabat-Kenitra), which constitutes 40 percent of the urban population, uncontrolled growth remains predominant.

In northern Algeria, 95 percent of the population inhabit one-sixth of the country's surface area (350,000 square kilometres). There, in areas found on arid coastal land 1,200 kilometres long and 100 kilometres wide, no less than 447 urban centres surveyed in the 1994 census house 50 percent of the population. This is in contrast to 211 centres in 1977, and an urban population which was only 31 percent of the total in 1966.

In Tunisia, urban development is focused mainly in the provinces of Tunis and Sahel, the country's mid-east. This area enjoys the most economic activity and contains more than 40 percent of the country's urban population.

In Egypt, where urban residents constitute about 50 percent of the population, the largest part of the urban network is to be found along the banks of the Nile. There, population density is high, with Cairo predominating. Between 1976 and 1986, the latest inter-census period, city populations had increased by 10 percent while the number of cities having more than 100,000 inhabitants had grown from 20 to 24.

The Crisis in Traditional City Centres

The spatial organization of North African cities did not resist strong growth surges for long. At the end of the colonial period, it showed three types of spatial units: *Medinas*, new suburbs *[villeneuves]* and bidonvilles (Berque 1974). Immediately following independence, socio-economic and cultural changes progressively led to a near-total loss of function in the traditional urban centres. In these cities of ancient urban traditions, the historical centres, or *medinas,* are marred by extreme economic difficulties. This collapse is due not only to the lack of safety-net projects, but also to migration strains and complete overuse of resources. These maghreb cities have witnessed a "shantification" of the *medinas* that accompanies the rapid expansion of newer settlements of *gourbi*.[3]

Once areas boasting a special and valuable role, the *medinas* began to attract and shelter a huge population of migrants. They are now the home of disadvantaged social groups: the unemployed, divorced women, widows without regular incomes, and so on. Insular squalor is substituting itself for the old community ways. The overpopulation of areas once devoted to economic activities, such as the *oukala*,[4] has by necessity reassigned new divisions of the architectural superstructure and created many one-room shanties. These changes have brought new tensions and difficulties to North Africa's cities, including violence, and the loss of traditional modes of urban regulation.

The medina of Tunis, after having attracted numerous settlers from destroyed neighbourhoods such as Borgel and Sidi Ali Rais, as well as from rural locations, is beginning to experience high levels of emigration due to the disintegration of its infrastructure. This abandonment can be seen in census results: in 1956, the *medina* had 168,110 inhabitants; in 1975, it had 141,170, and in 1984, 109,725. This demographic decline of some 34.7 percent between 1956 and 1984 has continued, and the *medina* today houses around 100,000 inhabitants. The current population has been drawn from the country's rural regions, and 10 percent live below the threshold of absolute poverty — defined as households in which no active member enjoys continuous work (Sethom 1992, 312–13).

The dilapidation of this built-up area has often been pointed out. An inquiry conducted in 1985 by the *Agence de Réhabilitation et de Rénovation Urbaine* (ARRU) shows that 75 percent of households live in quarters requiring renovation, 10 percent in housing unfit for human habitation and therefore destined for bulldozing, and 5 percent requiring other improvements. The official source of government information, *La Presse*, signalled on October 30, 1994 the need to rehabilitate 361 *oukalas* in the *medina* of Tunis. One example described eight families sharing a single sanitary installation. This meant that residents already living in difficult and dangerous situations were to be relocated.

In Morocco, the *medina* of Marrakech, for instance, is an entirely over-populated space, housing 650 people per hectare. Even though it was designed for 100,000 inhabitants, some 280,000 were counted as residents in the 1982 census. In Algeria, urban population growth and higher densities in old city centres have attained even greater proportions. The medina of Constantine now houses 40,000 inhabitants, and the Casbah of Algiers, 60,000. This means the density for these cities is respectively 1,200 and 1,900 persons per hectare (Côté 1993, 260–61).

An Acute Housing Problem

Urban areas increasingly betray grave social divisions in *maghreb* and Egyptian society. Cities are posing serious problems, especially in the area of housing. The pattern is familiar: the well-to-do place their homes on topologically advantageous land, while groups of more modest income must seek inexpensive areas, and the poorest are left to squat in shanties on low-quality public lands, hoping not to be removed. The shortage of housing which, until the 1960s, affected only the very poorest groups, now touches many other social classes. The petroleum crisis of the 1970s, linked to the end of an economic model founded on petroleum export and, notably in the Algerian case with the end of emigration to France, has aggravated these circumstances.

With 30 years of worsening housing problems, the *bidonville* and other spontaneous settlements constructed on non-residential land are a popular alternative recourse. Despite efforts to contain the growth of *bidonvilles* (following decolonization and independence, every North African public authority made the eradication of shanty-towns a symbol of restored national dignity), the construction of spontaneous and non-regulation housing has increased considerably since the 1960s, playing a significant part in urban growth throughout the entire region. Often situated within the perimeters of older urban municipalities, this type of housing creates a problem in the management and delivery of urban services. For example, urban services are needed by more than 665,000 persons in Morocco (Ameur 1993), and 200,000 in Tunisia. In Greater Cairo, 1,580,000 people, or 20 percent of the population, are living in settlements composed of illegal shelters and are in need of services (El-Kadi 1988).

In Algeria, the issue of housing fuels the greatest degree of tension between city populations and urban authorities. In 1966, the number of non-regulation homes was estimated at 1.98 million, housing 2.28 million couples, with a continuing deficit of 600,000 houses. In 1977, the inadequacy of housing had worsened — urban populations had grown to represent 40 percent of the total, but the number of dwellings had reached only 2.2 million. This inadequacy is in part explained by the 350 percent increase in the cost of building materials between 1964 and 1984 (Boudebaba 1994, 8). Out of 25 million Algerians, writes Ahmed Rouadjia (1994, 296), 17 million suffer the pernicious consequences of a level of overpopulation characterized as critical by the standards of international norms. The rate of occupation per shelter, identified in most cases as a single-room construction, can reach as many as seven persons. The personal and intra-household consequences of such conditions — fighting, foregone marriages, divorce, incest, infanticide and so on — are grave.

The current situation in Algeria seems to be the result of mismanagement by municipal politicians, who have often resorted to eliminating slum neighbourhoods by force, and to coercive relocation of individuals to their rural places of origin. The "legitimate" development of suburban housing has served only to satisfy the needs of company executives and people with legal permission to move. The limited number of units actually built were also acquired by inhabitants profiting from this distributive phase of state planning (Belguidoum 1994, 50).

In Morocco, the state's housing policy therefore responded more to the needs of middle-income individuals than to those who showed the greatest need, like the inhabitants of shanties. This latter group constitutes the most active sector in terms of spread of neighbourhoods (Naciri 1984,

90), partly because their shelters are quickly built of makeshift materials. Moroccan public authorities have tried to maintain control of this unregulated development. In 1984, the *Agence nationale de lutte contre l'habitat insalubre* (ANHI) was created with the objective of resettling shanty inhabitants. But the financial insolvency of most households, the increasing costs of land and a growth rate of shantytown populations reaching 5.7 percent per annum limited the effectiveness of public housing programs. Even if certain successes were to be made — such as those of US AID which obtained permission to construct 15,000 units between 1985 and 1992 — there were still 1,008 shanty-town sites in Morocco by 1992 (*Al-Asas* 1994, 34).

Following urban riots in 1984, Tunisian authorities have abandoned the previous policy of destroying the shanty-towns or *bidonvilles* and have begun to focus on increasing the number of new units built. Nevertheless, improvement in housing supply is far from evenly spread among the various social levels (Chabbi 1988). The state's efforts remain most beneficial to the fiscally solvent middle-income group of the population.[5]

In Egypt, Greater Cairo has faced rapid population growth and urban expansion and authorities have been unable to generate adequate housing. Spontaneous settlements have developed in a number of zones as a result of the complete saturation of central neighbourhoods. One extreme example is the permanent residence of 179,000 persons, according to the latest census figures, in former graveyards.

When the latest census results for Cairo became available in 1986, there were 11.3 million housing units, of which 52 percent were in urban zones, and 10.8 percent consisted of one room per family. Many families had to make do with tents, huts and other fragile or precarious shelters. Several households were forced to share sanitary facilities such as toilets and running water.

In response to the need to satisfy housing demands, Egyptian authorities have sometimes adopted a *laissez-faire* policy. The state has tolerated numerous illegal setlements on public land, and has turned a blind eye toward infractions of zoning and construction legislation on agriculturally zoned lands. Bulldozings are now rare but, when they do occur, are symptomatic of a high degree of tension between the local population and urban authorities. For example, in Cairo in 1982–83, the inhabitants of Ara Al-Mohammadi and of Echach Al-Turgumaan were forced to relocate.[6] This operation was an official response to the active participation of Echach Al-Turgumaan's inhabitants in the urban riots of January 18 and

19, 1977. The authorities also intervened in 1987, razing a housing lot of 3,000 square metres to the ground, including 200 units situated on state-owned land in the Mattariyya neighbourhood (Raymond 1993, 349; Al-Wali 1993, 12).

The renewed interest of the authorities in housing issues stems from the rise of a popular integration movement and the accordant political violence in Egyptian cities which has claimed more than 600 victims since March 1992. The growth of violent Islamic groups arising from situations of urban poverty has apparently been underestimated. The evolution of an Islamic opposition movement from a minority of ideologically motivated but marginalized youth into a more popular and violent political front has now been recognized. Thus, in his address to the nation on May 1, 1993, President Mubarak announced the mobilization of significant financial resources (4 billion Egyptian pounds) for the rehabilitation of informal urban housing settlements. This plan of action has clear political motivations as President Mubarak's government is seeking to regain control of those neighbourhoods.

III POVERTY AND SELF-EXPRESSION IN URBAN CIVIL SOCIETY

According to World Bank definitions, Morocco, Algeria and Tunisia are classified as belonging to the lower segment of middle-income countries, while Egypt is said to belong to the low-income group. Nevertheless, all of them are experiencing widespread urban poverty. Restructuring programs, which began in the Maghreb countries and Egypt in the early 1980s, have aggravated the problems of both the poorest and the intermediate social groups. This has occurred in spite of institutional help offered to the most disadvantaged.[7] Even in the absence of official inquiries, certain instruments — census surveys and studies of the budgeting and consumption patterns of households — still allow us to suggest that urban poverty is no longer merely a residual phenomenon in the city life of these North African countries.

In the case of Morocco, the structural adjustment programme initiated in 1983 included austerity measures, which cut social spending from 27.6 percent to 25.8 percent of public expenditures. This reduction in subsidies for essential services was accompanied by a slow-down in the hiring of public employees, and an additional 4 percent cut in public spending in education (Morisson 1992, 255–58). These cumulative cuts which actually began in 1981, contributed to the rural exodus and the 6 percent annual urban population growth rate of the period. One consequence has been the increased proportion of households living in sub-standard shelters, estimated at between 20 and 40 percent of the urban population (Naciri 1984, 72). The results of a 1993 study on internal migration by the Ministry of the Interior show that 1,452,887 peasants have left their birthplaces in the countryside to seek shelter in the 12 largest cities, including 653,638 in Casablanca.

Algeria has been a late entrant into the club of the "normally adjusted" economies. The impact of the new adjustments has been compounded by a commodities market dominated by speculators protecting many levels of monopolies. Thus, rising prices for meats, fruits and vegetables, and inadequate access to consumer goods has made life even more difficult for the thousands of families already suffering from the hardships of poverty. The riots of October 4, 1988 were provoked by a scarcity of necessities like semolina, but were also a response to the worsening standards of living. They translated into a serious obstacle for the *laissez-faire* agenda, which had led to economic chaos and was later followed by political antagonism and armed conflict.

The failure of a distributive economic model supported by petroleum-related revenues was clear by the mid-1980s, when numerous urban renewal projects were abandoned. Most notable among those dropped were the projects intended for the outskirts of the cities, the places inhabited by the poorest and those most in need of services and improved housing. This crisis was reflected in the municipal elections of June 12, 1990 and the legislative elections of December 5, 1991, both of which were marked by evidence of massive support for fundamentalist slogans in urban centres. Of 188 constituencies in which the *Front Islamique du Salut* (Islamic Salvation Front) won a majority, over 90 percent were located in urban regions. The larger cities were swept by the Front, which gained control of 15 of the 16 metropolitan regions with more than 100,000 persons, and 88 cities with 50,000 or more inhabitants.

In Tunisia, the nation-wide inquiry into individual consumption conducted by the *Institut National de la Statistique* in 1990 revealed a nation of households unable to meet their food-energy requirements. It defined the threshold of poverty as 208 dinars or less per person per annum, of which 102 dinars are devoted to the purchase of food. The study counted some 544,000 persons, or 6.7 percent of the total population, living in "absolute poverty." The situation is particularly desperate in the south and the interior which suffer from poor infrastructure and weak links to the other large metropolitan centres. Despite concerted efforts by the authorities to intervene, it is unclear whether the 90 billion dinars allocated to urban development programmes for 1992 to 1996 will be enough to defeat poverty in and around Tunisian cities, especially those of the interior and south.

With an income of US$ 600 per inhabitant, Egypt is one of the poorest countries of the North African Sub-region. Even if various studies on household revenue show a slight improvement overall in the standard of living between 1974–75 and 1981–82, they later reveal a decrease in consumption levels per household in 1990–91. This trend, linked to the gradual decline in subsidies for essential goods (such as bread, beans, oil, sugar, rice) — articles which constitute 47.5 percent of expenditures in family budgets among the poorest citizens — has affected most regions of Egypt. The exception is Cairo, where the rate of absolute poverty is slightly less than the rest of the nation (Al-Laithy and Al-Dine 1993, 118–23). However, it is estimated that 50 percent of Cairo's residents live beneath the poverty-line. In the current context of decreases in public expenditures there has been an appearance, in recent years, of spontaneous associations whose mandate is to work on problems in health and education.

IV SOMETHING NEW IN CITY GOVERNANCE?

During the last two decades, public policies of considerable amplitude have been developed, aimed at a strategy of decentralization and a desire to include citizens in the management of their own cities. Ongoing programmes of decentraliztion — *al-amarkaziyya* — have been undertaken in Algeria, Tunisia, Egypt and Morocco since 1970. Associated with the principle of liberal government, decentralization is supposed to inspire a renewal of relations between the people and the state.

In Egypt in 1974, in Tunisia in 1975 and in Morocco in 1976, important reforms at an economic and legislative level were announced concerning the life of local representative associations. These reforms involved changes in the entire political system, including electoral procedures, and the restructuring of municipal councils. In Algeria, the National Assembly was created in 1975, following the passing of the Commons Codes and the *Wilaya* in 1967 and 1969 respectively.

These reforms were intended to offer an alternative to the exercise of centralized power. However, in spite of their capacity to introduce reforms and other programmes, it remains true that these countries' authorities are still incapable of dealing with autonomous initiatives detached from their sensitivity to criticism and partisan politics. As a result, the development of a healthy political culture has been hindered considerably. It is also important to note that these societies, including every level of their elites, are sustained to a great degree by circles emanating from the structures of centralized power. Thus, social relations remain most conducive to authoritarian, hierarchical functioning.

In this context, popular associations are a vital means of social expression — they are instruments of integration, and vehicles through which civil society is able to manifest its existence and participate in the governance of the country. They represent an organized framework which allows citizens to express opinions about events affecting them, and which permits the counterbalancing of often abusive political powers. Nonetheless, it should be noted that a civil political society has been constructed only with extreme difficulty. The number of non-governmental organizations is limited, gender divisions persist, and free expression and free association continue to be difficult to achieve. Often, citizens maintain the viewpoint that any form of collective organization must be created through official channels, to have any chance of success. Moreover, official government agencies have yet to waive their strong mistrust of NGOs.

Nevertheless, a change in attitude is perceptible in the behaviour of North African governments. Following the events of October 1988, Algerian public authorities began to tolerate an openness which has allowed committees and organizations of many kinds to flourish. More associations were created during the first two months after these reforms than in the previous 25 years. The adoption of a liberal constitution, which ended totalitarian rule, has brought about greater freedoms of expression and association (Articles 39 and 40). Thus, by the end of 1991, 60 political associations were recognized as such, and 2,000 non-political ones had been brought into existence (Bou Shair 1993, 200).

In Tunisia, the fabric of popular association is still weak. Though they play an important role in the social and cultural animation of the country, restrictions are sometimes imposed upon those defending human rights. Indeed, a law passed on April 22, 1992 limits membership in associations to persons who have no responsibility or function within a political party. There is a one-month deadline to respect this condition, after which any violating group is forced to dissolve.

The presence of feminist movements has succeeded in bringing about the passage of a Code of Personal Status, representing a step ahead of other

North African countries. However, it has not been followed by an explosion in the number of women's groups, with only two formally recognized women's associations in existence — representing 0.09 percent of all Tunisian organizations. According to sociologist Ilhem Marzouki's (1993) defining criteria, women's voices as a whole do not yet constitute a veritable social movement.

In Egypt, the country in which North African Islamic political movements were born, religious associations are a popular means of expression. While Egypt also is distinguished for a large number of associations, the number with a religious character reached 21.2 percent of the total reported in the 1986 census. During the last two decades, Egypt and Algeria have been the stage for a proliferation of networks of mosques. This has been aided by their strong volunteer representation. These mosques have been important in the process of training, restructuring and expanding the Islamic movement into urban territory.

In Morocco, the movement towards popular representative associations is focused mainly in the cities — the two largest of which boast 52 percent of total membership of all associations — and involves a largely young and educated membership. At the end of the 1980s, there were 441 volunteer associations active in society. Of these 24.7 percent existed to care for the handicapped, 9.5 percent to care for families, 7.9 percent to conduct social work, 3.4 percent to work for children's aid and 1.4 percent for the aged. Beginning in the early 1990s, Morocco became host to a new generation of other associations. This is in addition to large regional associations created by the government (Fes Sais, Ribaat Al-Fath, Angaad, Bou Regreg and others) to represent human rights, women's rights, the environment, children and culture. They differ from popular associations in that they enjoy large financial resources, and they are run largely by powerful bureaucrats from the *Makhzen* (a department of the state).

V CONCLUSION

It is clear that the record of responsible governance in the countries on the southern coast of the Mediterranean leaves much to be desired. The reduction in state controls for regulating the economy and national finances has given rise to serious shortages. In the case of Algeria, these changes have resulted in the exhaustion of all legitimate means for dealing with such concerns. As long as urban populations continue to grow, traditional methods of regulation (subsidies on necessities, guaranteed employment, for example) which assume a balance and harmony between the population and available resources will become increasingly insufficient. Long before the application of social restructuring programmes, subsidies for necessities often were aimed at helping politically active segments of the population. This left the most disenfranchised without aid.

On a more positive note, the marginalization of large, poor populations, including those recently arrived from the countryside, eventually may evoke a consciousness of their plight among young city dwellers and a subsequent mobilization of resources in their aid. A disintegrating social consensus and failure to respect human rights may force the often silent majority to initiate changes in the current establishment.

The birth of democracy in North Africa has been difficult and painful, and has caused a crisis in the normative social structures which traditionally have eschewed public expression and action. It has also spawned revolutions which are shaking traditional structures and institutions like the family. Attentive observers are even able to discern the spread of new attitudes which can be seen in social unionism, the expression of new social demands, the role of the media, the status of women, not to mention a rise in the number of educated elected officials. There are visible improvements emanating from widely advertised political adjustments like the constitution of an electoral process (even if marred by irregularities); the relative intensification of local political life; and in the expansion of certain liberties. These changes may be a sign that a new urban landscape is emerging in the face of an increasingly totalitarian conception of Islam.

Notes

1 The chapter has been translated from the original French.
2 The concept of governance touches on many domains: urban politics, the role of municipalities and of the private sector in urban management, the relationship between the state and the civil society, the participation of the community in the management of the city, the role of women, etc. See McCarney, Halfani and Rodriguez (1995) and Stren et. al. (1992)
3 The *gourbi* is a small shelter made of diverse materials: wood, sheet metal and mud, with a low roof and rarely possessing more than two small contiguous rooms (from 4 to 5 m2 covered).
4 The *oukala,* an area situated near the centre of the *medina,* was once equipped for commercial activities and was often inhabited by single men

(in one-room houses). These spaces are now the home of mixed groups following the rural exodus: migrants, married in their home villages, are seen to bring their families there today.

5   On urbanization in Tunisia, see also Pierre Signoles (1985).

6   The first is situated on Ramses Avenue behind the building of the Press group Al-Ahraam. The latter can be found between the neighbourhoods of Ramses and Abbasiyya, near Madinat Al-Salaam, itself a zone situated at the height of the Airport in the north-western part of the city.

7   In the case of Egypt, this is the Social Aid Fund; in the case of Tunisia, it is the "solidarity trust" known as "26–26."

References

Al Laithy, Hiba, and Keir Al-Dine. 1993. "Evaluation de la pauvreté en Egypte en fonction des données sur les ménages." *Egypte-Monde Arabe*, no. 12–13, 4th quarter: 109–37.

Al-Wali, Mamdûh. 1993. *Les habitants des 'ichach': la carte d'habitat des gouvernorats.* Cairo: Syndicat des ingénieurs. (In Arabic)

Ameur, Mohamed. 1993. *Fès . . . ou l'obsession du foncier.* Tours: Fascicule de recherche no. 25. Tours: Urbama.

Belguidoum, Saïd. 1994. "Citadins en attente de la ville. Logement et plitique à Sétif." *Maghreb-Machrek* 143(January-March): 42–52.

Berque, Jacques. 1974. "Médinas, villeneuves et bidonville." In *Maghreb: histoire et société.* Paris: Duculot.

Boudebaba, Rabah. 1994. "Development policies and their effects on Urban Poverty. A case study of Constantine (Algeria)." Discussion at the round-table *Gouvernance et pauvreté urbaine en Afrique du Nord,* Tunis, July 15–16.

Bou Shair, Saïd. 1993. *Le système politique algérien.* Aïn Mlila: Dâr al-hudâ. (In Arabic)

Chabbi, Morched. 1988. "Politiques d'habitat et modèles de développement: Le cas de Tunis." In Pierre-Robert Baduel (ed.), *Habitat, Etat et société au Maghreb.* Paris: Editions du CNRS.

Côté, Marc. 1993. *L'Algérie ou l'espace retourné.* Constantine: Média-Plus.

Al-Asas 1994. Editorial. No. 119. Casablanca.

El-Kadi, Galila. 1988. *L'urbanisation spontanée au Caire.* Fascicule de recherche no. 18. Tours: Urbama.

Marzouki, Ilhem. 1993. *Le mouvement des femmes en Tunisie au XXème siècle. Féminisme et politique.* Tunis: Cérès Productions.

McCarney, Patricia L., Mohamed Halfani and Alfredo Rodriguez. "Toward an Understanding of Governance: The Emergence of an Idea and its Implication for Urban Research in Developing Countries." In Richard Stren with Judith Kjellberg Bell (eds.), *Urban Research in the Developing World: Vol. 4, Perspectives on the City.* Toronto: Centre for Urban and Community Studies, University of Toronto.

Morisson, Christian. 1992. *Ajustement et équité au Maroc.* Paris: OECD.

Naciri, Mohamed. 1984. "Politique urbaine et 'politiques' de l'habitat au Maroc: incertitude d'une stratégie." *Politiques urbaines dans le monde arabe.* Lyon: Maison de l'Orient, pp. 71–98.

Raymond, André. 1993. *Le Caire.* Paris: Fayard.

Rouadjia, Ahmed. 1994. *Grandeur et décadence de l'Etat algérien.* Paris: Khartala.

Sethom, Hafed. 1992. *Etat et paysannerie en Tunisie.* Tunis: Cérès Productions.

Signoles, Pierre. 1985. *L'espace tunisien: capitale et état-région.* 2 vols. Fascicule de recherches no. 14. Tours: Urbama.

Stren, Richard, with V. Bhatt, L. Bourne, J.E. Hardoy, P. McCarney, R. Riendeau, L.N. Tellier, R. White, J. Whitney. 1992. *Une problematique urbaine: le défi de l'urbanisation pur l'aide au développement.* Toronto: Centre for Urban and Community Studies, University of Toronto.

11 Governance and Urban Poverty in Anglophone West Africa

A.G. ONIBOKUN

I INTRODUCTION

This chapter focuses on governance and urban poverty in an area of Anglophone West Africa which comprises Nigeria, Ghana, Sierra-Leone and Gambia. Of the four states, Nigeria is the largest both in its size and its population, of over 80 million (see the 1993 Census), and Gambia is the smallest with a population of about one million (1,025,869). Great Britain has had a strong influence in the Anglophone states of West Africa, ruling over them for the better part of the 19th and 20th centuries. Even after attaining their political independence, these African nations maintained links with the British.

Today, virtually all the Anglophone countries in West Africa are under military rule. In February 1966, Ghana became the first Anglophone state in the area to experience a military coup. Ghana has recently re-entered the democratic fold, although the current head of state is the former military leader turned civilian. While Gambia and Sierra Leone have enjoyed a longer and more stable democracy than any of the other Anglophone states in West Africa, they have also been affected recently by the coup-d'état contagion. Of Nigeria's 35 years of independence, 26 have been under military rule.

Another common factor in all four countries is the predominance and increasing rate of poverty in both urban and rural settings. In the urban areas in particular most indicators of development point to the fact that these countries have not been able to cope effectively with the challenges posed by high urban growth rates. While other developing countries in Latin America and Asia appear to be making some progress, Anglophone countries in West Africa, like most other African countries, are sliding towards greater under-development. Yet, as West African governments appear increasingly less capable of coping with this situation, their civil societies seem to be emerging gradually as a source of hope.

The profile discussed above touches on a central factor of development —

good governance. Why has good governance become elusive in these countries? Or, put another way, how has governance, as it is practiced in West Africa, resulted in endemic urban poverty? Before addressing these questions, let us examine urbanization trends and briefly consider these countries' extreme poverty.

Urbanization Trends in Anglophone West Africa

There is no doubt that urbanization, especially in Anglophone West Africa, has become a more pressing issue within the last four decades. For example, in Nigeria in 1890 there were 25 urban centres (i.e., settlements with 20,000 and more inhabitants). By 1953, over a period of 63 years, this figure increased by 125 percent to 56 centres. Moreover, the number of urban centres in Nigeria grew astronomically between 1953 and 1963. During those 10 years the number of urban centres grew by about 228.6 percent until there were 185 in Nigeria. Between 1890 and 1953, the total urban population similarly increased by about 240 percent; and it increased further by more than 300 percent between 1953 and 1993. Current and reliable estimates put the share of urban population at over 35 percent of Nigeria's total population. According to the National Office of Statistics this proportion can be expected to reach 68 percent by the year 2020. Within the last 30 years, the population of most major towns in Nigeria has increased four-fold.

In Ghana, the picture is similar. The urban population has been growing at the rate of 4.41 percent per annum, which has led to a doubling of the urban population within a 30-year period. The urban population jumped from less than a million in 1960 to over three million in 1984 (Addo 1972, 243; Ghana 1984). One important feature of urbanization in Ghana, and in conformity with world trends, is that the largest urban settlement is growing very quickly, making urban growth a pressing social issue. Another striking feature is the overwhelming concentration of towns in the southern half of the country.

In Sierra Leone, with a population of about 4 million, the annual urban population growth rate is 5 percent. Sierra Leone is about 32 percent urban.

On the other hand, Gambia is the least urbanized, with only 3 percent of its population residing in cities. Banjul — Gambia's largest city — represents over a third of the country's total population. The population of Greater Banjul has doubled within the last two decades.

The rise of urban centres, especially in developed countries, is usually associated with the growth of industrialization. In theory, industry and its products stimulate urban growth. However, urban growth in Anglophone West Africa, and Africa as a whole, is an exception to this trend. Rather than industrialization, rural-urban drift and a high rate of natural population increase have been responsible for the rapid rate of African urbanization.

II POVERTY AS A CRITICAL URBAN CHALLENGE

There is nothing wrong with urbanization if the capacity to cope with the challenges it poses is assured. In Anglophone West Africa, the challenges seem to have overwhelmed the existing capacity to manage resources, and one of the major consequences of this is endemic urban poverty.

Urban poverty is difficult to define. A simple definition is that urban poverty exists in a society when people do not attain a level of well-being deemed to constitute a reasonable minimum for that society. The most common definition of poverty is in terms of a "poverty line." Two levels of the line have been established: "poverty 1," the absolutely poor; and "poverty 2," the hard-core poor. In all the countries of Anglophone West Africa, over 70 percent of the urban population are classified in these two categories. A recent study in the greater Banjul area (N'Jie 1995) revealed the following social class structure: 0.5 percent of the population were considered upper-class citizens, 9.5 percent fell within the middle-class category, and 90 percent were regarded as lower-class and poor. A similar study of 14 major urban centres in Nigeria (Onibokun and Faniran 1995a) revealed that the middle class is gradually being wiped out, as a large portion of the urban population (over 92 percent) has fallen below the poverty line. The phenomenon is directly related to the recent process of structural adjustment.

The Nigerian case represents perhaps the most distressing example of urban poverty in the region. Nigeria experienced considerable growth in post-independent years, particularly since the 1970s. Its gross domestic product grew at the rate of 3.3 percent between 1950 and 1955 and 2.1 percent between 1960 and 1970 (Lipton 1977, 428). The oil boom era brought tremendous growth: 8.2 percent per annum between 1970 and 1975 (Nigeria 1975). However, despite this economic growth the majority of people remained poor by all accounts; in terms of income, education, health, employment, nutrition and access to basic facilities.

TABLE 11.1: Selected Indicators of Development, Anglophone West African Countries

Indicator	Nigeria	Ghana	S/Leone	Gambia
Annual births per 100 women aged 15–19	15.0	13.0	21.0	—
Pregnant women with anaemia (%)	43.0	64.0	45.0	—
Women receiving prenatal care (%)	57.0	82.0	30.0	—
Births attended by trained personnel (%)	37.0	59.0	25.0	—
Infertility in women (%)	8.0	3.0	10.0	—
Average births per woman (TFR)	6.5	6.0	6.5	—
Maternal deaths per 100,000 births	800.0	1,000.0	450.0	—
Reproductive risk index	61.5	52.1	64.4	—
Infant mortality rate (IMR) per 1,000 (1985–90)	105.0	90.0	154.0	143.0
Children under 5 underweight (%) 1980–88	—	27.0	23.0	—
Female illiteracy (%) 1990	61.0	49.0	89.0	84.0
Total fertility rate (TFR) (1985–90) per Woman	6.9	6.4	6.5	6.5
Current GNP per capita ($ US) 1988	280.0	400.0	—	200.0
Access to local health care (%) 1985	—	65.0	—	—
School enrolment ratio ages 6–11 (1990)	74.0	60.0	58.0	43.0
Access to safe water (1985–88)	48	57	42	—
Access to safe sanitation (1985–88)	42	31	43	—

SOURCES: Population Action International (1995); United Nations (1994).

The indicators presented in Table 11.1 are quite revealing. In sharp contrast to Europe and North America, the four Anglophone countries in West Africa have among the lowest profiles in terms of virtually every indicator of development. Population Action International (1995) appropriately considers the reproductive risk index in these countries to be among the highest in the world. Most women lack access to basic health care in pregnancy and childbirth, and fewer than 10 percent of women use any method of family planning. Abortions are illegal or permitted only to save a woman's life. More than one-fifth of 15-to-19 year-olds give birth each year, and women have an average of 6 to 7 children. Women have a better than 1 in 20 risk of death from maternal causes over their lifetime, directly related to high-risk childbearing and poor general health coverage. Similarly, at least 10 percent of women are infertile, many due to highly prevalent sexually transmitted diseases.

Urban poverty in these countries also is manifest in the physical environment. In virtually all the towns in the region, the city centres are gradually and systematically decaying without any tangible programme of rehabilitation. The new urban peripheries emerged in an unplanned manner and without the necessary infrastructure. If the colonial era left a legacy of central slums in most Anglophone West African countries, post-colonial regimes have created suburban slums of greater dimensions. The urban environment in many of the urban centres in this region is characterized by over-crowding, complex land use, marginal employment and inadequate social infrastructure.

III URBAN GOVERNANCE AND URBAN POVERTY

Why have these countries failed in their attempts to improve the quality of life of their people? The concept of governance is likely to provide the most plausible answer.

The term "governance" has been defined differently by various scholars and according to several schools of thought. Two good attempts to define governance have been put forward, and shall be briefly examined here. The World Bank sees governance as:

> [T]he mechanisms whereby an institution incorporates the participation of relevant interest groups in defining the scope and content of its work, including the capacity to mediate among these interests when they enter into conflict and the means whereby it demonstrates accountability to those who support it through its mission mandate and the application of its resources in pursuit of these goals (World Bank 1993, 17).

The key words in this definition are "participation" and "accountability," which stand out as crucial elements of good governance. Another definition put forward by Dele Olowu and Shittu Akinola (1995) presents governance as being manifested through state and societal institutions and the relationships between them. They also believe that governance has to do with the way rulers are accepted as legitimate in society, so that values that are sought by individuals and groups within the society may be enhanced.

Governance has been perceived by the World Bank as "the manner in which power is exercised in the management of a country's economic and social resources for development" (World Bank 1992, in McCarney, Halfani and Rodriguez 1995). Depending on the way in which that power is exercised, governance can either be good or bad. Good governance should be defined as the presence of a government with good and legitimate leadership, having a lawful claim to its power and authority based on a mandate derived from the people's will. Good governance must also have vision, and a progressive socio-political agenda acceptable to and accepted by the people. Good governance implies that this vision will be implemented in partnership with the people in a transparent manner, with accountability at all levels. Good governance recognizes the existence of a government and the governed — the former drawing its legitimacy from the latter, and accountable to the latter. Governments should build the capacity of the governed with a view to harnessing people's abilities in a partnership which aims for the advancement of everyone involved.

According to the definition being put together here, vision, transparency, accountability, legitimacy, credibility, predictability and reliability (on the part of the leadership) combined with confidence and stability (on the part of the society) are the hallmarks of good governance. Good governance also emphasizes effective and accountable institutions, democratic principles, reliable electoral process, representative and responsible structures of government and the need to ensure an open and legitimate relationship between civil society and the state. It is important to note that there can never be a good government nor a good society without good governance. Sustainable and appreciable development also require the implementation of good governance practices. The question which remains is: how has governance been practiced in the four Anglophone countries of West Africa?

IV THE PRACTICE OF GOVERNANCE IN THE SUB-REGION

The practice of governance in Anglophone West Africa is characterized by the following common features: political instability, the absence of accountable government, arbitrary and irregular inter-governmental relations and poor coordination, fiscal dependence, inefficient and ineffective administration, and limited private-sector citizen participation. As a region, it is noted for its political instability, and this insecurity manifests itself in many ways. Perhaps the most obvious manifestation at the level of urban governance is the frequency of change in the system of administration operating in an urban centre. Unpredictable local administration, not to mention state and central governments, remains the norm in most of Anglophone West Africa.

For example, Nigeria became an independent nation in 1960. Between 1960 and the present the military has ruled for about 26 years, during which there have been four military regimes, each taking office by coup-d'état and each followed by complete changes in the hierarchy of top government functionaries. As a result, federal ministers, permanent secretaries and directors are changed so often that there has been no way of maintaining any consistency or predictability in government policy and programmes. This inconsistency has had particularly dire consequences for urban administration. At the state level, the governors are changed so frequently by the federal military government that there are frequent losses of confidence between the federal and state level military administrations. Each change of state governors is accompanied by new appointments to the state executive councils and to the senior management staff of state ministries. In one state, for example, there were six different state governors or administrators over a period of four years. In one state ministry responsible for urban planning, there were eight different commissioners over a five-year period.

In Gambia, Sierra Leone and Ghana the seizure of government by their militaries resulted in similar administrative instability and unpredicability. Once again, efforts to secure the roles and responsibilities of local and urban governments have suffered the most. In all these countries, the transfer of power has been associated with each new administration discrediting the previous one. More disastrous still, each change in government has meant the consequent abandonment of projects upon which colossal sums of money already have been expended. Similarly, most of the urban service agencies in the cities have, over the years, been subjected to frequent structural and functional changes.

In all these countries, there have been attempts to decentralize the power structure. For example, the Nigerians have more than doubled the number of states in the country. The 12 states that existed in 1976 are now divided into 30 states and a federal capital, and the creation of more states is currently being discussed. Local government councils have also increased in number, from fewer than 200 in 1976 to 588 at present. Similarly, there were only 65 District Councils in Ghana in 1986, and now there are 110. Sierra Leone and Gambia have also adopted the philosophy of decentralization, and the central governments have increased the number of local governments. However, decentralization has not been accompanied in any of these countries by a devolution of power and authority. The various localities still operate as mere appendages of the central/state authorities, directed at will by the central or state institutions and depending almost entirely on their central government for their resources and initiative.

In Ghana, all the chief executives directing the 110 district councils were appointees of the central government. In Nigeria, every one of the 588 local councils are managed by caretaker committees appointed by the central and state governments. These commitees are changed at will and thus, logically, they owe their allegance to the governments that appoint them. In Sierra Leone the elected mayor of Freetown was thrown out in 1994 and replaced by a government appointee. In Gambia, the central military government maintains an equally domineering influence on local government operators. Under the circumstances, local governments cannot be expected to operate with vision. They cannot achieve real accountability, nor can there be much progress.

Research has revealed that one consequence of the lack of governmental accountability and transparency is that it has become difficult for authorities to mobilize much needed revenue. Tax evasion is a norm in many of these countries. Apart from the taxes deducted under the "Pay As You Earn" system, people very rarely pay other forms of tax — including property rates. Denied many of the major sources of municipal revenue, the local and urban governments lack the necessary resource bases to perform their statutory functions. Instead of striving to achieve financial autonomy, many local government functionaries "lobby" the higher tiers of government for a greater share of the "national cake," as it is often referred to in Nigeria. Under such a situation, it should come as no surprise that most of the local governments and councils cannot meet the challenges posed by their rapidly expanding communities.

Previous research also revealed that most of the urban councils and municipal authorities in Anglophone West Africa were managed by men and women who had very inadequate experience or training. Projects and decisions requiring technical expertise were often manned by officers with no technical knowledge. M.U. Akpan (1982, 83) suggests that "one of the barriers of Civil Service efficiency is the retention in service of the people who have no work in their own special field to do, and then have to be fitted into other jobs like square pegs in round holes." This has been particularly true of West African administrations during the first two decades after independence.

Unfortunately, in spite of the known advantages of popular participation, it is rarely included in governance as it is practiced in West Africa. Politicians and the local elite are often hostile to, or suspicious of, efforts to organize and use non-state structures as vehicles for self-reliant development. Furthermore, protective legal environments, so essential to popular mobilization, organization and institutionalization, simply do not exist in most countries.

V THE EMERGENCE OF CIVIL SOCIETY

Nevertheless, there is a growing importance of civil society in Anglophone West Africa. This expansion can be traced to the vacuum of legitimacy which has resulted from local and urban governments' irresponsibility and lack of authority. People have grown accustomed to relying on self-help methods and on civil associations to meet their basic needs. Recent studies have shown that there are hundreds of community-based associations and NGOs now operating in each of the urban centres in the region. Onibokun and Faniran (1995b) have revealed that there are over 6,000 such organizations working in just 14 towns in Nigeria. These associations operate through transparent administrations based on accountability. As a result, most of them have succeeded in mobilizing to address people's perceived and real needs. In Ghana, the same phenomenon was recorded. According to P.Y.Z. Yankson (1995):

> [U]rban centres are becoming increasingly "informal" in appearance, organization and management, as the informal mechanisms have assumed such importance in a situation where the informal sector has the opportunity to operate in the niches left by the formal sector. The result has been such that in the last few decades the informal sector and the informal mechanisms have assumed dominant roles in the urban development process in West Africa. . . . Yet the informal sector and the various informal organizations have not been incorporated in the urban administration and management systems.

VI CHALLENGES FOR URBAN GOVERNANCE

Governance in Anglophone West Africa poses many challenges, not only to researchers but to policy-makers as well. This chapter has established that there is a direct correlation between urban governance and urban poverty. Urban poverty is exacerbated by managerial incompetence, inefficiency, ineffectiveness and unresponsiveness. Moreover, a lack of transparency, accountability, responsiveness, institutional legitimacy and popular participation, have combined to weaken the capacity of the state. Few states are able to face the challenges of urban growth effectively. However, the solution seems to be in the institutionalization of good governance.

Simply stated, current practices cannot lead to sustainable development. The requisite vision and commitment are lacking, the required popular confidence does not exist, and the partnership between government and civil society is a mirage. Further compounding this situation is the fact that the resources needed to cope with the challenges are on the decline. More often than not, any shred of accountability is lost to the authorities' deceit. While other nations in Africa are democratizing, the countries of Anglophone West Africa are wallowing in dictatorship and administrative chaos.

How may we then expect West Africans to live better? All of the conditions necessary for growth and development are being ignored or destroyed by central authorities. Rather than attracting development, most of the nations are unknowingly fostering conditions which make development difficult and unsustainable. Without real transparency and accountability, governments' unstable and inconsistent policy and administration are forfeiting many development opportunities in their countries. This will likely remain the case until these nations include meaningful citizen participation in their system of governance.

The challenge facing researchers, policy-makers and activists is the installation of democracy in West Africa — the only option which can harness the innate resources of the people. The global and the national plans of action for human settlements in the post-Habitat II era should focus on the development of democratic governance as the primary challenge.

References

Addo, N.O. 1972. "Urbanization, Population and Employment in Ghana." In Simeon H. Ominde and Charles N. Ejiogu (eds.), *Population Growth and Economic Development in Africa*. London: Heinnemann, pp. 243–51.

Akpan, M.U. 1982. *Public Administration in Nigeria*. Lagos: Longman.

Ghana, Republic. 1984. *Census of Population*. Accra: CBS.

Lipton M. 1977. *Why Poor People Stay Poor: A Study of Urban Bias in World Development*. London: Temple Smith.

McCarney, Patricia L., Mohamed Halfani and Alfredo Rodriguez. 1995. "Towards an Understanding of Governance: The Emergence of a nIdea and its Implication for Urban Research in the Developing Countries." In Richard Stren with Judith Kjellberg Bell, eds. *Urban Research in the Developing World: Vol. 4, Perspectives on the City*. Toronto: Centre for Urban and Community Studies, University of Toronto, pp. 91–141.

Nigeria, Federal Republic. 1975. *Third National Development Programme, 1975–1980*. Lagos: Federal Ministry of National Planning.

N'Jie, M.M. 1995. "The Politics of Urban Governance and Its Implications on Urban Poverty and Social Structure in the Gambia, the Greater Banjul Municipal Area Example." In A.G. Onibokun and A. Faniran (eds.), *Governance and Urban Poverty in Anglophone West Africa*. CASSAD Monograph Series No. 4. Ibadan: CASSAD, pp. 199–209.

Olowu, Dele and Shittu Akinola. 1995. "Urban Governance and Urban Poverty in Nigeria." In A.G. Onibokun and A. Faniran (eds.), *Governance and Urban Poverty in Anglophone West Africa*. CASSAD Monograph Series 4. Ibadan: CASSAD, pp. 20–42.

Onibokun, A.G. and A. Faniran. 1995a. *The Impact of Structural Adjustment on Housing, Environment and Urban Productivity in Nigeria*. Ibadan: CASSAD.

Onibokun, A.G. and A. Faniran. 1995b. *Community Based Associations in Nigeria*. CASSAD Monograph Series No. 7. Ibadan: CASSAD.

Population Action International. 1995. *Report on Progress Towards World Population Stabilization*. Washington, DC: Population Action International.

United Nations. 1994. *Statistical Chart on Children, Early Child Development and Learning Achievement*. New York: UN.

UNCHS. 1995. *Graphic Presentation of Basic Human Settlements Statistics*. Nairobi: UNCHS.

World Bank. 1993. *Federal Republic of Nigeria: Poverty Assessment Indicators*. Lagos: FOS/World Bank Resident Office.

Yankson, P.W.K. 1995. "Urban Governance and Urban Poverty in Ghana." In A.G. Onibokun and A. Faniran (eds.), *Governance and Urban Poverty in Anglophone West Africa*. CASSAD Monograph Series No. 4. Ibadan: CASSAD, pp. 43–70.

12 Urban Governance in Francophone Africa
KOFFI ATTAHI

I COUNTRY PROFILES

West and Central Africa's Francophone countries comprise some 15 states sharing an institutional and administrative history inherited from France, their former colonial power. These countries, which all achieved their independence in the early 1960s, have followed differing paths of institutional evolution since then. Nevertheless, they can be characterized by the following common traits:

- A strong concentration of power often wielded by a single political party, and a deconcentrated administration during the two first decades of independence;
- Two timid attempts at decentralization in the early 1960s and 1970s which met with very limited success;
- A third wave of decentralization at the end of the 1970s and the beginning of the 1980s provoked by lending institutions in search of improved national governance following economic collapses, and with the subsequent support of certain urban elite groups who were impatient to share power;
- A fourth wave of decentralization at the end of the 1980s and the beginning of the 1990s, supported by independent political forces and involved in the development of the powerful democratization movement which swept the Francophone regions of the continent.

An analysis of the recent political histories of these countries nevertheless allows us to discern two groups of countries: those which have seen relative political stability bolstered by a certain degree of economic success (Côte d'Ivoire, Senegal, Gabon, Cameroon); and those which have suffered long periods of military rule (Burkina Faso, Benin, Mali, Togo, Central African Republic, Niger, Congo) and which, with the exception of Togo, have not been able to develop a solid economic or a viable political base. The suppression of political liberties, along with poor domestic economies in the second category of countries, have pushed their urban populations into paralyzing strikes in an effort to bring about institutional reforms.

In certain of these countries, notably in Mali, Benin, Niger and the Congo, pluralist and democratic political administrations have been put in place following national conferences and transition governments. The successes of the democratization movement in more politically stable countries have been solidified through the installation of multi-party democratic governments. In certain cases, this democratization process has been harnessed by the status-quo elites in order to ensure their own political survival (Côte d'Ivoire, Burkina Faso, Senegal, Gabon and Togo). The hard political realities of this region and the painful process of learning democratic practices have resulted in a situation in which, despite plans of action and national conferences, the political apparatus has long remained in an unhealthy state of inertia. This is particularly true in the case of the Congo, Niger and Togo.

Trends in Urbanization

Sub-Saharan Africa, particularly in the western part of the continent, has witnessed a highly accelerated rate of urbanization. In fact, West Africa passed from a level of urbanization of 13 percent in 1960 to 40 percent in 1990. According to studies of urbanization patterns in this region, urban growth is presumed in some cases to result from economic prosperity — for instance, Côte d'Ivoire went from 7 percent urbanization to 47 percent between 1960 and 1990. Nevertheless, this rate of urbanization has been matched by unforeseen growth in countries that have suffered through ecological crises — Mauritania's level of urbanization has gone from 9 percent to 42 percent over the same period. This growth has also occurred with surprising vigour in countries suffering from political instability, such as Chad, in which the level of urbanization has gone from 6 percent to 24 percent between 1960 and 1990. Within this general pattern three subregional tendencies can be distinguished: the countries surrounding the Benin Gulf lead the way (Côte d'Ivoire, Togo, Benin, Cameroon) with a level of urbanization of 45 percent; the group of countries on the Atlantic coast (Mauritania, Senegal, Guinea) are behind them at 34 percent; and finally, the enclave states (Mali, Burkina Faso, Niger, Chad, Central African Republic) bring up the rear with 22 percent.

Between 1960 and 1990 the average annual rate of urban growth for all of this region was 6.3 percent. The projected rate for the period between 1990 and 2020 is 4.2 percent, with a level of urbanization estimated to reach 60 percent subsequently. In spite of these figures, urbanization has occurred in a relatively balanced manner in this geographic region. In fact, during the period between 1960 and 1990, the urban population has multiplied by 6.5 times, the number of cities with over 100,000 inhabitants has gone from 12 to 90, and the number of towns of over 5,000 inhabitants has increased from 600 to 3,000. This urbanization has also seen the advent of large metropolitan centres like Abidjan with 2,500,000 inhabitants and Dakar with 1,168,000.

The size ranking for cities on the national level indicates a strong bias toward the primacy of the largest centre — Dakar with 22 percent of the urban population compared with 3 percent for Thiès, Abidjan with 22 percent against 4 percent in Bouaké, and Cotonou with 11 percent as compared with 4 percent in Porto Novo.

II URBAN GOVERNANCE

Since the beginning of the 1990s, two conceptual models of urban management, inspired by two separate schools of thought, have been represented in debates as well as in actual practice in French-speaking Africa. These two models are represented by the notions of decentralization and urban governance.

The oldest of these models, decentralization, which was inherited from French tradition, refers to a new division of powers and responsibilities between the state and the municipalities in order to render the latter more autonomous and the management of urban services more efficient.

The second model, recently introduced (1990) and promoted by the international donor community, proposes a redistribution of responsibilities and powers between the state, local governments and members of the civil society. It also suggests a simultaneous process which introduces accountability and responsibility to these civilians, whose participation in urban management needs to be taken into consideration from the outset according to the principles of accountability and transparency.

In contrast to the notion of urban management espoused in management circles in the early 1980s — and these were also supported by these lending institutions — the concept of governance promoted by the political-economic milieux in North America is seen as a tool for democratization of local life.

Far from being in opposition or mutually exclusive as is generally first believed, these two management concepts are complementary. In fact, the principal objectives pursued by decision-makers in formulating and applying policies of decentralization are focused on the development, on a local level, of a representative and participatory democracy involving healthy and improved municipal practices. According to this criterion, any analysis of urban governance in Francophone Africa requires a study of the characteristics of decentralization before an attempt can be made at an evaluation of the conditions of good local governance. This is particularly true with respect to accountability and transparency, and to the "de-politicization" achieved in the management of local affairs, as well as the level of participation of the actors of urban society.

The Characteristics of Decentralization: Objectives, Size and Trends

Analysis of the general objectives of decentralization policies in the various countries of the sub-region suggests the following observations:

- Four countries — Senegal, Mauritania, Benin and Burkina Faso — consider decentralization a tool for promoting and learning about democracy and local development;
- In Mali, the aim is to attain control by the population of the management of their own affairs, implying a transfer of power to institutions which they themselves elect;
- Côte d'Ivoire retains only the aspect of sharing power between the central government and the local level as a means of promoting local development.

A review of the evolution of the decentralization process suggests that there is a break between the third wave of decentralization — successfully undertaken mainly in Senegal, Côte d'Ivoire and Cameroon in the early 1980s — and the fourth wave which results from national conferences (which has been spreading since the beginning of the current decade).

Indeed, while the third wave applied to *communalization* — the creation of municipal councils and the conditions necessary for their functioning, — the fourth phase relied on major concessions being made at national conferences. There, the plan to democratize society from the bottom up through the decentralization movement has been aimed at a veritable restructuring and repositioning of the state in order to leave more room for others involved, notably the municipalities ("communes") and civil society. One must note that this is the first time the laws governing decentralization in the region, specifically in Mali, Burkina Faso, Guinea and Benin, make explicit reference to the participants from civil society and to their role in the process, unlike the vague allusions to popular participation that had been made previously. While the restructuring of the State and of the administrative apparatus in Mali sets down its goals aiming to favour the emergence of initiatives in various sectors of civil society, in Benin the goal of decentralization is precisely to promote development from the ground up through the liberation of local initiatives and local energies.

Arising as it has from local political sources, and supported by the international donor community, this last wave of decentralization requires a systematic institutional restructuring. The ultimate aim of this process is the establishment of good local governance at the same time that the institutions are adjusted for national democratization and good governance. This process accompanies structural adjustment without any explicit mention of this element. It also differs from the preceding wave of decentralization in its participatory approach, and its constant search for consensus on its goals, processes and means of attaining decentralization. Others have followed the example set by Benin, which held conferences on decentralization in January, 1993 in Cotonou, with more than 300 participants representing all of Benin. There, the general orientation of the reform plans and subsequent recommendations regarding its course of action were made to the government. Afterwards, other countries also organized national conferences — Mali (1994), Guinea and Burkina Faso (1995) — designed to consult the people and find consensus on a plan of action for decentralization.

Decentralization: The Key Issues

In order to understand the various paths taken by different Francophone nations in Africa, the levels of decentralization and community autonomy must be addressed.

The level of decentralization refers both to the definition of the communal-municipal entity, its nature (urban, rural, regional) and the degree of coverage of the countries in question. Before evaluating the sizes and sociological content of the communities, there is the problem of defining an optimal size for such a local authority, one which will guarantee the functioning of a solidarity resulting from neighbourliness and the mobilization of resources essential to its development.

In sub-Saharan Francophone Africa, despite rather idealized theoretical definitions of the commune, the idea is mainly inherited from the colonial period, even adopted unchanged from colonial administrative entities. While the local population may accept these administrative divisions in general, their involvement in communal politics and especially their participation in its civic development cannot be taken for granted. This interest and action are brought about only through long processes of civic education, information and sensitization. Unfortunately, these kinds of initiatives do not often appear in municipal plans of action or in national decentralization programmes.

The region, the "commune" and the urban community are the only three levels of decentralization employed by the countries in this study. The commune may be either rural or urban, and with limited to full powers, or it can even be the size of a neighbourhood. Some communes within cities group together to form supra-municipal entities: the "urban community" or the "district." Since the recent creation of its 10 regions and subsequent elections, only Senegal retains all three categories: the region, the commune (rural or urban) and the urban community.

Côte d'Ivoire, Benin and Mauritania have kept the commune only, without distinguishing between the functions of rural or urban institutions. Guinea and Cameroon have the two rural and urban categories with differing processes for financial management (Cameroon) and the designation of legislative assemblies (Guinea). Burkina Faso lags behind again with two ex-colonial categories: communities with full powers (with elected legislative and executive branches) and communes with limited powers (having an elected legislature and a centrally appointed executive branch). Beyond semantic subtleties, the urban commune corresponds to a fully empowered municipality, while the rural commune corresponds to the second type, having an appointed executive.

Nearly all of the capital cities (economic and/or administrative) in these countries stand either in urban communities — formed as metropolitan agglomerations composed of several formerly autonomous communes (10 in Abidjan and 4 in Dakar) — or in smaller municipal zones split from older larger communes (Douala, Yaoundé, Brazzaville, Bobo-Dioulasso and Ouagadougou). In Niamey, Bamako and Conakry, the metropolitan government (district or urban community) is directed by a governor named by the central government while the communes within each metropolitan government are autonomous (with full powers) with elected mayors and councils.

Finally, by 1996, only Mauritania and Benin had achieved a complete level of decentralization covering the entire country.

The Political and Administrative Autonomy of Local Government

There are two criteria for evaluating the political and administrative autonomy of the communes. First is the free administration of the local institutions, the possibility that they might freely elect their legislative and executive bodies. The second is the absence of *a priori* control of these same procedures. From this point of view, only Cameroon's communes are fully autonomous and meet both criteria — and only since the latest reforms (1995). Communes in Senegal and Côte d'Ivoire, which meet only one of the criteria, can only be considered semi-autonomous.

The Financial and Fiscal Autonomy of Local Government

The legitimacy of the communes in the eyes of the population is increased whenever they initiate or support actions designed to contribute to the mitigation of urban poverty. More and more, communes seem to have understood this and are abandoning the trodden paths of traditional urban administration to try new approaches. Unfortunately, while such municipalities do not lack either ambitions or ideas on how to attempt this, they often do not have the necessary resources or they fall short at crucial moments. A recent study by the *Caisse Française de Développement* (French Development Fund) on local finances in five of these countries (Senegal, Côte d'Ivoire, Burkina Faso, Benin and Cameroon) shows that the financial weight of cities is only between 2 percent and 5 percent of total national budgets. This can be explained by the fact that in most cases, reforms have not been followed by the fiscal restructuring necessary to divide the pie equitably between national and local levels of government. The transfer of new powers to the municipalities has not been accompanied by the transfer of the resources necessary to make real use of them.

Moreover, the municipal communes have poor control over the fiscal resources that they receive from the state. From one financial law to the next, the state frequently reassigns financial resources in order to balance its own budget (for example, the case of Côte d'Ivoire in 1993). The same national government which has restricted municipal governments' recourse to credit and financial investment, has in many cases refused to develop a budgeting formula to guide the distribution of its aid to the communes.

Finally, the practice of the single account — a principle of public finance which obliges communes to deposit the totality of their holdings in an actualized public account, run by public accountants who give preference to payments of state expenses over those of the communes, but who nonetheless will acknowledge a positive balance on financial statements — only serves to worsen the financial crisis in which the communes find themselves, and damages their credibility with their suppliers. Although a concession was made by the government in Côte d'Ivoire to allow communes to operate a separate account for their projects, it was obtained only after high-level power struggles involving the donor community. Today, only one category of municipality in Cameroon enjoys real control over finances. Indeed, following the complaints of consecutive mayors over insolvency crises in the communes due to the single-fund policy, a reform implemented in 1995 ended this practice in 32 of the 339 communes in that country. In these communes, the municipal receiver is permitted to manage the communal resources separately in accounts opened at the Central Bank, in postal cheques or in a commercial bank. For the other 90 percent of the communes in which the single-account policy remains in force, the reform stipulates that only 50 percent of their resources may be borrowed by the central government to pay its debts, and then only after approval of the conditions of repayment by the mayor of the commune in question.

Although the obstacles to the free management of communal resources are currently numerous, the reform of financial management at the local level in Cameroon is leading in the right direction. This reform will almost certainly be followed by subsequent and similar reforms in other parts of the region.

III SPECIFIC ISSUES OF URBAN GOVERNANCE AND NEW CHALLENGES

In recent years, beyond municipal elections and the establishment of conditions necessary for the proper functioning of the communes (communalization and representative democracy), the debate on urban governance brings to light a number of specific issues. These are:

- The redefinition of the role of the commune in order to create the necessary room to manoeuvre for civil society;
- Accountability and greater transparency in administrative processes at the local level;
- The large-scale involvement of members of civil society.

Redefining the Role and the Place of the Communes in City Management

With democratization and decentralization, there has been a renewed interest in municipal life and the people are regaining hope that they can be involved in the management of city life. These demands for participation are the result of the communes' failure in the production and maintenance of urban services and they are often the subject of discussion at national conferences. Moreover, this interest in participation has resulted in central governments redefining the role of the communes. The new commune, a reflection of the method of the newly "adjusted" central government, is designed to allow participants from civil society to adopt roles and functions previously attributed to the communes. The latter in turn would be obliged to devote more of its resources to the foundation and evaluation of policy, evaluating needs, programming, monitoring, regulating and controlling of provision resources. This "new deal" for the communes leaves the mayors and municipal bureaucrats uncomfortable. The former fear for their political life now that their political visibility no longer will be tied to the creation and provision of much-desired services to the population. By the same token, abandoning production constitutes an enormous political favour to political opponents on the urban scene who, unable to participate officially in urban management structures, have chosen to invest their efforts in civic organizations such as the NGOs and CBOs. Municipal bureaucrats, on the other hand, are afraid they will be eliminated by a process which may only retain a lean skeleton of personnel.

Accountability and Transparency

Accountability and transparency are key concepts for good urban governance. The quest for them is motivated by a will to eliminate the practice of corruption. The best way to arrive at this is to produce and utilize policies and tools which prevent recourse to discretionary power in the hands of bureaucrats or which allow the collection and use of resources to be scrutinized.

Today, the numerous tools, procedural manuals and management policies necessary for fair and equitable use of urban resources — such as fairness in the awarding of contracts, and especially a non-partisan and non-patrimonial management of municipal infrastructure (markets, road-stations, slaughterhouses, undertakers, public washrooms) — still have not eliminated the possibility of considerable problems in public services. The desire for transparency must be accompanied by a judicious sharing of tasks between members of the municipal team. In fact, there have been reports of cases in which the mayor personally manages public works contracts while the engineer responsible for the technical department, who has been properly trained for such matters, remains outside the process.

The strengthening of transparency and accountability can also result in a de-politicization of urban management and the introduction of functional multi-party plurality at the local level. This, in turn, could act as a counterbalance to poor management. Indeed, the development of an opposition and of a free and independent press has contributed, through its critique of the system, to limit both deterioration from neglect and the poor allocation of national resources.

Active Participation in Urban Management by Civil Society

The participation of civil society in the production and management of urban services in the city occurs at two levels: at the level of social and political management, and at the level of socio-economic management.

Insufficient participation of such individuals in the political management of the city is the result of a certain weakness in the mechanisms of representative democracy. The principal cause of exclusion is the single-list ballot system. To counter this practice, Senegal has proposed a mixed system which combines the advantages of direct representation with those of the proportional method, guaranteeing the opposition representation while giving sufficient weight to the winning party to govern. Faced with inadequate representation of some civic participants (notably chiefs, religious leaders, and representatives of professional and economic associations), certain communes in Côte d'Ivoire have created "committees of wise men" or "elders' committees" or have arranged for the involvement of such individuals in statutory committees in order to benefit from their experience and popular legitimacy.

The participation of civil society in the economic management of the city is undermined by various situations and conditions. First, there is a lack of awareness of urban authorities with respect to their potential role in economic development. Second, local authorities do not trust many economic and associational groups. Finally, there are few organizations on the ground which are capable of responding to social demands, developing and managing projects competently and transparently. Nevertheless, several types of partnership and several modes of production and management of urban services by civic actors have already shown merit and deserve to be evaluated, improved and publicized.

IV THE CHALLENGES FOR URBAN GOVERNANCE

Our study has proposed some major challenges to ensure the establishment of good urban governance. They require the cooperation not only of governments but also assistance agencies and researchers. These are specifically:

- The continuation of the process of decentralization in order to cover all national territories.
- The political emancipation of the communes by an elaboration of representative democracy and the limitation of central control to include only after-the-fact scrutiny.
- The introduction of true financial autonomy for the communes, eliminating or softening the practice of the single account system and implementing formulas for fair sharing of resources, free from the potential manipulation of state resources received by the communes.
- The reinforcement of transparency and accountability in urban management through the participation of political parties and the introduction of tools and procedures which limit recourse to discretionary use of power, poor resource allocation and an arbitrary use of urban infrastructures.
- The strengthening of the participation of members of civil society in urban management by redefining the roles and goals of the various actors on the urban scene.
- The inclusion in metropolitan governance processes of action research on methods which will give civic participants a forum for participation in the new forms of production and management of urban services.

13 The Challenge of Urban Governance in East Africa: Responding to an Unrelenting Crisis
MOHAMED HALFANI

I INTRODUCTION

In 1989, a group of researchers published findings which suggested that African urban centres were passing through a severe management crisis (Stren and White 1989). Most of the data used in the analysis was based on trends that occurred in the period between 1979 and 1985. It is now 10 years since those data were collected and yet there is no evidence that the crisis has abated in Kenya, Tanzania or Uganda, or that the administrative capacities of these countries have developed sufficiently to deal with its effects.

Figures published by the United Nations in 1995 show that the East African sub-region has the fastest urban growth rate in the whole world (United Nations 1995, 38). At the same time, marginalization of primary exporting economies in the 1980s severely eroded the urban economic base. The cities' traditional function of providing rudimentary services for a raw-material based export-import economy has lost its value in the global economic exchange. The existing system for service delivery operates at a level which is less than optimal. Formal institutions that are assigned the task of managing cities are experiencing severe difficulties; they can neither execute their assigned functions effectively nor sustain themselves as institutions.

Even Nairobi, a city that is considered to be a "sub-metropolis" of the region, manifests elements of physical degeneration, social deprivation and managerial incompetence (Karuga 1993). All indicators suggest that the urban crisis in Kenya, Tanzania and Uganda remains unabated and intervention capacities have not developed.

By 1995, demographic projections indicate that the urban population in East Africa had grown to about 20 million people (United Nations 1995, 15). In each country, close to two-thirds of the urban populations live in unplanned settlements that have poor infrastructural and social services.

Close to 75 percent of the labour force is engaged outside the formal sector. Formal control mechanisms remain very limited, as less than 25 percent of activities taking place within urban boundaries are regulated by local municipal authorities. At the same time, there is a rapid depletion of energy sources, rampant destruction of water reservoirs, and heavy pollution of urban ecological systems.

Despite the apparent fragility of urban centres in East Africa, they still continue to attract and accommodate migrants at an average rate of 10 percent per annum. Between 1980 and 1995, 10 million more people had to be accommodated and provided with a means of subsistence in the urban centres of this region. The urban population has grown from about 5.6 million to 15.8 million people within a span of only 15 years. It is now estimated that by the year 2025, less than two decades from now, urban centres will have to take care of a population which will more than quadruple to 80 million people (United Nations 1995).

Since 1985, and in addition to this demographic burden, urban centres have had to cope with the acute stress of implementing structural adjustment programmes. The retrenchment of public service, shifting investment to tradeable goods, the removal of subsidies, and fiscal and monetary reforms are policies which, at least in the short run, have had a negative impact on much of the urban system in East Africa. This series of changes has aggravated unemployment, accentuated social strife, increased the cost of living, and impaired the delivery of public services.[1]

As if the above predicament is not enough, East African urban centres in the 1990s also have had to deal with the imperatives of political reforms. The tempo of democratic change is mostly determined by the urban centres; this has created a situation that has aggravated tensions, generated animosities and intensified demands on the managerial system. These urban centres are now the crucibles of political activism, propagating pluralism and liberalization. They promote civic engagement, even though it is still localized at this stage. At the same time, urban centres provide a fertile ground for recruitment to the new political parties, which makes these municipalities pedestals for launching activities in national politics. All the frictions associated with these political dynamics are borne by urban centres.

Despite the stringent effects of these changes, towns and cities continue to survive the challenges of demographic, economic and political transformation. Unlike the situation in Europe, whose equivalent transition had a higher human cost, there is no evidence of a pervasive social malaise in the development of East African cities. How can we explain this paradoxical phenomenon? Specifically, how are urban centres coping with all these challenges in spite of their fragility? What organizational system in the East African city provides this resilience, enabling its population to survive under such severe odds? How can this capacity for endurance be vitalized and employed in the creation of well-functioning urban systems in East Africa?

This chapter explores the institutional landscape underlying the resilience of the East African urban system.

II DEFICIENCIES OF STATE-DRIVEN MANAGEMENT

The survival of East African cities cannot be attributed solely to policy measures taken by the state. To a large extent, these measures have not been adequate, and in some cases they have even exacerbated the crisis.

Until the end of the of the 1980s, the governments of Kenya, Tanzania and Uganda had not even introduced innovative programmes for urban change. Failure to replicate the "sites and services/squatter upgrading" approach left a void in housing delivery. Between 1965 and 1986 the government of Kenya designed several policy strategies aimed at maintaining a rural-urban balance, assisting the informal sector, and de-concentrating administrative power to the lower level. None of these policies had produced positive results at the end of their implementation period. Similarly, the government of Tanzania promulgated a growth-pole strategy in 1969, and incorporated a Basic Industrial Strategy which gave a prominent role to urban investment. In 1983, several repressive measures attempted to control urban growth and employ the surplus labour. None of these measures was successful (Stren et al. 1994).

The new government that assumed power in Uganda in 1986, after an extended period of lawlessness and disorder, appointed a commission to look into the system of local government. The commission's recommendations exhibited a strong anti-urban bias, opposing the prevailing system of parallel administration between rural and urban, tracing the origins of such a division to the colonial period. For the Commission, ". . . separate planning, [of] urban and rural (districts) means an enormous duplication and wastage of resources. Combined with the fracture in services — local and central — the wastage can at times reach dramatic proportions . . ." (Uganda 1987a, 54). Although the government did not adopt this perspective, urban development was not accorded special attention, except for some isolated projects.

At an institutional level, Tanzania completed the restoration of urban authorities in 1982 after their abolition a decade earlier (Max 1991). In 1984, Kenya made substantial amendments to the 1963 local government statute that was the basis of urban management (Karuga 1993, 102). Both moves strengthened the power of central government in managing local affairs. Similarly, in Uganda, the National Resistance Movement (NRM) government introduced a non-partisan system of Resistance Councils (RCs) but also retained the watchful eye of a centrally appointed District Secretary who served as the central government overseer (Uganda 1987b; Ddungu 1989) The basic rubric of colonial local government traditions, expressed in the local government statute of 1967, were also maintained.

To a large extent, these states' failures in dealing with the urban crisis was caused by their resistance to changing the mode of urban governance. Existing modes emphasize state exclusiveness, maintain only a limited hegemony, and respond only to an enclave sphere of the urban socio-political system. Ironically, it was the very crisis of continuity which created a new scenario. It has provided a space for non-state actors to play a prominent role in the governance of urban development. While at this point (mid-1990s) the engagement of multiple actors in the system of urban governance has not been formally rationalized, the mere tolerance of this process by the state indicates that East African countries are now adopting a new mode of governance. The new model is characterized by *regime multiplicity.* This constellation of forces opens the way for the ultimate evolution of a higher mode of governance, one driven by empowerment, partnership, and enablement.

In the next section we shall examine the configuration of regime multiplicity in the system of urban governance in each country.

III REGIME MULTIPLICITY IN URBAN GOVERNANCE

Kenya: State Recalcitrance, Civil Engagement and Informal Resilience

In Kenya, civil society has fractured on the basis of ethnicity, class and regionalism. Coupled with an advanced form of capitalist development in urban industry and commerce, this fragmentation has created a highly pluralized society with vibrant civil associations. Over the last 20 years, however, the state has limited the political space for civil associations and dominated all agencies of governance. Nevertheless, the informal sector has remained resilient and maintains a significant degree of hegemony.

The early advent of multi-party participation (a process also fostered by the relative strength of the fractured civil society) further pluralized the urban authorities and exacerbated the tension between the state and autonomous institutions of civil society.

Kenya has maintained its inherited, British-style system of municipal authorities with much more stability than either Tanzania or Uganda. Local urban authorities are responsible for operating and regulating land use and primary services, and central government agencies manage the larger secondary functions. However, the aspiration of decentralizing authority, embedded in the District Focus for Rural Development programme (Kenya 1983), was extended to include urban centres. It has resulted in a dispersion of bureaucratic power towards the local level. In fact, the 1984 amendments of the Local Government Act 1963 (Cap 265) essentially wrested powers from the elected councillors and concentrated it in the central government, particularly in the hands of the Minister responsible for local government. The transferred functions even included minor issues like the naming of roads (Karuga 1993, 96).

By 1992, the administrative system for urban management in Kenya was a hierarchy composed of 30 municipal authorities, 17 town councils, 40 county councils and 27 urban councils. They were distinguished on the basis of size, powers, resource disposition and functions (Agevi 1992, 59). The main instruments of governance include: master plans and statutory controls, project investments, public delivery systems and fiscal mechanisms. Some of the major programmes undertaken have included the provision of shelter, land use planning, the development of micro-enterprises and improvements to infrastructure.

While most of these programmes did contribute to a modest increase in the physical stock, they did not lead to the establishment of a sustainable and duplicable system of delivery system for urban goods and services. As Stren and his colleagues observe (Stren et al. 1994), by the end of the 1980s urban planning policies were largely quiescent and inoperative in the face of institutional and resource deficiencies. Moreover, they maintain that slums and squatter settlements were more pronounced than ever, and poverty and squalor had become increasingly visible indicators of a decaying urban environment. This sentiment is confirmed in the report of a unique convention, called in 1992 to discuss the future of Nairobi as its residents desire to build it. The working group on the structure and system of city government reported:

The Group was concerned with the issue of the system and structures of City government in Nairobi. Most of us feel that governance (i.e. who rules, why, on whose behalf, and under what rules/laws) and accountability (who gets what, when, how, why, and under what rules/laws) are the key issues in City government. . . . The group observed first that the administrative and legal context (Local Government Act) in which the City Government finds itself is disabling. Secondly, the dynamics within City Hall (system of representation, consultation and public discourse) leave a lot to be desired. Thirdly, City Government, seemingly isolated from its own constituency, has been increasingly unable to deliver the services which provide the basis for its justification (Karuga 1993, 101).

The report identified the main problems to be: the deterioration of services due to inadequate resources, poor administration, bureaucratic lethargy, corruption and a lack of discipline among the workforce, the absence of clear lines of authority, the disregard for public opinion, ineffective representation at City Hall, and apathy among the people of Nairobi (Karuga 1993).

In strictly legal terms, municipal authorities are partners of central government agencies, and together they are the sole organs of urban governance. However, economic constraints combined with institutional inefficiencies have impaired their capacity to perform this duty and have reduced their domain of effective control. As a result, a large sphere of urban life has operated outside the regulatory and directive authority of the formal system. The proliferation of squatter settlements, the expansion of the informal economy, the rampant violation of rules and regulation, and the growth of alternative service delivery systems are all symptomatic of the formal governance system's ineffectiveness.

The main constituents of the formal governance system are a few private households, public agencies, corporate firms, and NGOs. Within the inherited traditions of the western municipal systems (the English system in particular), these sectors are supposed to be the only constituents of an urban system. The role of municipal authorities is to regulate their socio-economic activities, facilitate their accumulative functions, and provide them with collective services. However, by the 1980s, municipal authorities were not performing these functions reliably. This led to some of the urban sectors carving out a small domain of autonomy within the formal sphere of municipal governance.

In the first place, proliferation of housing estates expanded the pockets of autonomy that officially are supposed to operate within the framework of general municipal ordinances. In most cases these ordinances have not been enforced. Moreover, the housing estates have their own internal codes of conduct and alternative systems of service provision. Except for main roads, electricity, water and the enclaves of existing central sewerage systems, the estates have maintained a semi-autonomous relationship with Kenyan municipal authorities.

Secondly, the absence of coherent investment plans has created a situation whereby the overall initiative for urban development has been relinquished and subordinated to the interests of private developers and private suppliers of urban services. The fact that municipal agencies have weak institutional capacities for enforcing standards has bolstered the virtual autonomy of the corporate sector within the system of urban governance.

Straddling the margins of the formal system are the various categories of civil associations. In Kenya as a whole it is estimated that NGOs have an annual development expenditure of US$ 150-200 million. NGOs finance 30 to 40 percent of the total development expenditure, over 40 percent of all health care services, and between 40 and 45 percent of all family planning services (Ndegwa 1994). In the city of Nairobi alone, Ndinda Bubba and Davinder Lamba (1991) reveal that most of the major hospitals are run by NGOs. They also show that NGOs are responsible for 9 percent of Nairobi's primary education and 27 percent of its secondary education. In almost every sector (housing, income generation, welfare) and in most of the urban centres, there has been a proliferation of associations that operate independent of the state. These associations seem to have the most impact in determining the direction of urban development.

Of course, it is not simply the management of an alternative system of service provision that qualifies Kenyan urban civil associations to be a distinct regime of governance. After all, Kenya has had a long history of social movements that were seemingly outside state tutelage but whose activities bolstered state legitimacy and effectiveness — the Harambee movement for instance (Holmquist 1994). Since the 1980s, however, civil associations have begun to distinguish themselves from the state. Initially, they do so by devising alternative systems of urban sustenance and, later, by engaging in a contest for urban socio-political space. The early organizations were essentially survivalist, the main preoccupation being the maintenance of household and community self-preservation. Afterward, civil organizations evolved and began to play an intermediary role by linking the state and civil society through institutions such as professional and trade associations, churches and mosques, and hometown organizations.

As the impediments to efficient urban governance persisted, particularly as the municipal and central government agencies became more alienated from the people, civil associations transcended their survivalist mentality and began to seek the overall transformation of the system of urban governance.

The final statement of the Nairobi City Convention strongly reflected the transformation of civil society into an agent of change, reasserting its ownership of the city:

> We the Nairobians gathered in this first open forum for the direct participation by Nairobians, to consider the state and the future of our city; Looking forward to Nairobi's first centenary; Concerned about the present degradation of our environment; Anxious to arrest this situation; Mindful of the need to determine our future and to preserve and enrich our diverse cultures; Inspired by the new vision of change; Committed to joint and united action; Recognizing the efforts of all communities to solve our problems; We resolve to enhance dialogue and participation in policy reforms towards good governance of our city; We further affirm our commitment to the Action Plan endorsed by this Convention, towards making Nairobi a secure place to live in peace and dignity for all Nairobians (Lamba 1994, i).

Informalism

By the end of the 1980s, informalism was not simply a locus of urban survival, or a sector whose structure makes it amenable for increasing urban employment. Its resilience and expansion transformed it into a distinct regime of urban governance. More than half of urban life is effectively regulated and directed by informal-sector systems. After all, by the second decade of the independence era the informal domain of urban resource mobilization, deployment and allocation was larger than the equivalent managed by the state. For example, between 1977 and 1987, the formal public and private housing sector managed to provide a total of about 58,820 units, while the total number of households formed annually was estimated at 380,000 units. Accordingly, it is estimated that around 55 percent of the urban population live in squatter (informal) settlements (Kiamba et al. 1992).

The informal sector also is a major provider of urban employment and transport services. It is estimated that 40 percent of total urban employment takes place within the informal system. Between 1985 and 1988, two categories of the informal sector — small-scale enterprises, and self-employed and family workers — grew at an annual rate of 11.1 percent and 9.6 percent respectively. By contrast, non-agricultural wage employment during the same period grew annually by only 3.6 percent (Stren et al. 1994, 182).

In 1988, the Nairobi City Commission reported that pirate vehicles (*matatus*) carried the equivalent passenger load of 650 large buses. In the same year, the Kenya Bus Service (a registered private transport company) maintained a fleet of only 300 buses, and the government established Nyayo Bus Service operated another 75 buses (Stren et al. 1994, 184). All the above indicators reflect an increasing process of informalization in the management of the Kenyan urban system.

Underlying the relative robustness and resilience of the informal system of governance is an institutional framework which operates on the basis of minimum contractual procedures. It also relies on traditional enforcement mechanisms, minimized transaction costs, and a market mediated by the institutional remnants of traditional norms and procedures.

Despite the dominance of this sector and its coherent modes of governance, the activities which take place within it are considered to be illegal by the state. Even though the government initially promoted informal-sector employment by supporting small-scale artisans — the short-lived Jua Kali programme — and attempts like that of Eldoret to integrate some aspects of traditional organizational systems into the formal management of urban centres, informal activities are subjected to continuous harassment and they are often denied state assistance (Mitullah 1991; SINA 1991; Macharia 1992; Owuor 1994, 1). Generally, the relationship between the pervasive informalism and the formal municipal system of urban governance in Kenya remains hostile and antagonistic.

Tanzania: Institutional Incongruity, Benign Tolerance and the Resurgence of Associations

The case of urban governance in Tanzania represents a fusion of two systems. On the one hand, there are formal state institutions which monopolize legal authority over the entire urban space. Due to weak capacities, this system lacks the effective controls needed to enforce its power. On the other hand, there is a resilient informal system which directs a larger sphere of urban governance. As a result of its inherent deficiencies and state impediments, the informal sector's effectiveness in urban development is greatly undermined. The advent of pluralism and the reconstitution of the public realm in the 1990s, introduces a dynamic which makes the fusion of the two systems unstable. Currently, Tanzania is going through a phase in which the role of institutions and the relationship between (and within) the state and civil society is being redefined.

The revival of local government in Tanzania has coincided with profound changes in the economic and political spheres. Three years after the full re-establishment of urban authorities, the government conceded to an IMF reform package. This has led to the abandonment of previous socialist strategies and the adoption of a market-driven development system. At the same time, the vibrancy of the informal sector was unleashed, and restrictions imposed on civil associations were relaxed. Similarly, the single-party political system was abolished and major changes in the system of urban governance were introduced.

The legal revival of urban local government in 1982 re-established organizational and procedural systems based on the political and economic paradigms of the pre-1982 period. This reinstated the judicial principles of the Colonial Native authority system (Cap. 333), based on a segmentary local governance that treated the indigenous people as temporary residents in the cities. The new system also maintained the exclusiveness of state institutions in the formal governance of urban centres. The scheme was designed for an era when the segmented state was the provider and when resources were allocated on the basis of a bureaucratic rationality that was administratively driven. In institutional terms, the formal system of governance is composed of municipal councils, central government ministries and parastatals. Until 1992, it also included the ruling Party (Kulaba 1989, 228–43). The various pieces of legislation which were enacted to strengthen the re-establishment of urban authorities conferred a virtual monopoly of governance powers on the state institutions.

Now, in the 1990s, the incongruity of this system of governance and the prevailing reality has become more apparent. This system cannot cope with the main challenges of urban development, especially the problems associated with the highest population growth rate in the world. Recent research also indicates that the formal system of urban governance suffers from severe dysfunctions which limit its capacity to perform effectively (Halfani and Sendaro 1990; Kitula et al. 1990). State institutions poorly execute the regulative, facilitative and operational functions of urban governance, and this has provided a space for the informal system to thrive and has permitted the resurgence of community organizations. Researchers in the 1990s are even suggesting that the informal system of governance is so powerful that it has its own distinct patterns of space organization, overlapping the official version (Halfani and Stren 1994).

The Post-Arusha Paradigm of Urban Governance

The statutory framework for urban governance in 1982 incorporated only the formal agencies of state management. Powers and functions pertaining to urban development were allocated to municipal authorities, central government ministries and parastatals that were involved in housing and infrastructural management. Not only were non-state agencies excluded in the statutory allocation of urban functions but their association with the designated formal agencies was dependent on bureaucratic contingencies.

The overall character of the urban management system was defined by an effort to sustain the internal bureaucratic coherence of these three agencies; a strong emphasis given to reinforcing administrative control, organizational compliance, bureaucratic authority and a technocratic reification of the management process. The dysfunctional, inefficient and bureaucratic relations between local authorities and the central government were exarcebated by the ambiguity of the statutory definition of inter-governmental relations. While a few provisions emphasized the element of "self-governance" through a hierarchical structure of semi-autonomous authorities (with the central government retaining supervisory and coordinating powers), quite a few other provisions uderscored an "agency" linkage, implying an execution of functions on behalf of the higher body. In the same regard, some provisions emphasized a "departmental" linkage, suggesting that municipal authorities are simply departments of the central government.

A critical defect of the institutional framework for management pertained to the weak, and at times conflictive, horizontal linkage among the three agencies of formal governance. Parastatal organs were less inclined to be accountable to municipal councils, and for quite some time central government organs at the regional and district level grabbed projects (especially those which involved foreign funding) and involved themselves in operational activities at the city level.

Apart from these organizational deficiencies, the formal system of governance was also impaired by the lack of a clear definition of urban development. The last time Tanzania addressed the role and content of urbanization in national development was in 1969 when it included a "growth pole" strategy in the Second Five-Year Plan for social and economic development. In 1975 this plan was consolidated by the promulgation of a Basic Industrial plan that involved decentralizing all levels of industrial activities to the growth-pole zones and fostering forward and backward linkages in sectoral and macroeconomic systems. However, none of these plans left the ground and the skewed distribution of industrial activities remained unchanged. This, coupled with the apparent reticence toward the movement of the administrative capital to Dodoma, rendered the "central place" given to urban development in the growth-pole strategy of 1969 an empty slogan.

With the adoption of a series of adjustment programmes in the 1980s, the issue of defining a role for urban places was completely ignored. In fact, for quite some time, urban areas were considered a "soft sector" and not a strategic priority for investment during a crisis period. Furthermore, despite the promulgation of a Basic Industrial Strategy in the third five-year plan, the prevailing perception was that urbanization is a dysfunctional process which has to be forestalled. As late as 1983 the option of repatriating individuals to the rural areas was still considered to be viable (Shaidi 1984; Miti 1985). According to this physiocratic view, Tanzania's development base was to remain agriculture, and the dynamism of growth was to evolve from the rural areas!

The most glaring anomaly of urban governance within the framework of the 1982 revival was the exclusion of the private sector. All activities performed by individuals and households, as well as corporate investors and entrepreneurs — were totally excluded in the official framework of urban governance. This was despite the fact that a substantial level of urban investments were made by the private sector, and the fact that community groups (mosques, churches, neighbourhoods, kinships) had demonstrated a strong capacity for service and welfare provision. With more than 60 percent of the urban population investing in their own housing and relying on on-site infrastructure, and with more than three-quarters of income generated from the non-state sector, one would expect that the official framework for governance would accord some recognition to the non-state sector and establish an organizational mechanism that would promote a managerial linkage between the two sectors. The disjuncture was such that, until 1992, local urban authorities did not have a functional organ at the sub-municipal level (where a lot of non-state activities took place), except for the councillor, who was more or less a political representative. Communities and neighbourhoods had either to comply with the bureaucratic authority of the council, which is far away from them, or they had to create their own civil associations.

Civil Associations

The same factors that triggered the growth of informalism in Kenya also apply to Tanzania. The failure of the monopolistic state to meet the challenge of urbanization unleashed a dynamic of association which began as a survival mechanism and became a transformation force. Aili Trip captures this transition as she observes the early stages of civil association whereby,

> [D]uring the 1980s the state's increasing inability to provide a modicum of social and public services, to ensure livable income for the employed, and to offer viable police protection made it necessary for local organizations to fill some of these voids. In fact, the resiliency of society and its ability to reproduce itself with considerable autonomy from the state was one of the reasons the entire fabric of society did not fall apart during years of unprecedented hardship . . . (Tripp 1990, 56).

In a subsequent study, Tripp reveals how survival-driven associations such as rotating credit associations and local defence teams were gradually evolving into vehicles for empowerment and contributing to the reconstruction of state-society relations (Tripp 1992). Similarly, Abdul-Wahab Byekwaso focuses on three informal settlements in Dar es Salaam — Tabata, Buguruni, and Vingunguti — where he traces the growth of local institutions which empower the people to take charge of their own development, to engage the state in a more vigorous manner, and to mobilize resources which contribute to their own transformation (Byekwaso 1994).

In a different case-study, A.G. Kyessi and S.A. Sheuya re-affirm the capacity of community organizations to engage the state and extract its resources for improving community welfare. The residents of Hanna Nassif of Dar es Salaam organized themselves to find solutions to the water shortages, the lack of storm water drainage, the poor sewerage systems, improper roads and high unemployment. They mobilized their own local resources and they succeeded in forging a link with a Technical Support Team, composed of staff from the City Council, International Labour Organization, UNCHS-Habitat and the United Nations Volunteers. The various tasks under this initiative will be managed and executed by the local community (through a system of community contracting), while the other agencies will simply perform a supporting role (Kyessi and Sheuya 1993).

A large part of the socio-economic activities take place outside the purview of state authority. For instance, two decades of pursuing a social-ist policy in land ownership which acknowledged the customary freehold tenurial system implied an official disregard of the thriving informal land market. Similarly, the absence of a developed financial market relegated the bulk of capital investment (mainly through households) to the infor-mal system. And the small size of the formal industrial and service sectors drove the labour market to the informal sector.

The same can be said of civil associations. Despite the harassment and lack of consistent state support, by the 1980s one can discern distinct rules, organizational procedures and sanction mechanisms that drive these representative bodies. By deploying the traditional virtues of reciprocity and collective trust, the system is gradually interfacing with market dynamics. At present, transactions in the urban land markets operate without the contractual complications which inundate the formal system. Similarly, credit, commerce and services take place in an organized way despite the absence of formal mechanisms.

Uganda: Nurturing A Partnership between State and Civil Society

Between 1971 and 1985, Ugandans, and particularly the country's urban citizens, lived through a vicious reign of terror perpetrated by various regimes. Relatively benign structures of governance were re-established in 1986, after Museveni's National Resistance Movement took power. It was faced with the challenge of reconstructing a country torn apart by war and a population that had experienced betrayal by several regimes. The NRM government committed itself to creating a governance system character-ized by a devolution of power to the people while, at the same time, avoid-ing every element which would rekindle divisiveness. Thus, a system of decentralized governance was initiated only cautiously and gradually through a process of consolidation, and by nurturing a non-partisan sys-tem of resistance councils (Ddungu 1989).

Although urban centres are treated as distinct units of administration within the resistance council system, the legal framework does not assign any special powers or functions to urban authorities. Little attention is given to the specific details of urban planning and management. In fact, in all the enabling legislations, urban authorities are mentioned in the same category as their predominantly rural counterparts: the district authorities (Uganda 1993). More likely than not, it is assumed that the local specificity of urban development can be accommodated within the framework of the resistance council system. The premise is that an urban resistance council has been given enough latitude to function within the parameters of distinctive urban environments.

Notwithstanding these efforts, the initial devolution of power made through the resistance council system was encumbered by a significant degree of central government control — through the District Executive Secretary. In 1993, however, legislation made all district level functionaries accountable to the district councils and their role in decision-making is now strictly advisory. In the last three years, substantial powers over the recurrent district budget have been devolved to the district level. In fact, the national constitution includes a special schedule which directs the central government to provide unconditional grants to local governments for running decentralized services on the basis of a provided formula (Uganda 1995, 195). Organizationally, the whole process has extended the space for community initiatives, albeit in a context that has bureaucratized civil associations.

Uganda represents a unique situation in East Africa because traditional forms of governing have remained more powerful than in other countries. Traditional rulership is so strong that it has been re-integrated into Uganda's formal system of governance in the 1990s. Except for a brief interlude, the system of chieftainship has been part of the district administrative system in much of the country. The role of the chief has been to maintain law and order, to enforce measures in the interest of socio-economic development, to settle local disputes, to collect government revenue, and to provide communication channels between the government and the people (Uganda 1987a, 15–16; Chiluvane 1992, 32).

The existing documentation seems to suggest that the position of a chief prevails at the sub-parish, parish and county levels, especially in rural and urban fringe areas. Nevertheless, the fact that the Local Government Commission was forced to make the following recommendation suggests that the system of chieftainship also operates in urban areas:

Urban centres above Town Councils have policemen to effect an arrest, tax collectors to effect payment of government tax and enforcement officers to ensure compliance with government laws and local by-laws. The chief, after all, is an enforcement officer who carries out all these duties in the country-side and in those peri-urban areas where such a differentiated administrative enforcement machinery is either absent or deficient. But where there does exist an adequate administrative enforcement machinery — that is, in Town Boards, Municipalities, and Cities — we recommend all levels of chiefs should be removed and their positions abolished (Uganda 1987a, 20).

The role of traditional institutions is more visible in the governance of Ugandan urban centres in two main areas: the system of land management, and the controversial reintroduction of monarchism.

Originally, much of the urban land in Uganda was managed under the leasehold system in which the state and its immediate agencies acquired custody over designated areas of land which it leased to individuals and corporate bodies. However, as the urban centres expanded they incorpo-rated areas which were previously under the jurisdiction of chiefs and clans and managed under freehold and customary tenure. Currently, all three tenurial systems operate in most of the urban centres, creating a complex system of land management.

This issue of land ownership within customary tenure is more pertinent now with the revival of monarchism. In July 1993, the National Resistance Council passed the Constitution Amendment Bill which re-established traditional monarchs (the Ebyaffe Bill) and the Restitution of Assets and Properties Bill, which returned the appropriated assets of the former king-doms (Nsibambi 1993: 14). A significant share of these assets, including land, now lies within the boundaries of major urban centres such as Kampala. Unfortunately, no research has been done to analyze the complex impli-cations that the revival of traditional kingdoms has for the system of urban governance. At present, the discourse on local governance in Uganda focuses only on the cultural symbolism of the monarch, and yet the Restitution Act will have a bearing on resource management in urban Uganda.

The traditional system of governance is just as dynamic a regime as the informal system. In fact, Daniel Mwesigwa (1987) observed that during the 1980s the urban informal sector was one of the few areas of growth in an otherwise bleak economic landscape in Uganda. In 1989, the late Ernest Wabwire observed that groups of informal sector workers are becoming more organized by individual trade, and capable of regulating themselves and providing a number of services which the state does not otherwise provide (Wabwire 1989). This has led some analysts to argue that the effectiveness of urban governance depends on the manner in which the informal sector is organized socially and politically and articulated within the formal urban administrative structures (Nabuguzi 1989).

The vitality of the informal system and the civil associations in urban governance is vividly demonstrated in a study of the confrontation between the City Council and the legal and illegal vendors in and around the central market of Kampala. Tracing the history of the market (Owino market) Christie Gombay describes the formation of vendor associations and demonstrates how these organizations successfully engaged the Kampala city council (KCC) in a negotiation on raising market fees and permitting evening markets outside the market area. Concluding his analysis, Gombay observes that:

> 'Urban Management' is going on in Kampala, but it is being carried out by people in ways that bear little resemblance to institutional definitions being encouraged and supported by the international agencies. . . . There is strict land-use in the evening market. Plots are allocated, fees are paid, there is lighting and a footing which does not get muddy, even when it rains. There is tremendous revenue generation going on — it simply doesn't make it into public accounts. And vendors are able to sell and make a living doing it. . . . Urban management is going on but is being done by the urban poor, not by the Ministry of Local Government or KCC (Gombay 1993, 20).

Regime Multiplicity and the Challenge of Urban Governance in the 1990s

This chapter has demonstrated that in each of the three East African countries municipal governments form the most dominant authority for directing urban development. However, there are also other structures of authority which determine the content of urban change. These include the informal system of production and exchange, traditional institutions and civil associations. In the course of their operation, these structures have developed distinct organizational patterns and rules of behaviour which determine how urban centres in East Africa can develop.

Despite the marginality and structural weaknesses of non-state systems, the East African experience reveals that a large part of urban socio-economic life takes place within this sphere. Its lower transition costs, its high degree of responsiveness, and its amenability to interface with the emerging market endows it with enhanced dynamism and resilience. However, the survival of East African urban centres in the last two decades is largely a function of the buoyancy created by regime multiplicity in the system of governance. The composite system formed by the symbiotic coexistence of state-based and non-state regimes sustains a structural functionalist system whose parts feed into the total system.

The challenge of the 1990s is to maximize the synergy created from the interactions of the different parts. Uganda, despite its turbulent history, seems to be leading the way.

Note

1   While the impact of structural adjustment on urban development has not been systematically investigated, all accounts of the urban situation during the implementation of structural adjustment programmes tend to highlight negative social impacts on urban systems (see, for example, Stren 1994; Lugalla 1995; Macharia 1995).

References

Agevi, Elijah. 1992. "Community Participation and Responsible Urban Management." In Joyce Malombe (ed.), *Urban Management in Kenya.* Proceedings of African Urban Research Network for Urban Management (ARNUM) Workshop, Nairobi, August 20. Nairobi: Housing and Building Research Institute, pp. 59–71.

Bubba, Ndinda and Davinder Lamba. 1991. "Urban Management in Kenya." Environment and Urbanization 3(1): 37–59.

Byekwaso, Abdul-Wahab S. 1994. "The Role of Community Based Organizations in land Servicing: A Case Study of Tabata, Buguruni and Vingnguti." Unpublished dissertation, Department of Urban and Rural Planning, University of Dar es Salaam.

Chiluvane, Lourenco. 1992. Local Government in Africa: Brief Analysis of 8 Case Studies. Maputo: Friedrich Ebert Foundation.

Ddungu, Expedit. 1989. Popular Forms and the Question of Democracy: The Case of Resistance Councils in Uganda. Publication No. 4. Kampala: Center for Basic Research.

Gombay, Christie. 1993. "Eating Cities: Urban Management and Markets in Kampala, Uganda." Paper presented at the 22nd Conference of the Canadian Association of African Studies, University of Toronto, May 12–15.

Halfani, M. and A.M. Sendaro. 1990. "Towards the Enhancement of Local Government Management Capacities in Tanzania." Dar es Salaam: Institute of Development Studies, University of Dar es Salaam.

Halfani, M. and Richard Stren. 1994. "Civil Society in Tanzania." Development and Democracy 1: 10–18.

Holmquist, Frank and Michael Ford. 1994. "Kenya: State and Civil Society the First Year After the Election." Africa Today 41(4): 5–26.

Karuga, James G. (ed.). 1993. Actions Towards A Better Nairobi: Report and Recommendations of The Nairobi City Convention. Nairobi: City Hall.

Kenya, Republic of. 1983. District Focus for Rural Development. Nairobi: Office of the President

Kiamba, M., J. Malombe and R. Muchene. 1992. Urban Management Instruments for Neighbourhood Development in Selected African Cities: The Case of Kenya. Nairobi: University of Nairobi, Department of Land Development.

Kitula, A.J. Mogella, C.A. Mrina, B.E. Senge, F.K. 1992. Towards Achieving the Objectives of Local Government System in Tanzania. A research Report. Dar es Salaam: Ministry of Local Government, Community Development, Cooperatives and Marketing.

Kulaba, Saitiel. 1989. "Local Government and the Management of Urban Services in Tanzania." In Richard Stren and Rodney White (eds.), African Cities in Crisis: Managing Rapid Urban Growth. Boulder Colorado: Westview Press.

Kyessi, A.G. and S.A. Sheuya. 1993. "The Role of the Community Based Organizations (CBOs) and Non-governmental Organizations (NGOs) in Squatter Upgrading." Paper presented to 5th International Seminar on Construction Management for Sustainable Self-help Housing in Habinet Countries, Centre for Housing Studies, Ardhi Institute, Dar es Salaam, Tanzania, November 22–26.

Lamba, Davinder. 1994. Nairobi Action Plan: City Environment and Sustainable Development. Nairobi: Mazingira Institute.

Lugalla, Joe L.P. 1995. "Where the Majority Live in Tanzania: Why and How?" In Charles Green (ed.), The New Urban Challenge and the Black Diaspora. Albany: State University of New York Press.

Macharia, Kinuthia. 1992. "Slum Clearance and the Informal Economy in Nairobi." Journal of Modern African Studies 30(2): 221–36.

Macaharia, Kinuthia. 1995. "Meeting the Challenge in an African City: Nairobi's Informal Economy." In Charles Green (ed.), The New Urban Challenge and the Black Diaspora. Albany: State University of New York Press.

Max, John A.O. 1991. The Development of Local Government in Tanzania. Dar es Salaam: Educational Publishers and Distributors.

Miti, K. 1985. "L'Operation Nguvu Kazi a Dar es Salaam: ardeur au travail et controle de l'espace urbain." Politique Africaine 17: 88–104.

Mitullah, Winnie. 1991. "Hawking as a Survival Strategy for the Urban Poor in Nairobi: The Case of Women." Environment and Urbanization 3(2): 13–22

Mwesigwa, David. 1987. "The Structure and Spatial Significance of Small Scale Economic Sector in Kampala City — Uganda." MA Dissertation, Department of Geography, University of Dar es Salaam.

Nabuguzi, Emmanuel. 1989. "Development Perspectives on Petty Commodity Production in Uganda: The Case of Katwe Metal Workers." Ecole des Etudes en Sciences Sociales, Paris, December.

Ndegwa, Stephen N. 1994. "Civil Society and Political Change in Africa: The Case of Non-Governmental Organization in Kenya." International Journal of Comparative Sociology XXXV(1/2): 19–36.

Nsimbabi, Apolo. 1993. "Facilitators and Inhibitors of Decentralization in Uganda." In Donald Rothchild (ed.), Strengthening African Local Initiative: Local Self-Governance, Decentralization and Accountability. Hamburg: Institute of African Studies.

Owuor, Otula. 1994. "Hawker Politics in Nairobi." The Urban Age 2(2): 1.

Shaidi, L. 1984. "Tanzania: The Human Resources Deployment Act 1983, a Desperate Measure to Contain a Desperate Situation." Review of African Political Economy 31: 82–7.

SINA (Settlement Information Network Africa). 1991. Newsletter, No. 22, November.

_____. 1992. Newsletter, No. 24, July.

_____. 1993. Newsletter, No. 29, February.

Stren, Richard et al. 1994. "Coping with Urbanization and Urban Policy." In Joel D. Barkan (ed.), Beyond Capitalism vs. Socialism in Kenya and Tanzania. Boulder, Colorado: Lynne Rienner, pp.178–200.

Stren, Richard E. and Rodney R. White (eds.). 1989. African Cities in Crisis: Managing Rapid Urban Growth. Boulder, Colorado: Westview Press.

Tanzania, Jamhuri ya Muungano. 1990. Katiba ya Jamhuri Ya Muungano wa Tanzania ya Mwaka 1977 (Constitution of the United Republic of Tanzania of 1977). Dar es Salaam: Government Printers.

Tanzania, United Republic. 1969. Second Five Year Plan for Economic and Social Development. Dar es Salaam: Ministry of Planning.

Tripp, A.M. 1990. "The Urban Informal Economy and the State in Tanzania." Ph.D. dissertation, Northwestern University, Evanston, IL.

_____. 1992. "Local Organizations, Pariticipation, and the State in Urban Tan-
zania." In Goran Hyden and Michael Bratton (eds.), Governance and Politics in Africa. London: Lynne Rienner, pp. 221–242.

Uganda, Republic of. 1987a. Report of the Commission of Inquiry into the
Local Government System. Kampala: Ministry of Local Government.

_____. 1987b. The Resistance Councils and Committees Statute (Statute 9,
1987). Kampala: Government of Uganda.

_____. 1993. The Local Government (Resistance Councils) Statute. Kampala:
Decentralization Secretariat.

_____. 1995. Constitution of the Republic of Uganda. Kampala: Government
of Uganda.

United Nations. 1995. World Urbanization Prospects. New York: United
Nations.

Wabwire, A.A. 1989. "Trends in Urban Growth and Administration: The Case
of Kampala City, Uganda." Paper presented at the International Seminar
on African Urban Management, Harare, Zimbabwe.

Glossary

ADB	Asian Development Bank
ANHI	National Agency against Unhealthy Housing (Morocco)
ARRU	Urban Rehabilitation and Renovation Agency (Tunisia)
BBS	Bangladesh Bureau of Statistics
CBO	Community-based organization
COMUL	Land Occupation Urbanization and Legalization Commission (Brazil)
CUS	Centre for Urban Studies
DIT	Dhaka Improvement Trust
EAP	Economically active population
FAP	Flood Action Plan
FIS	Islamic Salvation Front (Algeria)
FPM	Federal government revenues (Brazil)
GNP	Gross National Product
GPA	Global Plan of Action
GTA	Greater Toronto Area
GURI	Global Urban Research Initiative
HFA	Household financial assets
HVA	Hometown Voluntary Associations
IPTU	Urban building and property tax
ISS	Tax on services (Brazil)
IUPERJ	*Instituto Universitário de Pesquisas do Rio de Janeiro*
KCC	Kampala City Council
LGEB	Local Government Engineering Bureau
NEP	National environment policy
NGO	Non-governmental organization
NRM	National Resistance Movement
OGS	One-governor system
PL	Poverty line
PRI	Institutional Revolutionary Party (Mexico)
PRONASOL	National Solidarity Progamme (Mexico)

PT	Worker's Party (Brazil)
RAJUK	*Rajdhani Unnyan Kartripakkha* or the Capital Development Authority (later incarnation of the DIT)
RC	Resistance Councils
SIP	Slum improvement project
UBN	Unsatisfied basic needs
UDD	Urban Development Directorate
ULG	Urban local government
UNCHS	United Nations Centre for Human Settlements-Habitat
UNICEF	United Nations International Children's Emergency Fund
UPO	Urban poor organization
ZEIS	Special zones of social interest (Brazil)

Publications in Urban and Community Development

Urban Research in the Developing World:
Towards an Agenda for the 1990s
Richard Stren and Patricia McCarney
Major Report Series 26 October 1992 68 pp. ISBN 0-7727-1363-4 $7

Empowering People:
Building Community, Civil Associations, and Legality in Africa
Edited by Richard Sandbrook and Mohamed Halfani
Major Report 29 1993 209 pp. ISBN 0-7727-1364-2 $16

Seeing the Invisible: Women, Gender and Urban Development
Caroline O.N. Moser with Linda Peake
Major Report 30 September 1994 50 pp. ISBN 0-7727-1374-X $8

Financing Local Services: Patterns, Problems and Possibilities
Richard Bird
Major Report 31 February 1995 54pp. ISBN 0-7727-1204-2 $8

Urban Growth & Population Redistibution in North America:
A Diverse & Unequal Landscape
Larry S. Bourne
Major Report 32 May 1995 41 pp ISBN 0-7727-1402-9 $7.50

New Urban & Regional Geographies in Canada: 1986-91 and Beyond
Larry S. Bourne & Anthony E. Olvet
Major Report 33 July 1995 74 pp ISBN 0-7727-1404-5 $8.50

Urban Regions in a Global Context:
Directions for the Greater Toronto Area
Proceedings of a conference held at University of Toronto
October 18-20 1995
Major Report 34 March 1996 160 pp ISBN 0-7727-1405-3 $15

Price of Major Reports includes GST postage & handling.

Urban Research in the Developing World
Edited by Richard Stren
Volume 1: Asia
May 1994 *x,* 326pp. ISBN 0-7727-1368-5 $16 Cdn., $12 US
Volume 2: Africa
November 1994 *xii,* 378pp. ISBN 0-7727-1369-3 $20 Cdn., $15 US
Volume 3: Latin America
July 1995 *xiv,* 308 pp. ISBN 0-7727-1369-7 $16 Cdn., $12 US
Volume 4: Perspectives on the City
December 1995 *x,* 428 pp. ISBN 0-7727-1371-5 $20 Cdn., $15 US

An Urban Problematique:
The Challenge of Urbanization for Development Assistance
Richard Stren and others
September 1992 *xxxv,* 215 pp. ISBN 0-7727-1359-6 $16
(Also available in French)

The Changing Nature of Local Government in Developing Countries
Edited by Patricia L. McCarney
April 1996 *xii,* 314 pp. ISBN 0-7727-1406-1 $15

For book orders please add postage & handling, $5 for one volume $6.50
for 2 or more volumes by surface mail. Canadian residents please add GST.

Centre for Urban & Community Studies
University of Toronto, 455 Spadina Avenue
Toronto, Ontario M5S 2G8 Canada
TEL 416-978-2072
FAX 416-978-7162
E-MAIL cucs@epas.utoronto.ca